Mixed Rules, Mixed Strategies
Candidates and Parties in Germany's Electoral System

Philip Manow

ecprPRESS

First published by the ECPR Press in 2015

The ECPR Press is the publishing imprint of the European Consortium for Political Research (ECPR), a scholarly association, which supports and encourages the training, research and cross-national co-operation of political scientists in institutions throughout Europe and beyond.

ECPR Press
Harbour House
Hythe Quay
Colchester
CO2 8JF
United Kingdom

Typeset by Lapiz Digital Services

Printed and bound by Lightning Source

British Library Cataloguing in Publication Data

A catalogue record for this book is available from the British Library

ISBN: 978-1-785521-46-1

PDF ISBN: 978-1-785521-55-3

EPUB ISBN: 978-1785521-56-0

KINDLE ISBN: 978-1-785521-57-7

www.ecpr.eu/ecprpress

If you are interested in electoral systems, you may like to explore these other ECPR Press titles

Matching Voters with Parties and Candidates: Voting Advice Applications in Comparative Perspective
Edited by Diego Garzia and Stefan Marschall
The first comprehensive overview of the VAA phenomenon.
Paperback ISBN 9781785521416
Hardback ISBN 9781907301375

The Political Ecology of the Metropolis: Metropolitan Sources of Electoral Behaviour in Eleven Countries
Edited by Jefferey M Sellers, Daniel Kuebler, R Alan Walks and Melanie Walter-Rogg
An international comparative analysis of metropolitan political behaviour, covering eleven country cases.
Paperback ISBN 9781907301445
Hardback ISBN 9781907301377

Seats, Votes and the Spatial Organisation of Elections
Graham Gudgin and Peter Taylor
In many elections – especially those using single-member constituency systems – seat allocation is often incommensurate with each party's share of the votes. Gudgin and Taylor offer a rigorous analysis of this disproportionality.
ISBN 9781907301353

Identity, Competition and Electoral Availability
Stefano Bartolini and Peter Mair
The first systematic and conceptually sophisticated work to bring together the study of electoral change and cleavage persistence, which has since become one of the landmark volumes in the study of electoral politics in Europe.
ISBN 9780955248832

Electoral Change: Responses to Evolving Social and Attitudinal Structures in Western Countries
Mark Franklin, Thomas Mackie, Henry Valen *et al*
In the mid-1980s, an international team of leading scholars set out to explore the reasons for the shifts in voting patterns in sixteen western countries. This book reports their findings regarding the connections between social divisions and party choice, and the manner in which these links had changed over the previous two decades. The passage of time has not dated this classic text; this ECPR Press reissue carries a brand-new preface.
ISBN 9780955820311

Visit www.ecpr.eu/ecprpress for up-to-date information about new and forthcoming publications.

Contents

List of Figures and Tables

Figures

Tables

List of Abbreviations

BB	Brandenburg
BE	Berlin
BP	Bavarian Party (*Bayern Partei*)
BVerfG	German constitutional court (*Bundesverfassungsgericht*)
BW	Baden-Wurttemberg
BY	Bavaria
CDF	Cumulative density function
CDU	Christian Democrats (*Christlich Demokratische Union Deutschlands*)
CPD	Cumulative probability distribution
CSU	Christian Democrats, Bavarian branch (*Christlich-Soziale Union*)
DP	German Party (*Deutsche Partei*)
DRP	German Reich Party (*Deutsche Reichspartei*)
ENP	Effective number of parties (ENEP: effective number of electoral parties; ENPP: effective number of parliamentary parties; ENGP: effective number of government parties)
FDP	Liberals (*Freie Demokratische Partei*)
FPTP	First-past-the-post
HB	Bremen
HE	Hesse
HH	Hamburg
MM	Mixed-member electoral systems
MMM	Mixed-member majoritarian systems
MMP	Mixed-member proportional systems
MoV	Margin of victory
MP	Member of parliament
MV	Mecklenburg-West Pomerania
NI	Lower Saxony
NRQ	Number-ranking quotient
NW	North Rhine-Westphalia
OECD	Organization for Economic Cooperation and Development
OLS	Ordinary least square
OM	Optimal matching

PDS/*die Linke*	Ex-Communists (*Partei des Demokratischen Sozialismus*)
PR	Proportional representation
RDD	Regression discontinuity design
RP	Rhineland-Palatinate
SD	Standard deviation
SH	Schleswig-Holstein
SL	Saarland
SMD	Single member district
SPD	Social Democrats (*Sozialdemokratische Partei Deutschlands*)
SN	Saxony
ST	Saxony-Anhalt
TH	Thuringia

Acknowledgements

Institutions: Thanks go to the Universities of Konstanz, Heidelberg and Bremen, to the Max-Planck-Institute for the Study of Societies, Cologne. But in particular I would like to thank the Wissenschaftskolleg zu Berlin/Institute for Advanced Studies, which provided me with the time and rest necessary to finish this book. I will be eternally grateful.

Persons: Louis Massicotte and Valentin Schröder read the entire manuscript and provided many very helpful comments and ideas. It is only my fault that I have not followed all their suggestions. Both are superb experts and I am thankful for having been able to learn from them. I am also very grateful for the generosity with which Louis Massicotte shared his excellent book manuscript on mixed electoral systems with me. I also would like to thank two anonymous reviewers for ECPR Press for their valuable and encouraging comments.

At ECPR Press, Dario Castiglione, Kate Hawkins and Laura Pugh took care of the entire publication process in a highly professional manner. I also would like to thank Ildi Clarke and Simon Ward for very close reading and meticulous copy-editing. It was a pleasure to work with the ECPR team. I would also like to express my gratitude for the always responsive and cooperative attitude of the staff of the *Bundeswahlleiter* (Federal Returning Officer). In particular I would like to thank Gabriele Schömel for answering my various data requests. More specifically, for Chapter One, many thanks to Holger Döring for providing me with the comparative data. For Chapter Two I am quite indebted to Peter Selb for his valuable Stata tips and helpful comments. I am also grateful for the useful comments I received from André Kaiser, Susumu Shikano, and Thomas Zittel. My thanks go as well to Daniel Gallasch for his support in collecting and preparing the data and to Nick Borgwardt for his help with the cube rule function. I am also grateful to Dona Geyer, who translated a first version of this chapter into English. This is a corrected and extended version of (Manow 2011). An earlier version of Chapter Three was presented at the Political Economy Seminar of the University of Essex and I would like to thank all participants, especially Thomas Plümper and Vera Troeger, for their helpful comments. A previous version of Chapter Four was presented at the conference of the ECPR Political Economy Standing Group in Dublin, in 2010. I am very grateful for valuable comments by the participants, in particular by Nolan McCarty. I also greatly benefitted from Volker Lindhauer's advice and support in running the RDD analysis. Chapter Five is based on joint work with Valentin Schröder. For Chapter Six, helpful comments by André Kaiser, the late Peter Mair, Richard Matland, Donley Studlar, and Thomas Zittel are gratefully acknowledged. I am also very grateful that professors Matland and Studlar were kind enough to provide their original data set on legislative turnover, which allowed me to rerun their analysis with my additional turnover data. This chapter is a revised and corrected version of (Manow 2007). Chapter Seven is based on joint work with Martina Nistor. For Chapter Eight I am very grateful to Thomas Zittel and the editors of the *Zeitschrift für Parlamentsfragen* for their helpful comments. Chapter Nine benefitted from an excellent collaboration with Peter Flemming.

Inspiration: Roman Flügel and Daniel Ansorge (aka Barnt), among others for their inspiration.

Preface

Without noticing, work on this book started some seven years ago. It started with my replication of a study that had analysed the impact of electoral rules on parliamentary turnover, i.e. on the re-election probabilities of members of parliament. That Germany, in a comparison with twenty-four other established democracies with respect to parliamentary turnover, clustered mainly with majoritarian countries, but not with countries with proportional electoral rules, intrigued me. As it then turned out, the finding was largely based upon the analysis of (three) outlier elections, elections quite untypical for Germany's post-war electoral experience. Replicating the study with a more complete and balanced sample made the German turnover look much more 'well-behaved' and more 'proportional' – as expected (*see* Chapter Eight). A host of questions followed quite naturally from this first take on the functioning logic of Germany's mixed electoral rules – and to my great surprise, as of yet, the literature had addressed almost none of them in any satisfactory way. For instance, how do German parties combine list- and district-candidatures when they nominate their contenders for a seat in parliament? And why do parties and candidates combine the candidatures as they do – is it to hedge against electoral volatility and uncertainty (*see* Chapter Seven)? If yes, has electoral uncertainty increased lately and if yes, why (Chapters Two to Four)? Has increasing volatility something to do with rising disproportionality in the plurality tier of Germany's mixed electoral system? And is this rising disproportionality linked to the proliferation of parties since the early 1980s, first with the advent of the Greens, then with the establishment of a radical left party in the German party system in the late 1990s and early 2000s, i.e. *die Linke*? And so on, and so forth.

To address and answer these, and many more questions, I had to collect (of course with much support from others, *see* Acknowledgements) a lot of data since, and again to my great surprise, there was only very little relevant information available. I first collected encompassing data on all *Bundestag* members from 1949–2009, then on all candidates in all federal elections from 1949–2009. Finally, I extended these data sets with legislative information, for instance on committee membership and other features of MP parliamentary activity. The electoral data, however, were quite easily available, mostly already in digital form. Where they were not, the staff of the *Bundeswahlleiter* (Federal Returning Officer) proved to be very cooperative and helpful.

So, after some years, I suddenly had a book-length English treatment of the German case at my hands. Or so I thought. Turning the various papers into a coherent and updated book was, then, quite another challenging and, at some times, enervating task. Many helped me with this task (*see* Acknowledgements), but without a sabbatical spent at the *Wissenschaftskolleg* in Berlin, I wouldn't have been able to accomplish it.

Despite all the help and all the time that went into this book, it has its shortcomings and I am the first person to be aware of them. If the book substantially improves our understanding of the working of Germany's mixed electoral rules and of the effects of majoritarian and proportional rules more generally, which I think it does, then this has also something to do with the present rather poor state of that understanding.

I write these lines in my *Wissenschaftskolleg* office, 100 metres from where Walther Rathenau was shot in 1922, and very close to the *Schlachtensee*, where Carl Schmitt used to promenade first with Werner, and then later with Werner's son Nicolaus Sombart. It's a place full of German history, and a very important part of that history – yet rarely appreciated as such – is the German electoral system. In a new project I will therefore, together with my Bremen colleague Valentin Schröder, extend the perspective to the parliamentarisation and democratisation of Germany from the Imperial period via the Weimar Republic to early post-war Germany. Shall I mention that I was very much surprised to discover that we still today – after more than fifty years of debate about the *Kaiserreich* and the Weimar Republic – possess very little systematic information about the concrete electoral and legislative functioning of these two regimes?

March 2015, Berlin Grunewald

Chapter One

Introduction

The German electoral system

Mixed-member electoral systems (MM) have recently attracted increased academic interest. (Shugart and Wattenberg 2001b; Massicotte and Blais 1999; Moser and Scheiner 2004; Massicotte 2011; Moser and Scheiner 2012; Massicotte forthcoming). Regarding the number of studies treating these hybrid electoral systems, some have even spoken of an emerging 'cottage industry' (Nishikawa and Herron 2004: 753). That mixed systems attract this growing scholarly attention is explained by both a substantive and a methodological interest.

Regarding the substantive interest, MMs apparently combine the beneficial features of pure plurality and pure Proportional Representation (PR) systems (Shugart 2001b, 2001a; but see Bawn and Thies 2003). It, therefore, comes as no surprise that they have recently figured prominently in reform debates in many countries. Mixed-member electoral systems have become the 'most popular alternative to first past the post' systems (Blais 2008: 3) since they apparently meet the two prime goals of recent electoral reforms: proportionality and personalisation (Renwick 2010; Renwick 2011). They combine, as Moser and Scheiner note, the 'proportionality and small group representation commonly associated with PR and [...] the geographic representation of a particular locale and the large, catchall parties that are characteristic of SMD systems' (Moser and Scheiner 2012: 6). And – as at least the German case testifies – fair representation and personalisation does not need to come at the cost of lower government stability.

Today, around twenty-six countries apply mixed electoral rules for national elections. To this number one could add the state elections in the German and Austrian *Länder* (Massicotte 2011: 100–101), which increasingly emulate the two-vote proportional model of the federal level (Eder and Magin 2008). Overall, 'the use of majoritarian electoral systems has significantly declined while that of mixed systems has increased', as Bormann and Golder find in their recent overview of post-war electoral systems (Bormann and Golder 2013: 363).[1]

---

1. Whereas in 'the 1950s, majoritarian, proportional, and mixed electoral systems were employed in about 42 per cent, 50 per cent, and 8 per cent of democratic elections, respectively. By the 2000s, though, majoritarian systems were employed in only 33 per cent of elections, while mixed systems were used in 18 per cent of them' (Bormann and Golder 2013: 363).

True, the prediction that the switch to mixed rules will be the most frequent electoral reform in the twenty-first century (cf. Shugart and Wattenberg 2001c) appears today as having been prematurely judged when observing the decreasing number of countries that have recently undertaken such a switch. Yet, all still agree that mixed systems 'remain an important family of electoral systems worth scrutinising' (Massicotte 2011: 101). And among those, the German case is arguably the best suited for such scrutiny.

With respect to methodological interest, mixed systems have become a favourite object of study since they seem to offer the opportunity to examine the effects of electoral rules within a quasi-experimental setting (Stratmann and Baur 2002; Moser and Scheiner 2004, 2012: 44–61). They allow us to hold constant a number of intervening variables when studying particular effects of electoral rules – like the business-cycle, the political culture, party system characteristics (e.g. cleavage structures), and the institutional characteristics of the political system. The promise is that a 'mixed-member electoral system allows us to hold the environment constant and isolate the effects of different electoral rules' (Moser and Scheiner 2012: 46). If we are able to control for many factors with well-established impacts on political outcomes, this could help a great deal in ascribing causal effects to electoral rules.

However, the growing literature on 'contamination' has argued that whereas the study of mixed member electoral systems might allow for the controlling of a number of intervening variables, the analysis of the 'pure' effects of electoral rules is hindered by their interaction (Ferrara, Herron, and Nishikawa 2005b; Herron and Nishikawa 2001; Cox and Schoppa 2002; Ferrara 2004; Nishikawa and Herron 2004; Ferrara and Herron 2005). These interesting contamination effects then, themselves, have motivated many recent studies, which analyse the consequences of mixing majoritarian elements and principles of proportional representation in one electoral system.

This might also explain the renewed interest in the German electoral system that is reflected in a series of recent publications. One of the prominent features of the German electoral system that links its plurality tier to its PR tier is the possibility for candidates to run in a district and on a party list simultaneously (dual candidacy). Another feature is the way mandates won in districts and those won via the party-list are charged against each other in order to secure overall vote-seat proportionality. One empirical indication that the plurality tier and the PR tier of the German electoral system do indeed contaminate each other is the observable non-*Duvergerian* tendency in its plurality tier: the effective number of district candidates is regularly higher than two. The consequences of these institutional features of Germany's mixed system for the strategies of candidates, members of parliament (MPs) and parties will be the focus of the following analyses.

Mixed electoral systems combine (some kind of) plurality with (some kind of) proportional representation (Massicotte and Blais 1999). Being in place since 1949, the German electoral system appears as the 'archetype' (Saalfeld 2005: 209) or 'mother' (Carey 2009: 32) of this type of electoral system, as it is its 'oldest and most-copied' exemplar (Cappocia 2002; Sieberer 2010: 488).[2] The German electoral system combines regional closed-list PR with a nominal plurality vote in single-member districts (see also Nohlen 1978; Shugart and Wattenberg 2001c; Scarrow 2001; Klingemann and Wessels 2001b). Voters can cast two votes. With one vote they elect candidates in single seat districts with relative majority. With the other they vote for a closed regional party list. The list-votes decide the parties' overall seat shares for all – currently – 598 *Bundestag* seats, double the number of the – currently – 299 single member electoral districts. The candidate vote determines who will represent the district in parliament, and thereby, also the internal composition of each parliamentary party, especially the relative weights between district and list MPs. Since the districts won are subtracted from a party's overall seat share, calculated on the basis of all list votes, the higher the number of districts won, the lower the number of candidates that are drawn from the list. The seat-linkage between both components of the electoral system guarantees that proportionality dominates the translation of votes into seats. Accordingly scholars have labelled election systems, like the German one, Mixed-member *Proportional* systems, short MMP (Shugart and Wattenberg 2001c),[3] or – in a more critical vein – as 'simply a more complicated way of getting the same basic PR outcome' (Bawn 1999: 490). This also explains why many previous studies of the German system have tended to ignore its plurality-tier – as the following chapters will show, at the cost of failing to fully understand its working logic and its interactive effects.

The combination of a PR and a plurality tier in the German electoral system provides all those who are interested in the effects of electoral rules with an interesting testing ground. In particular, those interested in the differences between list-PR and nominal vote in single-member districts, but also those who are interested in the mutual impact of electoral rules on each other ('contamination'), can gain many new insights. Analyses are also facilitated by the fact that data on various aspects of theoretical interest is available, and also, by the high degree of continuity of electoral rules. This enables us to study 60 years of an almost unaltered electoral system in its impact on parliamentary behaviour, campaign strategies, re-election probabilities or on descriptive representation, amongst others.

As mentioned, the renewed interest in the German electoral system has not been only academic. Its apparent advantages – fair representation, i.e. a high degree of proportionality, a moderate effective number of parties (or a reasonable degree of party fragmentation), elections that regularly lead to stable coalitions,

2.   Germany 'still remains the country having the fullest experience of [...] [MMP], spanning over 60 years. The model was adopted there for federal elections in 1949. [...] numerous alterations have been brought since then. [...] none str[uck] at the heart of the model, whose essential features have remained' (Massicotte forthcoming ch. 3: 1).

3.   In contrast to Mixed-member Majoritarian systems (MMM), or superimposition (Massicotte and Blais 1999), in which no 'seat-linkage' between the PR tier and the plurality tier guarantees overall proportionality.

responsiveness of the party system to the representation of new societal interests due to moderate entry-thresholds (see the entry of the Green party in 1980 and of the PDS/ *die Linke* [ex-communists] after 1990; cf. Capoccia 2002), a combination of local and national interest representation, an element of 'personalisation' – have also qualified it to be a point of reference in electoral reform debates all over the world, from Japan, New Zealand, Great Britain, Italy, Canada, Scotland and Wales to Venezuela and Angola (cf. Shugart 2001b, 2001a; Massicotte forthcoming, chapter 2: 15–16; Moser and Scheiner 2012: 5). In Germany itself, the electoral system 'has been generally accepted since the early 1970s and carries a significant degree of legitimacy' (Saalfeld 2005: 226). It is generally considered to be 'tried and tested' (Nohlen 2014: 394).

This all, also, explains the increased need for an encompassing, up-to-date treatment of Germany's mixed-member electoral system in English. Yet, it does not exist. One important contribution to fill this lacuna will be Louis Massicotte's systematic and comprehensive study of mixed electoral systems (Massicotte forthcoming), in which German federal and state elections are covered in minute detail. Apart from this important and timely study, the last monographic study on Germany's electoral system in English has been published more than twenty years ago (Jesse 1990).[4] Yet, within these twenty years – not least due to German unification – electoral rules and electoral behaviour have changed in multiple (small) ways, and subsequently, the functioning logic of Germany's mixed system appears to have changed (quite profoundly) as well. Amongst others, we witness the following changes since unification:

- a higher number of effective parties (due to the entrance of the ex-communists),
- smaller districts and states with fewer districts in the East,
- lower turnout, higher voter volatility and less party-identification in East and West, and subsequently
- an increase in the disproportionality of the plurality tier, which led to a steeply increasing number of surplus seats (*see*, in particular, Chapters Two and Three).

These changes brought some features of Germany's mixed electoral system to the fore that had previously been attributed to the electoral rules as such, but were rather 'contextual' as now becomes apparent. But the effects of an electoral system – as Bingham Powell reminds us – depend on the interaction of

---

4. The text-book by Manfred G. Schmidt on the German political system (Schmidt 2003) treats the electoral system on four pages. We also have several country-chapters in edited volumes on electoral systems, electoral reform (Klingemann and Wessels 2001a; Saalfeld 2005; Gallagher and Mitchell 2005) or on candidate selection (Roberts 1988). But all these contributions fall far short of a full, both empirically and methodologically up-to date treatment of German elections and electoral rules. Some of them are rather dated, anyway. The recently increasing number of German books on the topic (Behnke 2007; Henning et al. 2009; Falter and Schoen 2005 [2014]) testifies to the need for a new systematic treatment of the German electoral system in English.

'(t) he decisions of parties as they offer candidates in the election; the decision of voters as they vote; [and] the rules that aggregate the citizen partisan choices to determine the winning representatives' (Powell 2000: 23). With changes in voters' and parties' strategies, we have recently observed changing effects of the electoral rules, too. These changes stress the necessity to re-assess an electoral system with such an exemplary status and to make another effort at uncovering its inner working logic. This is the aspiration of this book.

But promoting a better understanding of the German system is not the only, and not even the major, objective of the following chapters, it is rather the means to another end. The prime objective of this book is to address a number of current research controversies and debates in electoral and legislative studies – using the German case as an exemplary case that lends itself very well to their discussion. Therefore, the following chapters clearly reach beyond the German case as such. In particular, as I want to show in the following chapters, studying mixed systems promises to contribute substantially to at least five debates in political science: (1) the contamination literature, (2) the mandate-divide debate, (3) the literature on descriptive representation, (4) the debate on the cartel party and on decreasing democratic accountability and (5) pre-electoral coalition formation. I will briefly sketch these literatures and show how they relate to my study.

(1) *Electoral Contamination*: Recent literature has directed attention towards the possible contamination effects between the tiers of a mixed electoral system (Herron and Nishikawa 2001; Ferrara, Herron, and Nishikawa 2005b; Cox and Schoppa 2002). One central indicator that is said to indicate contamination is the number of parties competing in a district for the plurality vote. In a mixed member electoral system, this number does not follow Duverger's Law, that is, it does not converge into two (parties or candidates), but remains systematically higher. This effect, however, is debated (cf. Moser and Scheiner 2012; Chapter Two), and seems to depend, at least partly, on voters' information about likely election outcomes, i.e. on the stability of the party system (Herrmann 2012). The main contamination argument holds that more than two parties usually contest a district because smaller parties run constituency candidates in actually hopeless races with the expectation that candidates will positively influence small parties' list vote share (Hainmüller, Kern, and Bechtel 2006; Hainmüller and Kern 2008). However, as of yet, the literature has largely failed to demonstrate that running for a seat in a district indeed has a positive impact on the PR-votes gained in that district – at least for those parties that should be the most affected by the majoritarian rules in the district: small ones. This has given rise to the counter argument that causality is in fact reversed: it is not candidates entering district races that boost the PR-vote of their party, but where a party can count on stronger voter support it will also nominate district candidates. Below, I will present empirical evidence that a positive impact from the plurality towards the proportional tier and from the candidacy to the improved vote share (but not vice-versa) does in fact exist. This will also allow us to identify a kind of 'second order' contamination effect, that, as of yet, has not been noted in the literature. The higher the number of parties contesting a district, the stronger the disproportionality with which

nominal votes are translated into district seats in the plurality tier. This increase in disproportionality, in turn, has feedback effects on the functioning of the PR tier, which will be studied in more detail in Chapters Two–Four, and on candidates' strategies, which will be studied in more detail in Chapters Six–Seven.

(2) *Mandate-Divide*: With respect to the impact that electoral rules have on MPs' strategies and behaviour, the literature offers diametrically opposed views. Some claim that mixed electoral rules will induce mixed representation roles, while others assert that legislative behaviour depends on the way the members of parliament were elected. They thus identify two distinct legislator types in the German parliament and claim that list- and district-MPs show distinct parliamentary behaviour, that they employ different campaign strategies, and that they are differently willing to toe the party line (see Stratman and Baur 2002; Bawn 1999; Lancaster and Patterson 1990; Bawn and Thies 2003; Zittel and Gschwend 2007; Sieberer 2010). This is flatly denied by others: 'Contrary to widespread opinion, it is of absolutely no importance whether a mandate is obtained through the constituency or the Landesliste' (Burkett and Padgett 1987: 130; cf. Jesse 1988: 120).[5] The controversy points to a larger literature evaluating the incentives that electoral rules provide for the representation of constituency- *vs.*-party- or lobbying-group-interests (Bawn and Thies 2003; Andeweg and Thomassen 2005) or for MPs' legislative activities (Herron 2002). Because it renders both legislator types, Germany's electoral system seems particularly suited for looking closer into the arguments on either side, to assess empirically their relative explanatory power and to provide us with a more precise picture of the nexus between electoral rules and representative roles (see also Bailer *et al.* 2013; *see* Chapter Nine).

(3) *Descriptive Representation*: It is a well-established finding that PR is more favourable to women's parliamentary representation than majoritarian electoral rules (Rule 1987; Matland and Montgomery 2003; Salmond 2006; Diaz 2008; Wängnerud 2009). The much higher share of women elected into the *Bundestag* via the list, as compared to those elected in a district, fully confirms this finding. But what exactly causes these strikingly different success-rates of female candidates under different electoral rules: is it voters' social conservatism vis-à-vis female candidates running for a district mandate? Or does self-selection play the decisive role for fewer women running in districts? And could this self-selection, in turn, be explained by the anticipation of voters' antiquated views on gender issues? Or

---

5.   Many more similar judgments could be cited. For instance, Uwe Kitzinger notes in his study on the first two legislative terms: 'by and large, there was little difference in the *Bundestag* between the two types of members, and many probably were not sure which of their colleagues held constituency seats, and which did not. When local work was concerned the difference between constituency and list members was also less than might be thought' (Kitzinger 1960: 60–61). 'There is practically no difference – once elected – in the status or behaviour of constituency candidates and list candidates. Constituency candidates may have certain additional engagements and duties in the constituency, but, since most list candidates have contested constituencies – and perhaps hope to do so again – they, too, will 'nurse' constituencies and undertake engagements there' (Roberts 1988: 114).

is there something else that accounts for the significant impact of electoral rules on the political representation of gender (Iversen and Rosenbluth 2006, 2010)? Does PR allow parties to 'educate' their voters by placing more women on closed lists than voters like to see on them? And do we find here a 'contagion'-effect in that some parties advance in nominating female candidates and others feel forced to follow suite (Matland and Studlar 1996)? Again, looking at a mixed-electoral system and having complete information on both those running for office and those actually elected, while keeping constant a couple of additional variables that may also affect the extent of women's political representation, will help very much in identifying the electoral causes for a distorted descriptive representation. This is what Chapter Six does.

(4) *Democratic Accountability* or *the cartel party thesis*: But the German data does not only allow us to acquire a far better understanding of mechanisms of descriptive representation, it also helps in assessing the leeway that voters or parties have when it comes to the selection and election of representatives (Hazan and Rahat 2010). A complete data set on German candidates and – as a subgroup – MPs from 1949 to 2009, allows us to answer basic questions of democratic accountability: to what extent does the nomination of a candidate already ensure his or her election? How much can the voter decide on who will and who will not enter parliament? Who de-selects representatives – parties by not re-nominating them or voters by not re-electing them? And how has that changed over time or differs between different parties and between different types of candidatures (list-, district- or double-candidature; cf. Chapter Seven)?

According to the cartel party thesis, parties and candidates are faced with greater electoral volatility and, as a result, are increasingly turning away from the pursuit of electoral victory and are, instead, concentrating on minimising the costs of electoral defeat (Katz and Mair 2009, 1995). Analysing parties' nomination strategies is a promising way to test one central contention of the cartel party thesis – which, as of yet, has undergone only little empirical testing. Are the parties really sealing themselves off increasingly from voters, are they immunising themselves from an ever more volatile 'verdict of the people'?

(5) *Pre-electoral Coalitions*: In a mixed electoral system, parties can form pre-electoral coalitions basically in two-ways: either locally, in the district – that is in the plurality tier – or on a nationwide scale – that is in the PR tier – by announcing their intention to form a government coalition following the election (Ferrara 2004; Ferrara and Herron 2005; Golder 2005, 2006a, 2006b). These strategies depend on (and usually come with an appeal to) voters' willingness to support either the district candidate or the list of the potential coalition partner. In a mixed system with a double ballot like the German one, parties regularly ask their voters to split votes between the prospective members of a coalition. But when and why do parties pursue the local or the national strategy (Ferrara and Herron 2005)? The importance of answering this question may be gauged from the fact that district-level party agreements were quite a common feature in the first post-war *Bundestag* elections, but since then have

completely given way to nationwide pre-electoral arrangements – with the concomitant national campaign asking party followers to split their nominal and list vote between the larger and the smaller coalition partner, respectively (Pappi and Thurner 2002; Pappi *et al.* 2006; Gschwend 2007). Yet, coordination within the PR-tier became an ever costlier option. Since the 1990s, we observe an increasing number of surplus seats from election to election, lately up to an equivalent of about four per cent of the votes. These kinds of seats are won in the plurality tier, and district-level pre-electoral coordination might have been a way to reduce the number of surplus seats that political rivals can claim. So, although contamination motivates even small parties to participate in – for them hopeless – district races in order to boost their PR-vote share in that district, the net benefit of this strategy may turn negative if it leads to too many (surplus) districts won by the political adversary. We therefore, again, need to take a closer look at the relative advantages of these two strategies of pre-electoral coordination (*see* Chapter Five).

As can be gathered from the previous paragraphs, the German electoral system has an exemplary status which has also qualified it to be a point of reference internationally for many electoral reforms over the last twenty years. It has also an interesting institutional setup that suits it as a test case for various research questions. In addition, good data availability plus the thorough research recently undertaken, but often published in German only, allows it to appear worthwhile to devote a new book-length treatment to the German mixed member electoral system. This also seems warranted since many features of its functioning still remain rather poorly understood. Our still incomplete understanding mirrors certain long-held intellectual preconceptions, if not to say prejudices, of experts on Germany's electoral system, namely the dominant dogma that Germany has a PR system with an only adjunct, clearly less important and therefore negligible, feature of personalisation (or plurality).

Covering seventeen *Bundestag* elections since 1949, the book is based on various encompassing data sets: firstly, on a data set covering all candidates that ever ran in an election to the German federal parliament, with information on the mode of candidacy (list only, district only or double candidacy), on the list rank and/or the district, the votes won in the district, and the ways in which candidates were elected into the *Bundestag*, plus information on gender and age etc.; secondly, on a subset of this data, that contains all MPs who ever were elected into the *Bundestag*, including information on their tenure and their committee-membership (again plus biographical data such as gender and age), thirdly, on data of the results of all federal elections at district level, i.e. candidate or nominal votes and list votes plus abstentions and invalid votes from 1949–2009, including data on socio-economic district characteristics for the latest elections; finally, on data at the voting district level with almost 90,000 observations for the 2009 federal elections (Wahlleiter, *et al.* 2010). An extension of the analysis of the 2013 *Bundestag* election will be provided in the concluding chapter (*see* Chapter Ten).

Plan of the book

Chapters Two and Three start the analysis by looking at that component of Germany's mixed system that has been the most neglected in previous studies: its plurality tier. The first two chapters highlight the disproportionality introduced into the German electoral system by its plurality tier and its determinants. Further, its consequences for the internal composition of government and opposition parties, for parties' nomination strategies and for the growing number of surplus seats in recent *Bundestag* elections will be analysed. The chapters, moreover, show that the well-known cube rule, i.e. the disproportional effect of majoritarian rules on the seat distribution among parties, is clearly present in the plurality tier, but plays out differently due to the peculiar composed character of the German electoral system. It is a 'contaminated' cube rule, in which the high effective number of district parties lead to a significant 'left-shift' of the cube rule, i.e., the disproportionality in the translation of constituency votes into district mandates starts way before the traditional 50 per cent vote threshold. This has various consequences, as is shown in detail in those two starting chapters. Later chapters will again refer to these consequences of disproportionality.

Chapter Four asks why small parties enter hopeless district races. As is demonstrated in Chapters Two and Three, a high (and increasing) effective number of district parties is the main explanatory factor for the increasingly disproportional vote/seat translation in the plurality tier of Germany's mixed electoral system. This also explains the increasing number of surplus seats. Chapter Four expounds why exactly the plurality tier in a mixed member proportional system does *not* reveal *Duvergerian* tendencies toward an effective number of two parties. As we will see, again the cause lies in contamination: small parties field candidates in what, for them, are completely 'hopeless' districts in order to boost their 'second', party-list vote share. Chapter Four will show that such an often claimed, but rarely proved positive vote effect from one tier to the other can, in fact, be detected when looking at small parties' candidates.

With more parties entering district races, the vote-seat translation in the plurality tier turns more disproportionate. One upshot is the higher number of surplus seats in recent elections, i.e. the number of mandates won via the constituency-vote that surpass the number of seats that would have been allocated to a party based on its PR-vote share. Because of this, the overall seat shares in the German system increasingly deviate from the purely proportional outcome. That 'district races … do not affect aggregate seat shares' (Bawn 1999: 489) has become less and less true for recent elections. But the more the plurality-tier dominates the PR-tier, the more attractive it becomes for parties to form local electoral alliances in order to restrict the number of surplus seats which the political adversary can claim. This leads to the question: why don't German parties coordinate locally? With the help of a couple of counterfactual scenarios, Chapter Five will present alternative seat distributions that would have resulted from local electoral alliances of different composition and with different formulas for dividing the seats among the partners. The main result of these counterfactual scenarios is that local electoral coordination would not have affected the overall seat distribution a great deal, but that it can be used as an instrument to hinder smaller parties from entering parliament. The more interesting effects of centralised vs. decentralised electoral coalitions therefore materialise with respect to the effective number of parties, not with respect to parties' varying seat shares. This again shows that one effect of Germany's MMP lies in an effective number of district parties that is higher than in a pure Single-Member-District (SMD)-system and in an effective number of parliamentary parties that is lower than in a pure PR-system, due to the effective exclusion of regional parties from parliamentary representation.

Chapter Six investigates how candidates become MPs. Based on a complete sample of all individuals who ever ran for a seat in the *Bundestag* in any of the seventeen national elections since 1949,[6] the chapter asks to what extent parties' nomination strategies already predetermine the actual election outcomes. As we will see, candidates of the established parties rarely run for office unsuccessfully. Around 75 per cent of *Bundestag* MPs of these parties entered parliament upon their first attempt, and only around 25 per cent of the Members of Parliament ran again for office without actually being elected. But if the nomination itself means that one has already gone a long way towards being elected, parties possess a strong disciplining device vis-à-vis 'their' candidates. Chapter Six will also address the interaction effects between the two basic modes of being elected into parliament: in the district or via the list. I will particularly focus on the effects on women's representation and explain the fact that female parliamentarians almost exclusively enter the *Bundestag* via the list and not via districts.

Chapter Seven looks at the consequences of parties' strategies to hedge against electoral volatility. In this respect another 'contamination' feature of Germany's electoral system becomes relevant. Given the (increasing) disproportionality of its plurality tier and given that seats from the plurality and the PR tier are charged against each other, parties in the German mixed-electoral system have to insure themselves and their candidates against two scenarios: vote losses, which put a (disproportionally) high number of their district seats at danger, and vote gains with their 'cannibalistic' consequences, since, in this case, a higher number of successful district candidates threaten to eat into the party's number of promising list positions (*see* Chapters Two and Three). Recent elections frequently led to situations in which, for many state lists, not even a single list place proved safe in the sense of providing its candidate with a position in parliament.[7] The ideal instrument to confront both scenarios is the double candidacy, i.e. running simultaneously in a district and on a list. This displays another feature that links the plurality and the PR tier in Germany's MMP-system. Chapter Seven examines how parties have used the double candidacy in response to what can be described as a secular decrease in the number of safe seats and safe list positions. A precondition for this analysis is first to define what can count as a safe list rank and a safe seat.

6.   The last election in 2013 is analysed in the Conclusion.

7.   This is simply the mirror image of the increasing number of surplus seats.

Chapter Eight investigates the effects of electoral rules on the re-election chances of Members of Parliament. It compares MPs and the various ways they have been elected into the *Bundestag* and examines whether MPs fare better when running as a list- or as a district- or as a double candidate. The German case again proves to be well suited to assess the effects of electoral rules on parliamentary turnover. Several hypotheses in this respect have been derived from comparing aggregate national data. An individual-level data set on all German MPs, with detailed information on candidatures, allows a much more fine-grained analysis and the application of more appropriate statistical methods, in particular, survival analysis.

With so many contamination effects, one wonders whether MPs voted into parliament (either via the party list or via the district) will pursue different parliamentary strategies and adopt different representational roles. Are district-MPs different from list-MPs? Are they less easy to discipline? Do they orient themselves towards their constituency rather than to their party? Does the one legislator type deliver 'pork', whereas the other is open to interest-group influence? Chapter Nine presents a replication of a study which examined committee membership in the German *Bundestag*, finding differences between district- and list-MPs. As a first step of the analysis, however, Chapter Nine discusses the all, but trivial, question how to code district- vs. list-MPs and shows that for the large number of MPs who entered parliament via the list but at the same time contested a district, much points to them being oriented toward the party as well as toward their district.

I will begin, however, in the following section by providing the reader with a short introduction into the German electoral rules and assess their working by comparing Germany with other established democracies along a number of established criteria from comparative politics: disproportionality, polarisation, effective number of electoral and legislative parties etc.

The German electoral rules

Let us start with a brief overview of German electoral rules. As already mentioned above, Germany's MMP system combines regional closed-list PR with a nominal plurality vote in single-member districts. Voters cast two votes,[8] a nominal ('direct', personal or district) vote (in German '*Erststimme*' = first vote). With it, voters select candidates in single seat districts with relative majority. The second vote is cast for the closed regional party list. This party vote (or list vote; in German '*Zweitstimme*' = second vote) decides the parties' seat shares, whereas the nominal vote determines the internal composition of the parliamentary party, especially the relative weights between district and list MPs within the parliamentary party. Since the seats won in the districts are subtracted from a party's overall seat share, calculated on the basis of all list votes, the higher the number of

---

8.   With the exception of the first election in 1949 in which voters had only one vote.

districts won, the lower the number of candidates that are drawn from the list. The seat-linkage between both components of the electoral systems guarantees that proportionality dominates the translation of votes into seats. However, two small – legal – deviations from proportionality have to be mentioned: parties will only participate in the PR tier allocation of seats if they have received at least five per cent of list-votes or have won at least three seats. The other major deviation from proportionality results from the fact that parties that win more districts than what their share of list votes would have allowed, can keep these surplus or 'overhang' seats.

But how exactly are the two votes charged against each other? Half of the seats of the German parliament, the *Bundestag*, are assigned to candidates who gain a relative majority of district votes in one of the – currently – 299 single-member electoral districts. The other half of the seats are distributed among the parties according to the relative vote share that the regional party lists receive – after subtracting the number of seats already won by candidates in that state. In other words, starting from the first position on the party list, a party can send candidates from the list to parliament until the combined number of its district and its list candidates matches the party's relative vote share received via the list vote. This 'seat-linkage' is supposed to compensate for the disproportionality generated by the plurality tier. However, if the number of directly won districts in a state surpasses the number of parliamentary seats that would have been allotted to a party according to its relative share of list votes, the party can keep these so-called surplus or overhang seats (*Überhangmandate*). As a consequence, small (but lately increasing) deviations from the total number of distributable parliamentary seats occur after elections. The 15th German *Bundestag*, for instance, had 603 members, five more than the $2 \times 299 = 598$ regular seats.[9] In the 17th *Bundestag*, the number of MPs has increased to 622, with a total of twenty-four surplus seats, the highest number ever. It is roughly equivalent to four per cent of all seats, almost as high as the nationwide five per cent nominal electoral threshold in the German electoral system since 1953.[10] In other words, we not only observe deviations from the 'normal' number of parliamentary seats, but also from proportionality. It seems as if the German MMP electoral system increasingly deviates from the 'basic PR-outcome' (see above). As we will see during the analysis, the increased number of surplus seats is itself linked to 'contamination', since it is the upshot of an increased disproportionality in the vote-seat translation in the plurality tier of Germany's mixed member electoral

9. Since a ruling of the constitutional court in 1998, district candidates who leave parliament for whatever reason will not be substituted from the list as long as the party has a positive number of surplus seats.

10. Besides the five per cent threshold in the PR-component (applied nationally since 1953, before that time relevant for the state level, only), there is also a three seat-waiver rule in the plurality-component (increased from one seat since 1957). A party that wins at least three districts will be represented in parliament with a number of mandates equal to their share of second, i.e. party-list votes, even if this share is below the five per cent threshold.

system. This increasing disproportionality, in turn, is caused by the increased number of parties that compete for seats at the district level in the hope that being present with a district candidate will have a positive effect on their list vote outcome (*see* Chapters Two, Three and Seven).

The entire process is complicated by the fact that party lists are formed at the state level. This entails that each party participates in the election with as many state lists as there are states in which it enters the race. As an informal rule, the established parties have always submitted party lists in every state. This also means that the compensation of district and list seats takes place at the state level. Votes are translated into seats in a two-staged process:

> seats are first distributed nationwide among parties that have crossed the five per cent threshold,[11] on the basis of the number of valid party votes cast nationwide for each. The seats won by each party are in turn re-allocated among its respective land lists, based on the number of votes cast for each. In the first stage, parties are competing against each other for seats, while in the second, the land lists of each party are competing against each other for their share of the seats assigned to the party (Massicotte forthcoming, ch. 5: 6).[12]

The first stage in which seats are distributed among parties nationwide is called 'superdivision' (in German: *Oberverteilung*; cf. § 6 para. 1 and 2 together with § 7 para. 2 Federal Election Law), the second, in which seats are distributed among the different state lists of the same party 'subdivision' (in German: *Unterverteilung*; cf. § 6 para. 2 together with § 7 para. three Federal Election Law). This somewhat complex procedure may, as we will see below, contribute to the occurrence of surplus seats.

This translation of votes into seats means that while the share of list or party votes determines a party's total seat share in parliament, the relative weights of district and list candidates within the parliamentary groups of the larger parties CDU/CSU (Christian Democrats) and SPD (Social Democrats) depends on how

---

11. Or, alternatively, the three seats threshold.

12. Kathleen Bawn's description of the vote-seat translation is therefore incorrect: 'The second votes (Zweitstimmen) are totaled at the state *(Land)* level. In each state, each party that received at least five per cent of second votes nationwide receives a fraction of seats proportional to its second-vote share' (Bawn 1999: 489). Votes are first totaled *nationwide*, the seats are then re-allocated to the land-level depending on actual turnout in the states, where the number of districts won by a party are then subtracted. This introduces complex interactions between differences in turnover (at the land-level, determining the number of seats per *Land*) and district size (determining the number of seats subtracted in each state) that also partly explains the increase of surplus seats after 1990. Lower turnover in the new Eastern states *(Länder)* meant a lower seat total was re-allocated to the *Länder* and smaller districts in these states meant that more (direct) seats were subtracted from this total – the probability of surplus seats increased. An electoral reform in 2002 lowered the number of districts in the new *Länder* (increased their size), reducing *this* cause of the increase of surplus seats after 1990.

Table 1.1: Numbers and types of governments in thirty-six OECD countries, 1945–2012

Country	Minority Government	Minimum Winning	Surplus Government	Total	Minimum Winning as % of Total
Australia (AUS)	2	29	4	35	0.83
Austria (AUT)	2	24	2	28	0.86
Belgium (BEL)	4	19	15	38	0.50
Bulgaria (BGR)	2	2	2	6	0.33
Canada (CAN)	10	17	0	27	0.63
Switzerland (CHE)	0	2	16	18	0.11
Cyprus (CYP)	6	7	5	18	0.39
Czech Republic (CZE)	3	8	1	12	0.67
Germany (DEU)	**0**	**21**	**4**	**25**	**0.84**
Denmark (DNK)	33	3	0	36	0.08
Spain (ESP)	7	5	0	12	0.42
Estonia (EST)	4	9	0	13	0.69
Finland (FIN)	9	5	29	43	0.12
France (FRA)	13	19	28	60	0.32
Great Britain (UK)	3	21	0	24	0.88
Greece (GRC)	1	16	0	17	0.94
Croatia (HPV)	4	3	2	9	0.33
Hungary (HUN)	2	3	5	10	0.30
Ireland (IRL)	8	15	2	25	0.60
Iceland (ISL)	3	23	3	29	0.79
Italy (ITA)	22	8	30	60	0.13
Japan (JPN)	8	26	20	54	0.48
Lithuania (LTU)	8	4	5	17	0.24
Luxembourg (LUX)	0	16	3	19	0.84
Latvia (LVA)	8	7	6	21	0.33
Malta (MLT)	0	15	0	15	1.00
Netherlands (NLD)	1	11	11	23	0.48
Norway (NOR)	19	11	0	30	0.37
New Zealand (NZL)	7	24	0	31	0.77
Poland (POL)	5	8	4	17	0.47
Portugal (PRT)	5	9	3	17	0.53
Romania (ROU)	12	2	4	18	0.11
Slovakia (SVK)	3	8	3	14	0.57
Slovenia (SVN)	3	8	4	15	0.53
Sweden (SWE)	20	10	0	30	0.33
Turkey (TUR)	3	13	0	16	0.81
ø	**6.67**	**11.97**	**5.86**	**24.50 (32.15)**	**0.52 (0.53)**

Source: Döring and Manow 2014, www.parlgov.org

successful the party was locally. Small parties, like the Liberals (FDP) or the Green party (*Die Grünen*), almost exclusively send list candidates to parliament since their chances of winning a simple majority of the votes within one of the districts are very small.[13] Nonetheless, they regularly enter races in districts with the hope of increasing their party votes. In contrast, larger parties may send more district- than list-candidates into parliament, especially if the party has gained vote shares nationwide, due to the well-known 'winner's bonus' of plurality rules.

How does the German system compare to other electoral systems? In the following section I give a brief comparative assessment of Germany's electoral system along some established indicators.

Comparing the German electoral system

I start the short comparison of electoral systems with reporting one very crucial 'output' variable, namely the frequency with which electoral rules have produced stable 'minimum-winning' coalitions, i.e. neither minority nor oversized governments. Table 1.1 reports the total numbers of governments for thirty-six OECD-countries over the period of full democratic rule, i.e. over the 1945–2012 period. The table also reports the frequency of minority, minimum winning and surplus governments (*see* Table 1.1; source www.parlgov.org; Döring and Manow 2015).

As can be read from Table 1.1, we count twenty-five German post-war governments until 2012, and more than 80 per cent of them were minimum winning. This compares to an average of roughly twenty-five post-war governments in all thirty-six OECD countries over the same time span, or to thirty-two governments when we restrict the comparison to only those other twenty OECD countries that had, like Germany, been democratic over the entire post-war period. About only half of these governments were minimum-winning in both country samples. As a first finding, we can therefore say that in this most important 'output' dimension the data clearly testify for a well-functioning electoral-*cum*-political system – without, of course, *causally* linking electoral rules to government type and frequency.

Figure 1.1 provides us with information not about the sheer frequency with which certain types of governments occur, but their duration. Again, the German case (country code DEU) is one in which minimum-winning coalitions ruled for about fifty-seven years of the sixty-three years (1949–2012) under consideration here. Exceptions were the Grand Coalitions between Christian and Social Democracy from 1966–1969, and again, from 2005–2009.

What if we consider other established comparative indicators like average turnout, party fragmentation at the electoral and parliamentary level (ENP votes

---

13. In the 2002 elections the Green Party, for the first time, won a district mandate – in Berlin (election district 84, *Friedrichshain Kreuzberg/ Prenzlauer Berg Ost*). It successfully defended this mandate in the 2005, 2009 and 2013 elections. The last district mandate for the FDP was won in 1990.

Figure 1.1: Types of governments in thirty-six OECD countries, 1945–2012

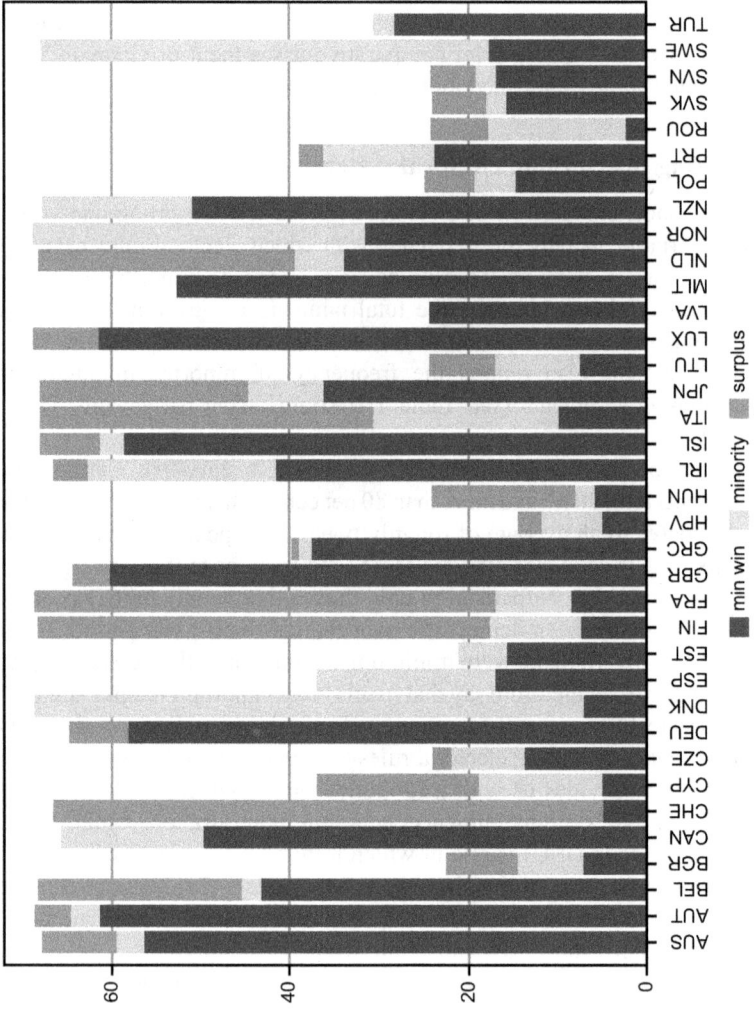

Source: Döring and Manow 2015; www.parlgov.org

and ENP seats),[14] and the disproportionality[15] and polarisation[16] of the electoral system?

These indicators give us a similar picture (*see* Table 1.2). With above average turnout, below average party fragmentation, with a very low degree of disproportionality, a small advantage ratio[17] as well as little polarisation, the German electoral system outperforms the OECD-average in all these dimensions, sometimes slightly, sometimes substantially. There is therefore considerable evidence that the German electoral system combines favourable characteristics like fairness (proportionality) and responsiveness (i.e. it allowed for the entry of new parties like the Greens and the ex-communists in the 1980s and 1990s, but also helped in the consolidation of the party system in the 1950s), that it has produced stable majorities and brought about the moderate alternation of power. As we will see below, there is also very ample evidence that the German electoral rules helped to keep the balance between centralisation and decentralisation, between parties and candidates, or between party- and district-orientation (Shugart 2001b, 2001a) or functional and territorial representation (Bawn and Thies 2003). All in all, it might be not that surprising that the German system over the years has inspired reform debates in many countries – except that it inspired a very lively reform debate in Germany, too (*see* Chapter Ten).

So, in a comparative perspective, and on the basis of various performance criteria, the German electoral rules apparently have performed reasonably well. But let's now turn to a more in-depth treatment of those electoral rules, starting with an analysis of the vote-seat translation logic in the plurality tier.

---

14. We measure party fragmentation as *the effective number of [electoral or parliamentary] parties* (ENP, see Laakso and Taagepera 1979):

$$ENP = \frac{1}{\sum_{i=1}^{n} v_i^2},$$

with v_i as the vote or seat share of party i.

15. Disproportionality is measured as the *Gallagher-index of disproportionality* (see Gallagher 1991):

$$Disproportionality = \sqrt{\frac{1}{2}\sum_{i=1}^{n}(V_i - S_i)^2},$$

with V_i and S_i as the vote- and seat-shares of party i, respectively.

16. Polarisation is measured with Dalton's (2008) index of polarisation:

$$Polarisation = \sqrt{\sum_{i=1}^{n} v_i \left(\frac{LR_i - \text{ø}LR}{5}\right)^2},$$

with LR_i the left-right score of party i, (on an index running from zero to ten), $\text{ø}LR$ the average left-right score over all parties, and v_i as the vote share of party i.

17. We measure the Advantage Ratio following Taagepera and Shugart (1989: 68) simply as:

$$Advantage\ Ratio = \frac{s_i}{v_i^2},$$

with s_i and v_i as the seat share and vote share of party i, respectively. To get a number for the entire electoral system the absolute value of the ratios are added and divided by two.

Table 1.2: Turnout, effective number of parties, disproportionality, advantage ratio and polarisation in thirty-six OECD-countries, 1945–2010

Country	Turnout	ENP votes	ENP seats	Disproportionality	Advantage ratio	Polarisation
Australia	94.39	2.98	2.54	9.31	1.89	0.36
Austria	82.94	3.18	2.94	2.75	1.08	0.37
Belgium	91.96	7.14	6.34	3.78	3.9	0.39
Bulgaria	58.01	4.86	3.58	7.95	1.26	0.36
Canada	71.52	3.27	2.52	11.58	1.88	0.36
Switzerland	47.93	5.83	5.23	2.69	1.39	0.45
Cyprus	85.17	3.7	3.46	5.22	1.33	0.62
Czech Republic	63.29	5.55	4.04	7.4	1.24	0.51
Germany	**74.86**	**3.91**	**3.39**	**3.43**	**1.1**	**0.35**
Denmark	78.31	5.21	4.92	2.58	1.26	0.43
Spain	67.27	3.55	2.71	6.17	1.27	0.42
Estonia	56.09	5.92	4.49	6.77	1.33	0.4
Finland	68.7	5.7	5.06	3.46	1.64	0.36
France	67.59	5.56	3.89	11.42	1.76	0.5
Great Britain	61.39	3.25	2.39	11.92	1.78	0.35
Greece	74.33	3.44	2.72	6.72	1.43	0.41
Croatia	56.66	4.5	3.67	8.18	1.65	0.43
Hungary	58.52	3.83	2.84	7.23	1.27	0.42
Ireland	67.77	3.73	3.07	5.86	1.47	0.32
Iceland	88.52	4.06	3.76	3.92	1.22	0.45
Italy	84.33	4.47	4.52	3.36	1.85	0.45
Japan	69.98	3.86	2.9	8.91	1.61	0.53
Lithuania	52.83	6.59	4.63	9.58	1.47	0.38
Luxembourg	89.7	4.05	3.32	7.06	1.35	0.41
Latvia	65.17	6.3	4.84	5.96	1.32	0.45
Malta	85.91	2.36	2.18	3.64	1.12	0.18
Netherlands	74.55	5.22	4.85	1.91	1.12	0.38
Norway	79.91	4.32	3.68	4.53	1.28	0.43
New Zealand	87.1	2.81	2.31	8.93	1.31	0.29
Poland	42.02	6.28	4.42	7.03	1.67	0.35
Portugal	63.93	3.5	3.14	4.4	1.08	0.43
Romania	55.6	4.58	4.31	6.64	1.21	0.26
Slovakia	61.83	6.04	4.47	6.85	1.24	0.36
Slovenia	59.44	6.39	5.27	5.11	1.29	0.37
Sweden	78.01	4.15	3.81	2.34	1.17	0.4
Turkey	86.04	4.57	2.99	13.24	1.44	0.36
Ø	**70.88**	**4.57**	**3.76**	**6.33**	**1.46**	**0.40**

Source: (Döring and Manow 2015: www.parlgov.org)

PART I

PARTIES IN GERMANY'S MIXED-ELECTORAL SYSTEM

Chapter Two

The Contaminated Cube Rule

That plurality voting systems translate votes into seats in a nonlinear (disproportional) way, in which the ratio of seat shares of two parties corresponds roughly to the ratio of their vote shares cubed, has long been known and was first described for the British electoral system of single-member-district plurality (Kendall and Stuart 1950, 1952).[1] This finding is referred to as the cube law or the cube rule in the literature (King and Browning 1987; Taagepera and Shugart 1989; Taagepera 1986).[2] Looking at the nexus between votes and seats in the German electoral system, we find the cube rule confirmed to a surprising degree when we focus solely on its plurality tier, i.e. on the connection between constituency votes and district mandates (*see* Figure 2.1 and Table 2.1). However, this nexus has been treated rarely in the literature on Germany's mixed member electoral system,[3] presumably because its PR-component was, and is, perceived as ensuring a full neutralisation of the disproportional seat distribution caused by the plurality component. Hence it was believed unnecessary to pay any greater attention to disproportionality.

Yet, as will be shown below, the party-list vote does not completely neutralise the disproportionality caused by the constituency vote; in fact, it can even enhance this effect. This happens particularly in cases where a large number of (small) parties strive to increase party-list votes by putting up candidates in district races although they have no reasonable prospect for success – a connection that has been described extensively in the recent literature on 'contamination effects' between the various electoral components in mixed member electoral systems. However, as the effective number of constituency parties rises, the disproportionality of the distribution of district seats to constituency votes also increases, as I will demonstrate. Moreover: if vote shares between 30 and 40 per cent in the *constituency vote* are already

---

1. An early identification of this regularity reaches back to a Royal Commission in 1904.

2. The rule can most easily be described with the following formula: $s_i/(1-s_i) = (v_i/(1-v_i))^3$ with s representing the share of seats for party *i* and v its share of votes (Taagepera and Shugart 1989). Empirically, the slope of the vote-seat translation function in majoritarian systems often came close to the factor of 3; for the reasons see (Gudgin and Taylor 2012 [1979]). But even for the British plurality electoral system, the slope, as a rule, is closer to 2.5 than to 3 (Laakso 1979). Therefore, the cube rule should be understood, and is here understood, rather as a simple guiding rule than as a 'law.'

3. It is interesting that the proposal for a 'cubic election system' was made during the German electoral reform debate in the 1960s; see (Hermens and Unkelbach 1967). According to this proposal, the calculation of mandates would not be based on the number of votes won by the parties, but on the cube of this number.

enough for winning a high number of district mandates, then this, at the same time, also increases the probability of a gap between the *list votes* share for any given party and the number of district mandates it wins – and thus the probability of the so-called *Überhangmandate* or surplus seats.

Since it facilitates the understanding of the working logic of Germany's mixed-member electoral system, and since disproportionality has profound consequences both for parties' and candidates' strategies, I will delve deeper into the issue of increased disproportionality in the plurality component in this and the following chapter. How has disproportionality developed over the course of time? What factors have chiefly influenced disproportionality? To examine these questions, I will compare the ratio of constituency votes to the percentage of district mandates over time for the two major parties at the national and state (*Land*) level. Firstly, in the second section, the disproportional distribution of district mandates in the German electoral system will be investigated against the background of the new debates on contamination effects in mixed electoral systems. I discuss the cube rule and suggest its modification when applying it to the German electoral system. This modification accommodates the circumstance that in mixed member electoral systems the effective number of constituency parties regularly do *not* converge into two, i.e. that 'Duverger's Law' does not apply (Cox and Schoppa 2002).[4] Following this, the third section offers an overview over the development of disproportionality in *Bundestag* elections since 1953 at the level of German states. Finally, in the fourth section the focus becomes the study of determinants of disproportionality – particularly the influence of the effective number of parties and of the 'district size', meaning here the number of districts per state. The final section concludes with a summary of the argument.

Contamination and Disproportionality

Figure 2.1 presents the nexus between the constituency-vote shares for the CDU/CSU and SPD in the last sixteen *Bundestag* elections[5] on the x-axis and the corresponding shares of district mandates awarded to both parties on the y-axis. We see the well-known nonlinear pattern with higher disproportionality – that is, with a steeper slope of the curve – near the 50-percentage mark for constituency votes (*see* Figure 2.1). The curve of the votes-to-seats-ratio dissects the diagonal depicting the ratio of perfect proportionality at about 50 per cent. Close to this point, smaller vote gains lead to disproportionate increases in the number of seats and smaller vote losses to disproportionate decreases. Formulas 2.1 and 2.2 (footnote 6 and page 29) express this nexus between votes and seats as a logarithmic function (King and Browning 1987: 1253). The classic cube rule in which the main gradient

---

4.   See (Calvo 2009) for a similar approach. Whereas Calvo is interested in an increase in the partisan bias of majority rule in cases where the number of parties is higher than two, I am, however, interested in changes in disproportionality.

5.   Excluded is the first *Bundestag* election of 1949, in which voters only had one vote.

Figure 2.1: Share of constituency votes and district mandates, CDU/CSU and SPD, 1953–2009 at the national level[6]

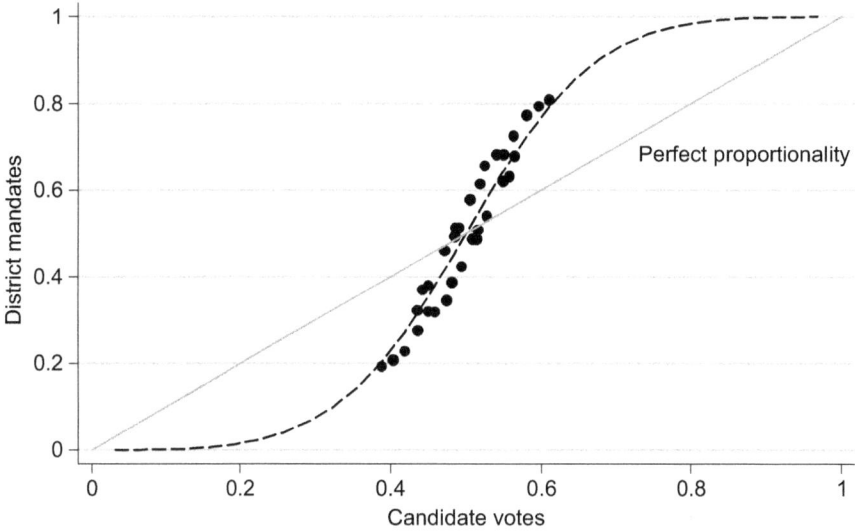

parameter *rho* [ρ] is set equal to three predicts the disproportionality pattern in the plurality component of the German mixed voting system almost perfectly. If one estimates ρ according to the German data, it equals 3.32 with an explained variance of 0.993 (*see* Table 2.1).

In the literature on the German electoral system, this disproportionate distribution pattern within its plurality component is rarely debated. As the prevalent reference to 'personalised proportional representation' already indicates (*see* § 1 par. 1 Federal Election Law), the prevailing view is that the plurality component in the German electoral system is only of secondary importance and, at most, introduces an element of personalisation in a voting system otherwise shaped by proportional representation (Schreiber 1994). However, this viewpoint disregards the fact that the impact of the disproportionality 'produced' by the constituency vote is not completely neutralised by the party-list vote. On the contrary, this impact can even be enhanced. Therefore, I argue that it is quite worthwhile to examine in depth the ratio between constituency votes and district mandates.

---

6. The cube rule used for this and all the following estimations in this chapter follows the transformation by King and Browning (1987: 1253):

$$(2.1) \quad s_i = \left\{1 + exp\left[-\rho ln\left(\frac{v_i}{1-v_i}\right)\right]\right\}^{-1}$$

Table 2.1: District mandate shares for CDU/CSU and SPD in the Bundestag *elections from 1953–2009, dependent on their share of the constituency vote; estimation of the parameter* ρ

ρ [rho]	3.32
	(0.000)***
Observations	32
R^2	0.99

p-value in parenthesis, * significant at the 10%-level; ** significant at the 5%-level; *** significant at the 1%-level.

It is also apparent in Figure 2.1 that the degree of disproportionality varies from election to election. Disproportionality is dependent on at least two factors: on the one hand on the 'district size' (1), and on the other, on the effective number of parties (2).

(1) Here district size refers to the state or *Land* level, specifically to the number of constituencies and thus district mandates *in each German state* (*Land*). Here we are talking simply about an 'arithmetic effect' in converting votes into seats that can be easily demonstrated: in a single-member district, a party can receive only zero or 100 per cent of the seats; in a total of two districts, 0, 50, or 100 per cent; in three constituencies, 0, 33, 66, or 100 per cent, etc. In other words, the more constituencies there are, the more exact the seat distribution of the respective vote distribution can be approximated – whereby the maximal number of seats always defines the upper limit of proportionality (Taagepera and Shugart 1989). At the same time, with a higher number of districts, their variance of vote shares should increase. Small swings in vote shares should then lead to only small changes in seat shares (Gudgin and Taylor 2012 [1979]; Taylor and Johnson 1979). With only a few districts, variance decreases and disproportionality increases. Therefore, it should make a difference for the proportionality of seat distribution whether the vote/seat-translation takes place on the base of two constituencies (as in Bremen 2002 and 2005) or on the base of seventy-three constituencies (as in North Rhine-Westphalia in the *Bundestag* elections between 1965 and 1976). But this does not only apply to the synchronic comparison of states of different size, but also to a diachronic comparison of parliamentary elections: when we compare the *Bundestag* elections over time, we find that it can make a difference whether or not the number of states with comparably few constituencies increase, as was the case after the German unification.

(2) With regard to the second factor, namely the number of parties,[7] it is logically not necessary but indeed probable that disproportionality grows as the number of participating parties increases. When only two parties are competing,

---

7.   Measured as the effective number of parties (Laakso and Taagepera 1979).

a party needs at least 51 per cent of the vote in order to win 100 per cent of the seats in a (single-member) constituency; with three parties, it needs at least 34 per cent; with four parties, at least 26 per cent, etc. Consequently, a large number of parties, particularly a strong third party (Behnke 2007), can lead to a constellation in which a party with a relatively low constituency vote share still wins many constituencies. Continuing this argument, however, the probability also increases that a discrepancy will emerge between the percentage of *party-list votes* and the percentage of the district mandates won in a state, and thereby the probability of surplus seats (Behnke 2003a, 2003c). These surplus seats are criticised because they appear to base parliamentary majorities on a moment of arbitrariness in the conversion of votes into seats. The discrepancy between the percentages of party-list votes and of district mandates can probably be attributed also to the increased possibility of the vote being split when a higher number of parties contest districts (Bawn 1999; Gschwend 2007). With many smaller parties entering district races, voters are still more likely to decide against 'wasting' their constituency vote and will cast it for a promising local candidate instead. Presumably, therefore, the discrepancy between the percentages of constituency votes and party-list votes for the two major parties – CDU/CSU and SPD – also increases as the effective number of parties competing in a constituency rises.

In the end, this indicates that the PR-component of the mixed system, which was actually designed to balance out the disproportionality caused by the plurality component, can – on the contrary – even enhance its disproportionate effect. This points to the debate on possible 'contamination' effects between the different electoral rules of mixed member electoral systems (Herron and Nishikawa 2001; Ferrara, Herron, and Nishikawa 2005b; Cox and Schoppa 2002). In this recent literature, one central indicator is usually considered to be the number of parties competing in a constituency for the plurality vote. In a mixed member electoral system, this number does not follow Duverger's Law, that is, it does not converge into two, but remains systematically higher. This is because smaller parties send constituency candidates into what are actually hopeless races for district mandates in the hope of positively influencing their percentage of the party-list vote by the presence of candidates running for district mandates (Hainmüller, Kern, and Bechtel 2006; Hainmüller and Kern 2008; *see* Chapter Four). This displays a classic case of contamination, defined as existing

> whenever at the micro-level, the behaviour of a voter, a party, a candidate or legislator in one tier of the election is demonstrably affected by the institutional rules employed in the other tier. At the aggregate level, contamination is observed when a particular outcome produced in one tier (like the number of parties) is affected by the institutional features of the other tier (Ferrara, Herron, and Nishikawa 2005b: 9).

If, however, these contamination effects at the same time give parties a systematic incentive to compete in constituencies where they have no hope of winning, the number of competing parties influences the degree of

Figure 2.2a: Disproportionate conversion of votes into seats, dependent on various values for ρ (when β = 0)

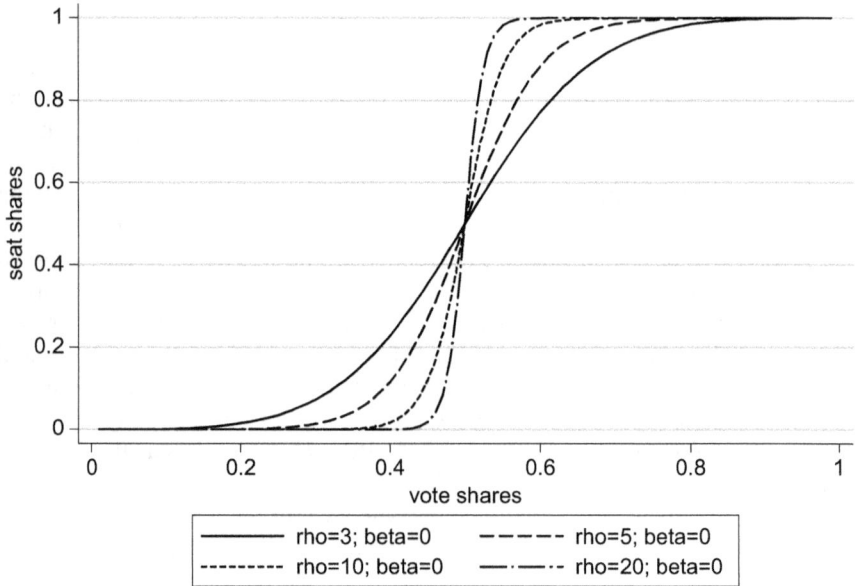

disproportionality and if this eventually promotes the likelihood of the parties' percentages of district mandates considerably deviating from their share of the party-list vote, then we are dealing here with a contamination effect that has not been noted previously. As of yet, work on contamination effects have highlighted the effects that strategic party action within the plurality component have had on the results within the PR-component – namely, *more party-list votes due to the (even if hopeless) party candidatures for a district mandate in constituency races.* Here, however, we are being confronted with an effect in which a party's strategies, geared towards the proportional representation component, have an impact on the results within the plurality component – namely *an increased disproportionality caused by a higher effective number of parties competing in a constituency.*

This has a methodological consequence for the context considered here. The cube rule was formulated in view of the strictly (British) single-member district voting system and therefore assumes, implicitly, the existence of a two-party system. It is precisely this that is foiled by Germany's mixed electoral rules. We, therefore, have to account for the high effective number of constituency parties in the cube rule formula. It needs to be modified. I supplement it here by the additional parameter ß. This parameter allows the estimated function – unlike the 'classic'

Figure 2.2b: Disproportionate conversion of votes into seats, dependent on various values for β (when ρ = 3)

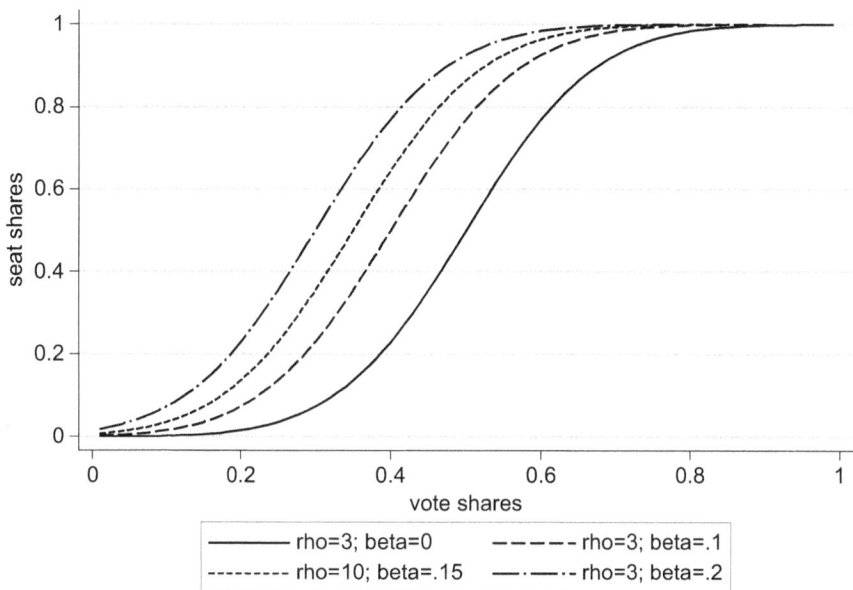

cube rule – to predict a seat share above 50 per cent, way before a vote share reaches 50 per cent. The modified formula, the extended cube rule, on which the following estimations and figures are based, is then (cf. King and Browning 1987):

$$(2.2) \qquad s_i = \left\{ 1 + exp \left[-\rho ln \left(\frac{v_i + \beta}{1 - v_i - \beta} \right) \right] \right\}^{-1}$$

This adopted formula contains two parameters that measure on the one hand, the slope of the curve (ρ) and on the other hand, its shift to the left (β). Figure 2.2 shows, by way of illustration, the course of the curve of the function for different values of ρ (3, 5, 10 and 20) and β (0, 0.1, 0.15, 0.2).

We therefore have two parameters to describe the vote-seat translation: The parameter ρ determines the degree of 'electoral responsiveness' (Gary King) of an electoral system and illustrates the system's 'amplifying effect' (Eckhart Jesse) or 'exaggerative quality' (David Butler). If ρ = 1, we are dealing with a perfectly proportionate election system. If ρ → ∞, we have a 'winner-takes-all' system, in which the party with the relative majority of votes wins *all* seats (King 1990; King and Browning 1987). The parameter β describes where ρ reaches its maximum. If β = 0, ρ is at its maximum when the vote share is at 50 per cent.

In the following sections, I apply the just derived extended cube rule formula in order to estimate ρ and β for *Bundestag* elections, over time and as a basis of comparison among the German states.[8] In turn, these estimated parameters serve as dependent variables in the next section, in order to study the effect of district sizes and of the effective number of parties on the degree of disproportionality within the plurality component in Germany's mixed electoral system. I expect the district size to primarily affect the slope of the curve, while the effective number of parties is expected to chiefly impact the left shift of the curve, i.e. β.

Constituency Votes and District

When we consider the plurality component on the national level separately for the only two parties that, as of yet, have proved able to win the vast majority of constituencies – the CDU/CSU and the SPD – several regularities become apparent immediately (*see* Figure 2.3).

First of all, Figure 2.3 confirms the established finding that the SPD suffers from a structural disadvantage with regard to constituency votes and district mandates. In the majority of the *Bundestag* elections, the CDU/CSU won substantially more constituencies than the SPD. To what extent this is the consequence of electoral geography disadvantaging the left is open to debate and will be addressed more extensively in the next chapter (Rodden 2005). We know that working class parties in majoritarian systems often tend to win several constituencies (industrial zones and big cities) with strong leads, but also lose many (rather rural) constituencies by a much narrower margin (Rodden 2010). From the parties' point of view, the number of 'wasted votes' might therefore be higher for the SPD than for the CDU/CSU. This is a general pattern in plurality voting systems for parties with a regionally concentrated electorate (Taylor and Johnson 1979). Especially in the context of the British system, it has long been recognised that if 'the supporters of one party tend to be more concentrated than those of the other, the former may squander many more votes than the latter in building up huge majorities in safe seats' (Butler 1953: 196). It seems plausible to assume that this factor is at work here, too, but it is of course unclear whether this tendency puts Social Democracy with concentrated worker voters, or Christian Democracy with concentrated Catholic voters, at a disadvantage.

Also evident in Figure 2.3 is the connection between the general electoral success of a party and its disproportionate gain of district mandates. The figure would enable us to tell the story of the alternating electoral successes of the two major parties in German parliamentary elections. In it, the first two *Bundestag* elections examined here – in 1953 and 1957 – would mark the positive and negative extreme points in outcomes for the CDU/CSU and the SPD. It is not

---

8.   Stata command nl (nonlinear).

Figure 2.3: Constituency votes shares and shares of district mandates in the Bundestag elections from 1953–2009 for the CDU/ CSU and SPD

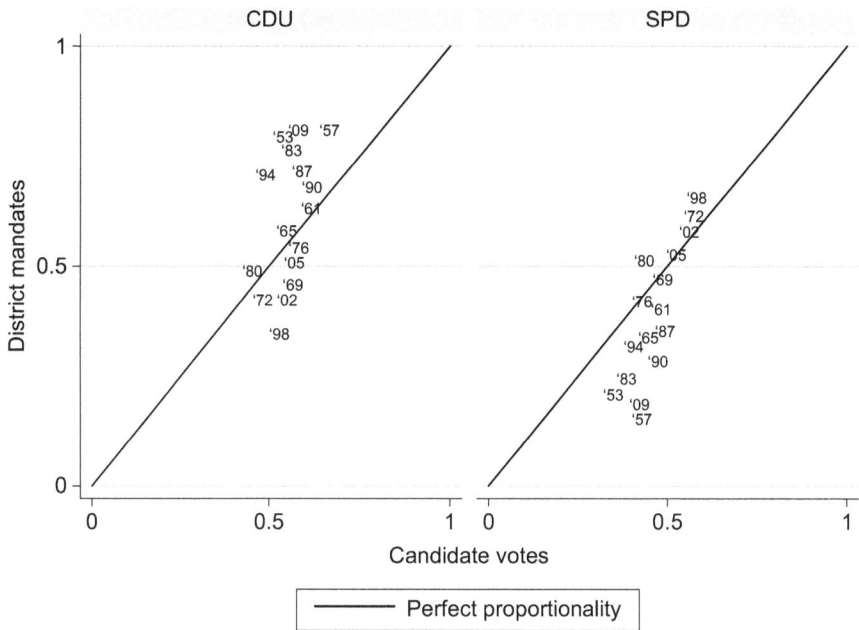

particularly surprising that the extraordinary election of 1957, in which a German party won an absolute majority of votes and seats for the first and – so far – last time, was also the election in which the distribution of district mandates was out of proportion to the most extreme degree observed to date. Just as unsurprising are the *Bundestag* elections in which the SPD was particularly successful – namely, the elections of 1972, 1998, and 2002, which propelled the Social Democrats over the line of perfectly proportional representation with regard to district mandates.

Yet we find no proof of a secular trend toward ever greater disproportionality in the ratio between votes and seats when talking about constituency votes and district mandates. This supports the presupposition that the degree of disproportionality for the plurality component of the German election system is possibly influenced by the number of parties competing for votes. In the early elections of 1953 and 1957, and once again in recent *Bundestag* elections (particularly those of 1998, 2002 and 2009), a relatively high degree of disproportionality is evident. In the interim period, however, the ratio between the percentage of constituency votes and district mandates lies closer to the ideal line of proportional representation. Whether this finding can actually be attributed to the relatively high (effective) number of parties in both the early and the more recent elections will be examined in the following section.

To conduct this endeavour, however, we first need to look at the ratio between the vote and seat shares at the *level of the German states*, because an examination at the national level can give a misleading picture. (On the national level, the disproportional seat distribution in one state – for instance, an SPD stronghold – is possibly offset by the disproportional seat distribution in another state – for instance a CDU stronghold.) Yet it is at the state level, in the course of the so-called *Unterverteilung* or 'sub-distribution' (according to §6 of the Federal Election Law), where the actual adjustment between the district mandates won, and the seats entitled to a party based on its party-list votes, takes place. Consequently, at this stage a very disproportionate ratio of party-list votes to the number of constituencies won, can lead to surplus seats. Furthermore, the state level offers the chance to test whether disproportionality varies with district size and with the effective number of (district) parties. This is the subject of the following section.

Disproportionality in the Plurality Component of the German Electoral System at the State Level: Elections

Since both votes – the plurality and the PR vote – are charged against each other at the state level for national German elections, this is the level at which we need to study the relations between the shares of constituency votes and district mandates. In proceeding this way, we can pay particular attention to the impact of the factor 'district size,' meaning the number of constituencies or seats, because in this dimension we see significant variance among the states – from two seats in Bremen in the *Bundestag* elections of 2002 and 2005, to the 73 district mandates in North Rhine-Westphalia in the elections from 1965–1976. From the literature, we know that district size is important for proportionality or disproportionality of the conversion of votes into seats (Taagepera and Shugart 1989). To determine accurately how much it actually influences proportionality or disproportionality, however, is an empirical question. Comparing states of varying size allows us to give an answer.

In the following, I estimate ρ and β for the sixteen *Bundestag* elections since 1953, based on a dataset that includes the percentages of constituency votes for the CDU/CSU and the SPD, as well as their percentage of district mandates at the state level for each of the elections. The variable 'Constituency Vote Share' indicates the percentages of *the total number of valid constituency votes* that were won by the SPD and the CDU/CSU, respectively. The variable 'District Mandate Share' represents the percentages of *the total number of district mandates* awarded to each of these two parties. Furthermore, the dataset contains information on the effective number of parties at the state level in each of the *Bundestag* elections, ('Effective Parties') (see Laakso and Taagepera 1979) as well as data on the total number of district mandates to be won at the state level, the 'District Size'. The data on the votes is based on the results of the *Bundestag* elections at the constituency level (aggregated at the state level), as they were made available by Germany's Federal Returning Office. The data on the district mandates at the state level has been taken from the *Datenhandbuch zur Geschichte des Deutschen Bundestags* (Schindler 1999; Feldkamp 2005, 2006). The number of observations is based on a total of sixteen elections (excluding the one in 1949), in which one election had only nine states participating (1953),[9] nine elections included ten states (1957–1987),[10] and six elections consider 16 states (since 1990). Constituency votes and district mandates are calculated for the CDU/CSU and for the SPD, so that the data set includes a total of $2 \times (9 + 9 \times 10 + 6 \times 16) = 390$ observations. When considering individual *Bundestag* elections or individual states, the number of observations is limited accordingly: in the case of *Bundestag* elections, to a minimum of eighteen and a maximum of thirty-two observations; in the case of individual states, to a minimum of twelve and a maximum of thirty-two observations.

When we observe the *Bundestag* elections at the state level over the course of time and based on the modified cube rule formula (*see* overview in Figure 2.4), several important regularities can be seen already in the graphic depiction. In Figure 2.4, the two major political parties are represented with distinct symbolic markers [CDU/CSU (*), SPD (+)], which enables us to follow the relative success of both parties in each of the national elections. Compared to the national level (*see* Figures 2.1 and 2.3), the seat distribution at the state level is clearly more disproportionate. The entire (value) scale of the y-axis is covered with states in which the CDU/CSU and the SPD obtain either all, or none, of the district mandates. At the same time, Figure 2.4 shows a relatively high disproportionality in the early *Bundestag* elections and then again after 1990, whereas the elections for the sixth to the eleventh *Bundestag* (1969–1987) display less 'polarised' results. The slope of the curve is flatter, and the line for perfect proportionality is crossed near the 50 per cent mark for vote share. Overall, the deviation from the line of an exactly proportional distribution of votes and seats at the state level is far more pronounced and ρ always lies over three (the range of values for each of the *Bundestag* election lies between 3.5 and 9.3; *see* Table 2.2a). In addition, we can see that the supposedly more important effect in converting constituency votes into district mandates at the state level is based on a shift to the left of the curve – that is, in a β that is clearly distant from zero (which varies between 2.8 and 12.8 percentage points for individual *Bundestag* elections, *see* Table 2.2a). Here – as it appears – a greater number of parties make a noticeable difference. Finally, the effect of a consolidation of the German party system until 1961 can be seen in Figure 2.4 in the diminishing scattering. After 1990 there are nearly two different functions of the votes-to-seats ratio, a western and an eastern distribution – and the estimated cube rule function lies in the middle of this (*see* Figure 2.4, especially the *Bundestag* elections of 1998 and 2005). Besides, after German unification, distributions become rather polarised again, whereby the CDU/CSU or SPD win either all, or no, district mandates in a state.

---

9. The Saarland was excluded.

10. The representatives for Berlin in the *Bundestag* were selected by the Berlin *Abgeordnetenhaus* (House of Representatives) according to the sizes of parliamentary parties there.

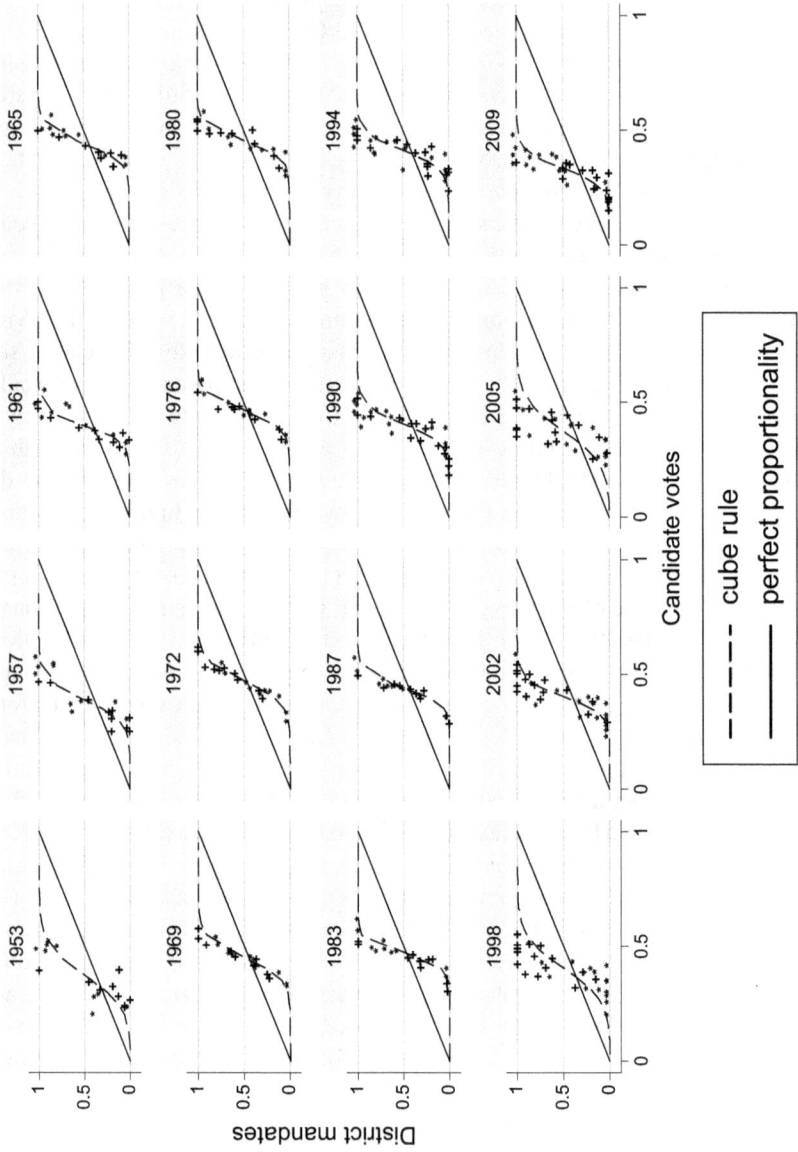

Figure 2.4: The cube rule in sixteen federal elections – the election level

Likewise, the elections in which a party was successful can be clearly identified, such as the unification election of 1990 in which the CDU/CSU was particularly successful in winning district mandates, compared to the election of 1998 in which it was the SPD that was able to win the vast number of district mandates. Once again the pattern in which the general electoral success or failure of a party, measured on its gain or loss of party-list votes, is reflected in the plurality component which to a very disproportionate degree becomes evident. This, in turn, leads to a high percentage of representatives who entered the *Bundestag* via the district mandates within the majority parliamentary party and, hence, probably in the governmental coalition.

Disproportionality in the Plurality Component of the German Electoral System: The States

When we shift the level of our study to the individual states, the presupposition that the 'district size,' meaning the number of constituencies in each state, clearly influences the proportionality of the conversion of votes into seats is first confirmed. Bremen represents an extreme case because it is split into three constituencies in some elections and only two in others (which were always won by the SPD). As a result, the curve for this state is extraordinarily steep – the estimated ρ equals 417! The city-state of Hamburg offers evidence of a similar situation.

The increase in comparatively small constituencies that occurred following German unification is considered to be, in the literature, one reason for the frequent appearance of surplus seats. Likewise, a higher probability of 'polarised' seat distribution (100:0) can also be reported from several of the new German states, particularly Saxony-Anhalt and Thuringia. It is also characteristic for the new German states that the estimated function of the modified cube rule crosses the diagonal of perfect proportionality long before the 50 per cent mark of the share of constituency votes. This can especially be attributed to the impact of the large percentage of votes cast for the PDS/*die Linke*. It is hardly surprising to find that the CDU/CSU is particularly successful in the former West German states of Baden-Wurttemberg, Bavaria, and even Rhineland-Palatinate when it comes to winning constituency races. In Hesse, the SPD is more successful, while the states of Lower Saxony, Schleswig-Holstein, and also North Rhine-Westphalia offer an inconsistent picture.

Figure 2.5 (see next page) offers an overview of the sixteen states. Once again, the parties are separately designated with CDU/CSU (*) and SPD (+).[11]

---

11. BB = Brandenburg; BE = Berlin; BW = Baden-Wurttemberg; BY = Bavaria; HB = Bremen; HE = Hesse; HH = Hamburg; MV = Mecklenburg-West Pomerania; NI = Lower Saxony; NW = North Rhine-Westphalia; RP = Rhineland-Palatinate; SH = Schleswig-Holstein; SL = Saarland; SN = Saxony; ST = Saxony-Anhalt; TH = Thuringia.

Figure 2.5: The cube rule in sixteen federal elections – the state level

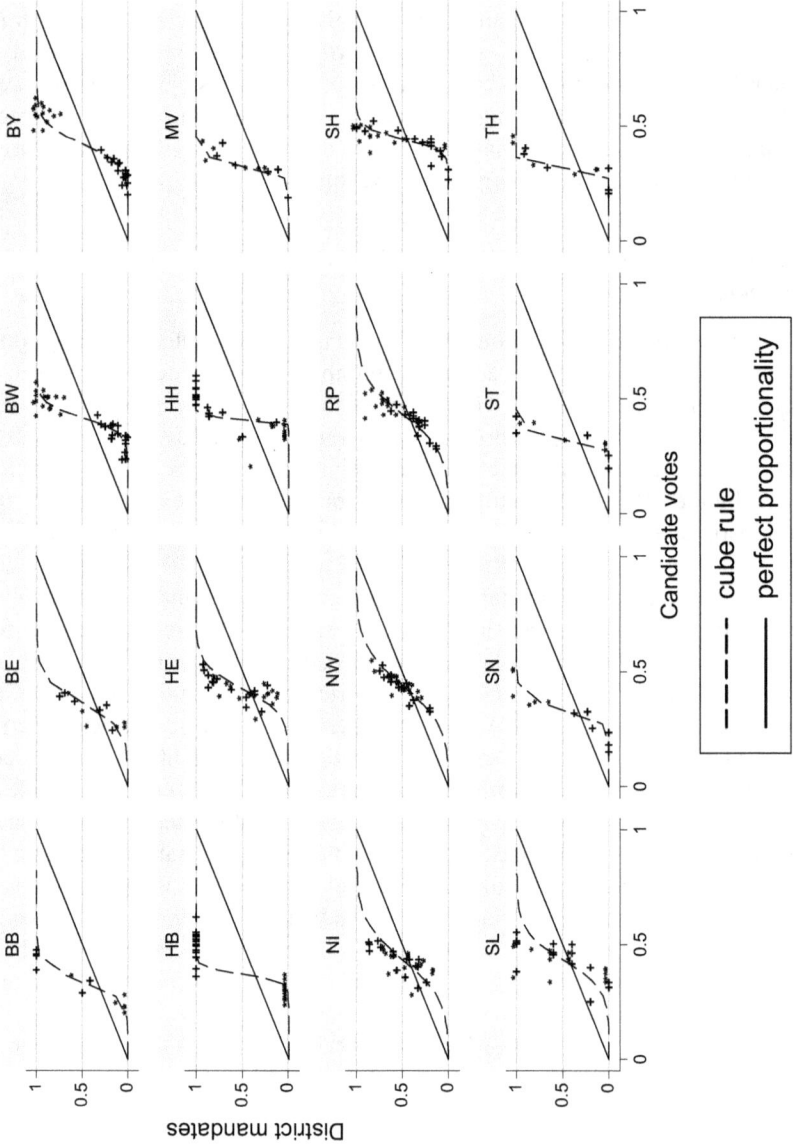

Determinants of Disproportionality – District Size and the Effective Number of Parties

Let us now treat the degree of disproportionality itself as a factor in need of explanation, that is, as a dependent variable. One specific aspect in this two-step regression design needs to be addressed briefly beforehand. In the case of disproportionality, we are dealing with an estimated variable acting as a dependent variable, which in turn is to be estimated as a function of two independent variables: district size and the effective number of parties. One problem with this is the possible heteroscedasticity of the dependent variables that could be caused by different sample sizes, for example (Lewis and Linzer 2005). In the case presented here, state-election parameters are estimated in one case on the basis of thirty-two observations ('old' German states), and in another case, on the basis of only twelve observations ('new' German states). Meanwhile, national-election parameters are based on at least eighteen and at most thirty-two observations. At first glance, one possible solution for the varying accuracy of the estimation would be a Weighted Least Square Regression, in which the (dependent) variable is weighted with the inverse of its standard error. As Lewis and Linzer have shown, this 'cure' is often worse than the actual 'illness' because it treats the entire accuracy of estimates for the second regression as being caused solely by the inaccuracy of estimates for the first regression. Yet a part of the error term of the second regression is genuine uncertainty, which can indeed be homoscedastically distributed (Lewis and Linzer 2005: 346). One of the solutions suggested by Lewis and Linzer consists of an OLS-estimate with heteroscedastic consistent standard errors – a procedure that is particularly applicable when, as in the case at hand, the uncertainty of the estimate of the dependent variable in relation to its variation is not large and does not vary greatly between the samples. Therefore, in the following regressions I will report White's standard errors.

Tables 2.2a and 2.2b show the coefficients of the ρ and β-parameters for the *Bundestag* elections and the German states.

As Figure 2.6 clearly shows, the development of the β-parameter closely corresponds to the effective number of (district) parties from 1953–2009.

We can now regress the β-parameter for each of the *Bundestag* elections and for each state on the average number of parties and the average district size (*see* Table 2.3). With the accession of the new German states, comparably small 'districts' – measured against the number of constituencies/district mandates per state – were added, which lowered the average district size in the *Bundestag* elections starting in 1990. The effective number of parties – measured by the absolute number of constituency votes – developed from 3.7 in 1953, to 2.2 in the 1972 *Bundestag* elections, to 3.7 in the 2009 election. We can run the same for the ρ-parameter (*see* Table 2.4). For the states, I calculated the logarithm of ρ because of the large range of fluctuation of the coefficient caused by certain outlier states (Bremen, Hamburg, Saxony-Anhalt).

Table 2.2a: Estimated ρ and β, Bundestag elections

Election year	ρ (standard error)	B (standard error)
1953	3.679 (0.946)***	0.127 (0.020)***
1957	5.530 (1.322)***	0.112 (0.011)***
1961	7.812 (1.573)***	0.102 (0.007)***
1965	6.805 (1.010)***	0.059 (0.007)***
1969	5.605 (0.723)***	0.049 (0.005)***
1972	5.439 (0.578)***	0.028 (0.005)***
1976	6.855 (1.212)***	0.037 (0.005)***
1980	7.314 (1.393)***	0.047 (0.006)***
1983	9.318 (1.493)***	0.034 (0.004)***
1987	8.057 (1.217)***	0.061 (0.003)***
1990	6.204 (1.424)***	0.094 (0.008)***
1994	6.361 (1.487)***	0.088 (0.008)***
1998	3.590 (1.166)***	0.096 (0.018)
2002	6.760 (1.627)***	0.097 (0.008)***
2005	3.536 (1.013)***	0.125 (0.016)***
2009	6.502 (1.419)***	0.166 (0.074)***

Source: own calculations; * significant at the 10%-level; ** significant at the 5%-level; *** significant at the 1%-level.

Table 2.2b: Estimated ρ and β, German states

German state	ρ (standard error)	B (standard error)
Schleswig-Holstein	12.333 (2.417)***	0.054 (0.004)***
Hamburg	55.339 (16.706)***	0.086 (0.002)***
Lower Saxony	3.497 (0.747)***	0.061 (0.009)***
Bremen	417.125 (0)***	0.118 (0.000)***
North Rhine-Westphalia	3.379 (0.326)***	0.054 (0.004)***
Hesse	5.646 (1.305)***	0.069 (0.008)***
Rhineland-Palatinate	3.363 (0.409)***	0.059 (0.006)***
Baden-Wurttemberg	6.408 (0.907)***	0.074 (0.007)***
Bavaria	3.712 (0.638)***	0.066 (0.017)***
Saarland	5.156 (1.446)***	0.056 (0.012)***
Berlin	6.018 (1.446)***	0.133 (0.008)***
Brandenburg	11.065 (1.943)***	0.157 (0.006)***
Mecklenburg-Western Pomerania	5.859 (1.438)***	0.152 (0.009)***
Saxony	15.442 (4.913)**	0.152 (0.005)***
Saxony-Anhalt	58.219 (31.397)*	0.169 (0.009)***
Thuringia	6.343 (2.126)**	0.165 (0.011)***

Source: own calculations; * significant at the 10%-level; ** significant at the 5%-level; *** significant at the 1%-level.

Figure 2.6: The 'left-shift' of the cube rule curve over sixteen Bundestag *elections*

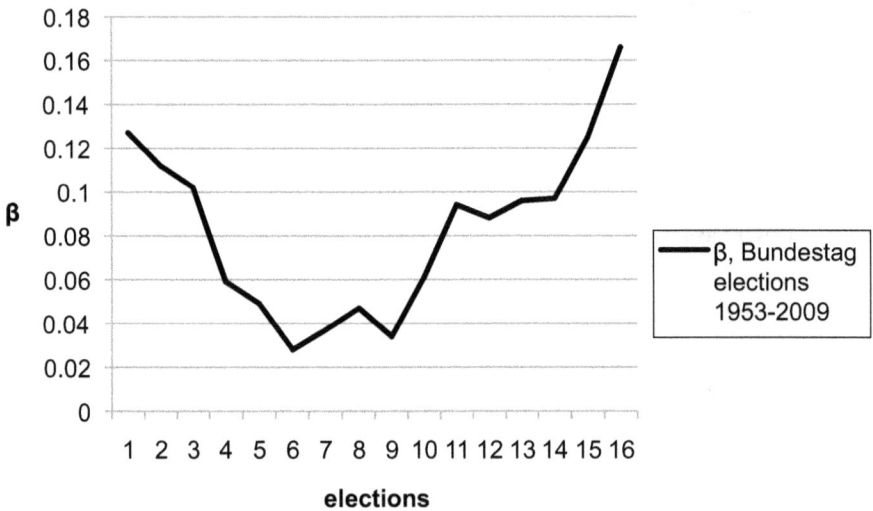

The findings reported in Tables 2.3 and 2.4 are clear-cut. The variable Effective Parties has a very robust and strong influence on the left shift of the cube rule function. When the effective number of parties rises from 2–3, for example, the β increases by 7.5 (*Bundestag* elections) and nine percentage points (German states). Both the β-parameter and the Effective Parties coefficient from Table 2.3 can be interpreted directly. β indicates where the cube rule function crosses the line of a perfectly proportional vote-to-seat ratio. As becomes evident in Table 2.2b, a high percentage of votes won by a strong 'third party' such as the PDS/*die Linke* in the new German states, is reflected in a β that lies well above ten per cent. We can ascertain an increase in this parameter since the mid-1980s when the Green Party established itself in the German party system. It is the effective number of parties that explains the vast amount of the variance of this dependent variable. For the ρ-parameter on the level of the states, the theoretically expected 'arithmetic effect' in the conversion of votes into seats is confirmed – the smaller the district size, that is, the smaller the number of constituencies per German state, the steeper the curve of the cube rule function. In other words, as the number of constituencies increases, the value of ρ decreases, and the slope of the curve for the cube rule function becomes flatter and therefore closer to the diagonal line of perfect proportionality. However, due to the logarithmic calculation of ρ, the coefficient cannot be interpreted directly. Overall, the explanatory power for variance in the disproportionality is less in case of the ρ-parameter than in the case of β.

Generally, the regressions substantiate the presupposition of a strong contamination effect in Germany's mixed election system. In this system, the

Table 2.3: Determinants of disproportionality – the β-parameter (OLS regression)

	β *Bundestag* elections	β German states
EFFECTIVE PARTIES	**0.075**	**0.090**
	(0.000)*	**(0.000)***
DISTRICT SIZE	−0.002	−0.000
	(0.027)**	(0.189)
Constants	−0.079	−0.157
	(0.031)**	(0.000)***
Observations	32	32
Adj. R^2	0.945	0.815

p-values in parentheses; * significant at the 10%-level; ** significant at the 5%-level; *** significant at the 1%-level.

Table 2.4: Determinants of disproportionality – the ρ-parameter (OLS regression)

	ρ *Bundestag* elections	ρ German states (logarithm)
EFFECTIVE PARTIES	−1.69	−0.202
	(0.01)**	(0.693)
DISTRICT SIZE	0.01	**−0.041**
	(0.919)	**(0.012)***
Constants	10.698	3.750
	(0.001)***	(0.051)*
Observations	32	32
Adj. R^2	0.243	0.217

p-values in parentheses; * significant at the 10%-level; ** significant at the 5%-level; *** significant at the 1%-level.

effective number of parties running in each constituency is greater than two because smaller parties also set up constituency candidates in actually hopeless races for district mandates. By doing this, they hope that the presence of the candidates will positively influence their share of the party-list vote (Hainmüller, Kern, and Bechtel 2006; Hainmüller and Kern 2008). As has been shown, the number of participating parties strongly influences the degree of disproportionality, especially in the form of a left shift of the cube rule function. Finally, this also increases the probability of the percentage of district mandates won by a party and its party-list percentage of the vote diverging considerably, which consequently increases the probability that surplus seats will be created.

Therefore, we have identified a contamination effect that has not been taken into consideration in the literature to date: the impact of the effective number of parties on the degree of disproportionality in the plurality component of the electoral system. In previous discussions on contamination effects in mixed member electoral systems, a high number of parties running in a constituency was interpreted *as an indicator* of the mutual influence of the various components in the electoral system (Cox and Schoppa 2002; Herron and Nishikawa 2001; Cappocia 2002), but not *as a variable* itself that has a distinct influence on the election behaviour or the election results in the plurality component.

A Contaminated Cube Rule

It is now appropriate to summarise the findings of this chapter. The previous analysis of the plurality component of Germany's mixed election system has identified two parameters that allow us to make a systematic longitudinal and cross-sectional comparison and with which we can ascertain the way the plurality element works. These two parameters – designated β and ρ – were determined by applying a modified version of the cube rule function to the German election system. They explain the left shift and the slope of the function respectively. As has been demonstrated, they are in turn influenced by two key dimensions of the electoral system: the effective number of parties on the one hand, and district size on the other. Since the effective number of parties competing in a constituency is greater within the plurality component of a mixed election system than it would be in a strict plurality voting system, the β-parameter, which describes the left shift of the cube rule function, is particularly well suited to measure an important contamination effect between the two electoral components.

According to the definition of contamination (see above, page 27), we can speak of both a micro-effect as well as an aggregate effect in the case presented here. On the level of voter behaviour, a greater number of parties evidently leads to a smaller share of district votes for the two major parties at the constituency level. In other words, Duverger's 'psychological effect' – the anticipation that the constituency vote for a small party could be 'wasted' – does not completely neutralise the impact of an increase in the number of parties competing in a constituency. Thus, the proportional representation component clearly influences the plurality component. As an aggregate effect, the larger effective number of parties leads to a greater disproportionality of the plurality vote. In this regard, the two electoral components in the German mixed election system do *not* moderate each other (Shugart and Wattenberg 2001c). Whether the greater disproportionality within the plurality component is actually 'neutral' with regard to the political parties involved, or if the impact differs for the SPD and the CDU/CSU, will be asked in the next chapter (*see* Chapter Three).

Finally, I would like to shortly address a series of implications linked to the finding of 'contaminated disproportionality'. Firstly, the identification of this contamination effect supports a point of view that refuses to consider the German election system simply as being one of proportional representation with a rather insignificant, negligible element of personalisation (e.g. Jesse 1990: 71). Both the PR- and the plurality-component in the German election system function differently than they would without any interaction. Contamination occurs due to party strategies, voter behaviour, and the mechanics of the vote-seat translation that targets the two components of Germany's MMP (Kaiser 2002). In order to understand these interactions better, we have to pay greater attention to the plurality element, which to date has tended to be ignored in political science literature on the German electoral system (but see Behnke 2007; Shikano 2007).

The argument with respect to proportionality, that 'personalized proportional representation does [...] not [differ] from 'simple' proportional representation systems' (Kaiser 2002), or that the German electoral system simply represents 'a more complicated way of getting the same basic PR outcome' (Bawn 1999: 490), has become less and less true in recent elections. The share of surplus seats amounted to roughly four per cent of all parliamentary seats in the 17th, term. Apparently, for the latest elections it was *not* anymore true, that 'only the second vote [that] affects seat shares' (Bawn 1999: 493). This, in turn, should have affected parties' electoral strategies, because with an increase in the number of district seats won, local instead of national pre-electoral coordination, should become more attractive (Ferrara and Herron 2005). Chapter Five will look closer into the relative advantages of local, plurality tier coordination as compared to central, PR tier coordination.

With the recent electoral reform which secures full compensation of surplus seats and, therefore, almost perfect list-vote proportionality (*see* Chapter Ten), parties' calculations have become simpler. Since, if a mixed system

> generate[s] fully proportional outcomes, parties face little incentive to coordinate. Even those parties that have no hope of winning any single-member district [...] are not at all damaged by the electoral formula because the compensatory mechanism guarantees that their total seat share will be proportional to their vote share. Hence, there is no reason for parties to form pre-electoral alliances in the single-member district elections of MMP systems, because the outcome is inconsequential for the maximization of their seat total (Ferrara and Herron 2005: 20; *see* Chapter Five).

Yet, in pre-reform times the higher incidence of surplus seats has less and less resulted in proportional results. How did the parties react?

But before looking at parties' coalitional strategies, I first have to analyse the effect of disproportionality on surplus seats. This issue will be addressed in more detail in the next chapter.

Chapter Three

Of the Cannibalistic Consequences

Twenty-four surplus seats in the election of the 17th German *Bundestag* in 2009 – never has a *Bundestag* election resulted in such a large number of these additional mandates. The foreseeable and very accurately predicted number of surplus seats[1] had rekindled the political (and academic) discussion even prior to the election, especially since, for a long time, it appeared plausible that such mandates could be the decisive factor in determining the governing majority in the new parliament. Specifically the Green party and the SPD called for electoral reform before the election of the 17th *Bundestag*, in particular to avoid a situation where the high number of surplus seats would lead to a 'manufactured majority' (Jesse 2009). A decision by the Federal Constitutional Court stipulated that legislators had to undertake an electoral reform by 2011 to correct for the possibility that more votes for a party might lead to fewer seats (so-called negative voting weight) – a problem linked to surplus seats. However, the discussion on surplus seats had been revived even before the election campaign of the preceding *Bundestag* election. Since the number of these additional mandates have started to increase dramatically – especially following German unification (1990: 6; 1994: 16; 1998: 13; 2002: 5; 2005: 16; 2009: 24) – surplus seats have again become the focus of academic interest, both in political science and law (Naundorf 1996; Mager and Uerpmann 1995; Behnke 2003a, 2003b, 2003c, 2009; Grotz 2000; Fürnberg and Knothe 2009; Jesse 1998; Bücking 1998; Mann 1995; Lang 2014).[2]

In the German mixed member electoral system, surplus seats *ceteris paribus* are becoming more probable as the translation of constituency votes into district mandates becomes more disproportional. If a strong third party exists, a party can win a large number of electoral districts in a state (*Land*) even with a relatively low percentage of constituency votes (Behnke 2003a, 2003c). In many German states, this condition prevails, particularly since reunification (Grotz 2000). Thus, the probability increases that a party gains far more district mandates than it should according to its *share of party-list votes*: the results are surplus seats.

However, a closer look at the disproportionality in the plurality component in the German mixed member electoral system is not only occasioned by the current debate on surplus seats. Regardless of whether or not surplus seats are

---

1.   Behnke's simulation calculations for the 2009 *Bundestag* election, published just prior to the election, predicted an average of 23 surplus seats (Behnke 2009).

2.   In 1990, the year of unification, Eckhard Jesse could still write: 'Surplus seats [...] in practice [...] are very rare' (Jesse 1990: 72; see also Bawn 1999: 489).

created, the issue of disproportionality in plurality voting is of interest as such. As will be shown in the following, it is important for the internal composition of both the largest ruling parliamentary party and the largest oppositional one. Should the gains in constituency votes translate into a disproportional gain in district mandates (and vice versa, losses in constituency votes translate into an over-proportionate loss in district mandates), this is reflected in the internal composition of the parliamentary parties. The one of the two major parties, the CDU/CSU or the SPD, that proves more successful in a *Bundestag* election, is likewise disproportionately successful in winning district mandates. As a rule, this is also the party that will be part of the next government. Thus, the major ruling parliamentary party in the *Bundestag* is made up of a majority of directly elected (i.e. constituency) candidates, while the majority of members of the major oppositional parliamentary party are party-list candidates (below). Amongst others, this implies consequences for the nomination strategies of the parties, which not only have to insure their constituency candidates against vote losses by providing them with safe list rankings, but also have to 'protect' their party-list candidates from the success of their own constituency candidates in the case of vote gains. This consequence of the disproportionality in the plurality component in the German mixed member electoral system will be examined more closely in the following. Chapter Seven will then investigate how parties manage to provide their candidates with this double protection.

In the first part of this chapter, I provide a brief empirical overview over how constituency votes are translated into district mandates in *Bundestag* elections. This description is structured to answer three empirical questions: How has the average share of constituency votes necessary to win a district mandate changed? Over the course of time, have 'polarised' results for constituency votes, in which one party wins all the possible district mandates in a state and the other party none of them, been occurring more often? Does disproportionality also bring about distorting effects in party politics, meaning that it disadvantages or benefits the CDU/CSU or the SPD?

As in the previous chapter, the period studied encompasses all of the 16 *Bundestag* elections between 1953–2009 in which the voters could directly elect candidates from an electoral district with their first vote and state party-lists with their second vote. The very first *Bundestag* election is, again, not included because of its different electoral set-up. Furthermore, I study only the outcomes of the two major parties, which in the vast majority of cases have been in a position to win district mandates – the SPD and the CDU/CSU – and ignore the FDP, the *Grünen*, and the PDS/*die Linke*. Since compensation between first and second votes takes place at the state (*Land*) level, we – as before – have a total of 390 observations (2 parties × ((1 election × 9 states) + (9 elections × 10 states) + (6 elections × 16 states))) = 390 observations see above, Chapter Two).

In the second part of this chapter, I examine the consequences of disproportionality. How does it affect the make-up of the parliamentary parties of both the largest ruling party and the largest oppositional one? How does it influence the safety of party-list and constituency candidatures? Does it impact the occurrence of surplus seats? The question of how parties have reacted to the different degrees of disproportionality (and therefore volatility) in the PR and plurality tier with their nomination strategies is subsequently addressed in more detail in Chapter Four.

The Disproportionality in the Plurality Components of the German Electoral System

As we have seen in the preceding chapter, the cube rule does apply – with an important modification – to the plurality tier of Germany's electoral system.

In order to study the disproportionality of its plurality tier I added an element to the conventional cube rule (3.1) that took into account the non-*Duvergerian* tendency at the district level, i.e. the fact that the number of district parties does not converge into two (cf. Calvo 2009). Formula (3.1) therefore changed into (3.2):

(3.1)
$$\left(\frac{s_i}{1-s_i}\right) = \left(\frac{v_i}{1-v_i}\right)^{\rho}$$

(3.2)
$$\left(\frac{s_i}{1-s_i}\right) = \left(\frac{v_i + \beta}{1-v_i - \beta}\right)^{\rho}$$

Consequently:

(3.3)
$$s_i = \left\{1 + exp\left[-\rho ln\left(\frac{v_i}{1-v_i}\right)\right]\right\}^{-1}$$

Changes into:

(3.4)
$$s_i = \left\{1 + exp\left[-\rho ln\left(\frac{v_i + \beta}{1-v_i - \beta}\right)\right]\right\}^{-1}$$

With the two parameters ρ (rho) and β (beta) we can analyse three dimensions of disproportionality. This analysis takes place not at the national, but at the state level because this is the level the distribution of seats is calculated on, based on the number of second votes won in the state compared to the number of district mandates won there. When we examine the translation of constituency votes into district mandates at the state level, we find two typical deviations from the cube rule that are inherent in the nature of the German electoral system as a mixed system (Manow 2010). These deviations are caused, first, by a steeper slope of the cube rule function (that is, by a larger ρ) at the state level, which is influenced, in particular, by the number of electoral districts in each German state (in the terminology of Taagepera and Shugart, by the 'assembly size'; see Taagepera and Shugart 1989; or in Cox's terms, the size of the 'secondary district'). A second reason is the rapidly rising number of victories in electoral districts where the percentage of first votes is clearly under 50 – because usually more than two parties are competing for the district mandate in the district, or in other words, because Duverger's law only rarely applies, if at all, to the plurality components of the German mixed member electoral system (Cox and Schoppa 2002).

Methodologically, to ensure that the results are not skewed, it is important *not* to estimate each individual parameter of the cube rule function in isolation. An estimation of rho without the simultaneous estimation of beta would produce erroneous values *if* it results in a clear left shift of the cube rule function and/or to a significant partisan bias in the translation of votes to seats (see King 1990; King and Browning 1987). Whether this is the case, can only be determined empirically.

The Majority Cut-off β

Let us now examine the effect of the number of parties on the 'critical majority value' β. According to the hypothesis, the value should be significantly smaller than 50 per cent as the number of parties increase, with the result that a slight

Figure 3.1: Shares of constituency votes and of district mandates for the CDU/CSU and the SPD at the German state level for the Bundestag elections of 1983 and 2009

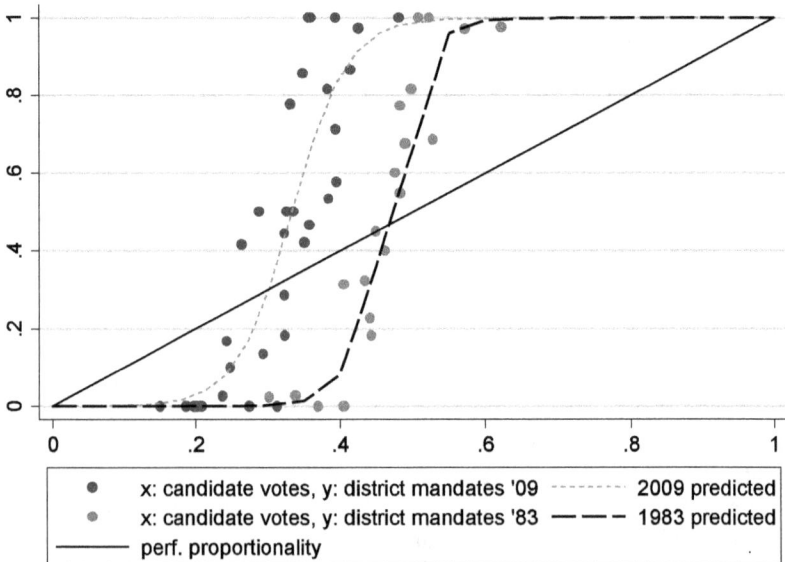

• x: candidate votes, y: district mandates '09	········· 2009 predicted
• x: candidate votes, y: district mandates '83	— — — 1983 predicted
—— perf. proportionality	

increase in the number of constituency votes leads to a considerable gain of district mandates and, a slight decrease, to a considerable loss. The comparison of a 'pre-unification election' (the 1983 *Bundestag* election) with a 'post-unification election' (the 2009 *Bundestag* election) demonstrates the effect of the left shift quite well (*see* Figure 3.1).

Figure 3.1 shows, with utmost clarity, that the average share of constituency votes needed to win a large number of district mandates has dropped considerably over time. Whereas in 1983 the cube rule function dissected the line of perfect proportionality just slightly below the 50 per cent mark of vote share, the crossing point in 2009 is only around the 30 per cent mark. The striking left shift that we observe when comparing these two curves, is verified also from another perspective. When we compare the share of the constituency votes needed to win an electoral district and thus to gain a seat in the *Bundestag*, a clear trend becomes evident. Figure 3.2 compares the density functions of the constituency-vote share of all members of parliament holding a district mandate for two pre-unification *Bundestag* elections, namely, those for the eighth and ninth legislative periods, with the constituency-vote share of all directly elected members of parliament in two post-unification *Bundestag* elections, namely, those for the thirteenth and fourteenth legislative periods.

Figure 3.2: Density functions for the constituency-vote shares of directly elected Bundestag representatives, a comparison of the 8th and 9th legislative periods (1976 and 1980 Bundestag elections) with the 13th and 14th legislative periods (1994 and 1998 Bundestag elections)

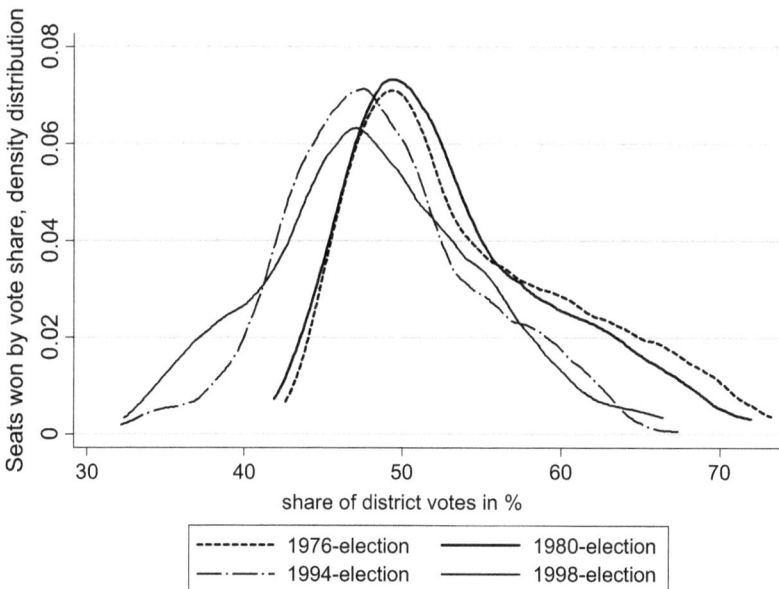

In Figure 3.2, a corresponding 'left shift' for later *Bundestag* elections also becomes clearly evident, which means that mandates in the *Bundestag* are achieved by markedly lower average numbers of constituency votes. In particular, the comparison shows an increase in the number of directly elected representatives whose share of the constituency vote is low, precisely within the realm of 35–45 per cent. At the same time, there is an increase in the dispersion of the constituency-vote share needed to win a *Bundestag* mandate. This also leads to a flatter, broader distribution.

Over the course of the sixteen *Bundestag* elections, the (rounded) beta value drops at first and then rises again (*see* Figure 2.6). β can be interpreted directly. If $\beta = 0$, then the maximal slope of the curve lies at 50 per cent of the constituency vote. A β-value greater than zero indicates a vote share of less than 50 per cent at which ρ reaches its maximal value. Thus the number of (constituency) parties proves to be a very strong and robust explanatory factor for the left shift of the curve (*see* Chapter Two in this volume). Should the effective number of constituency parties increase by 1, β increases by about 0.07–0.08. In the first *Bundestag* elections, the average number of constituency parties was 3.7, in the 1960s and 1970s, 2.2 and in the most recent *Bundestag* elections, 3.7 again.

The soaring increase in the number of surplus seats after 1990 is, among other things, an indication for the peculiarities of the party system in the new German states in the east. There, the vote shares of the two major parties, CDU and SPD, fall noticeably short of the values reached in the old German states in the west because of the position of the PDS/*die Linke* as a strong third party there. Hence, it makes sense to compare the disproportionality between East and West in the *Bundestag* elections starting in 1990 (Figure 3.3).

Figure 3.3 clearly verifies that the third-party effect is particularly pronounced in the new German states due to the strong position of the PDS/*die Linke*. In the comparison of all *Bundestag* elections since 1990, the β-parameter in the new German states is more than twice as high as in the old German states (0.1587–0.0727), whereas the ρ-parameter does not show any differences between East and West (Moser and Scheiner 2012; Herrmann 2012).

In the next section, we ask whether the translation of votes into seats in the plurality components of the German mixed member electoral system is neutral or skewed when it comes to political parties. It has been argued that the CDU/CSU experienced an adverse bias in the 1960s. I will examine whether such an effect can be verified and if it can be substantiated for the subsequent decades.

Is There a Partisan Bias?

Are parties benefitted or handicapped in the plurality components of the German mixed member electoral system? Hermens and Unkelbach (1967) argue that the CDU/CSU suffered a relative disadvantage in the 1960s, but the authors fail

Figure 3.3: The cube rule function for the Bundestag elections 1990–2009, a comparison of the new and old German states

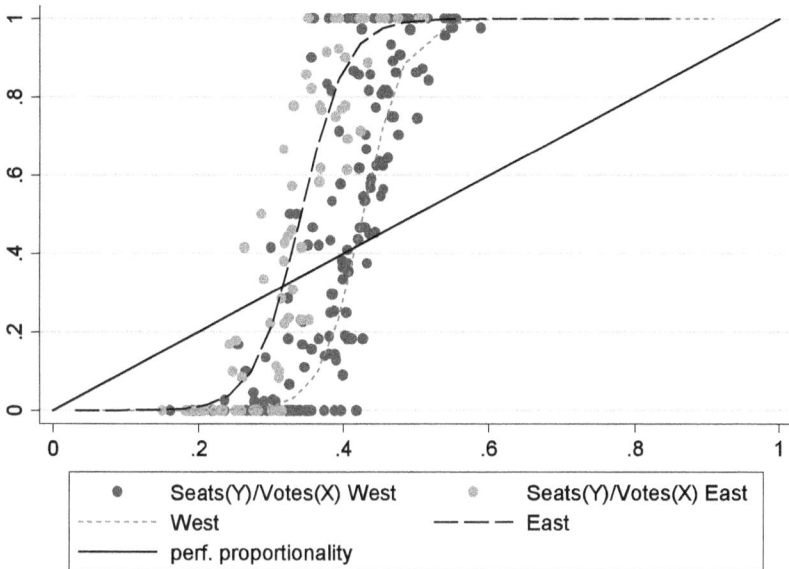

to offer empirical evidence to support their argument. The bias of an electoral system can be caused by the geographical layout of the electoral districts, the varying district sizes (measured by the number of eligible voters), or the regionally unequal distribution of electorates (cf. Rodden 2010; Gudgin and Taylor 2012 [1979]). Since the Federal Election Law requires an automatic adjustment of electoral districts to changes in population numbers (§ 3 Federal Election Law, esp. para. 2, pts. 2 and 3; Schreiber 1994), this determinant of disproportionality should not play a particularly decisive role in the German electoral system. It is to be assumed that the regional differences have a far greater influence in each of the respective electorates.

Partisan biases can be detected by comparing the party-specific cube rule functions for SPD and CDU for all 16 *Bundestag* elections and all German states (estimated on the basis of 195 observations per party; *see* Figure 3.4). If at all, a slight electoral advantage for the SPD over the CDU, that is contrary to expectation, is evident: when the two parties gain the same percentage of constituency votes, the percentage of district mandates won by the SPD is slightly higher than that of the CDU for the entire length of the curve. This finding is confirmed when comparing the average vote share of directly elected MPs of the SPD and the CDU/CSU (*see* Figure 3.5). Earlier findings by Gudgin and Taylor point to the same direction (Gudgin and Taylor 2012 [1979]: 190-192).

Figure 3.4: Partisan bias in the plurality components of the German mixed member electoral system, constituency-vote shares of the CDU/CSU and SPD in the Bundestag elections from 1953 to 2009

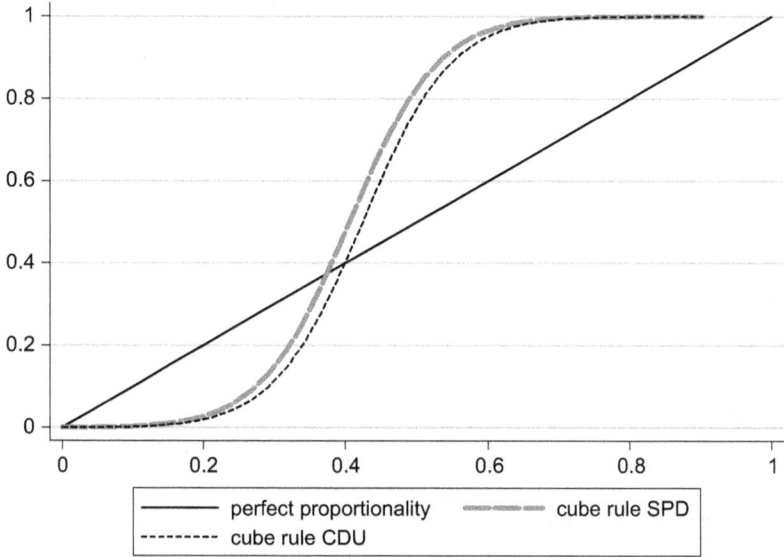

Figure 3.5: Density distributions of district votes, successful district candidatures of CDU/CSU- and SPD-candidates, 1953–2009

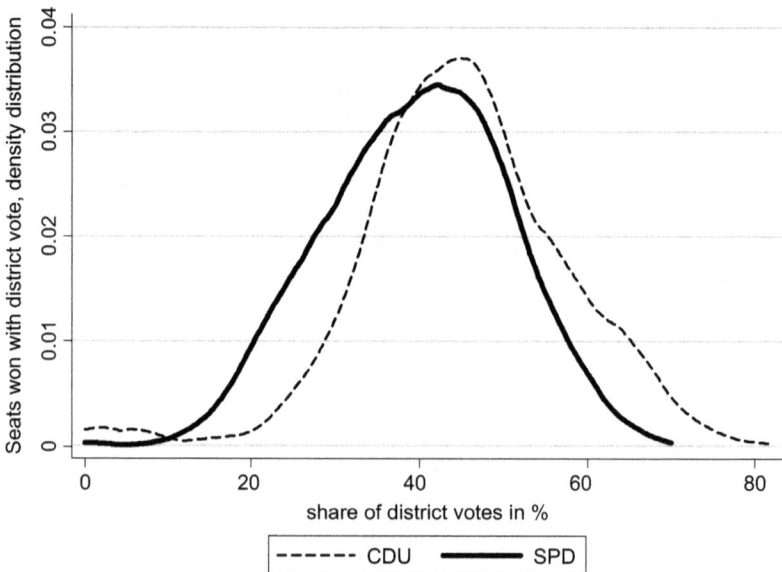

The slope of the cube law function – ρ

A computation of the slope parameter for each of the 16 *Bundestag* elections since 1953 shows no apparent trend over time comparable to that of the β-parameter (above, second section). The only regularity that appears in the comparison of individual *Bundestag* elections is a (rounded) ρ-value of (sometimes well) over 3 (*see* Table 2.2a, above). However, when we compare each individual German state, the results reveal a stronger systematic variance of this parameter (*see* Chapter Two, Table 2.2b, in this volume). As expected, the curve of the cube rule function is very steep especially in states with just a few electoral districts, as in the city-states of Bremen and Hamburg (cf. Taagepera and Shugart 1989, ch. 15). This mirrors the correlation between proportionality and the 'assembly size,' meaning the number of electoral districts per 'secondary district', i.e. the German states (see Cox 1997). At work in the translation of votes into seats, is simply the 'arithmetic effect' briefly explained above (*see* page 14): the higher the number of districts, the better can the vote share be approximated by the seat distribution. Actually, a strong, systematic effect of the number of electoral districts on the slope of the curve is evident in the comparison of the cube rule function *between the German states*. With each additional electoral district, the slope parameter drops by 0.32 (*see* Table 2.2 with ρ varying between 2.9 in North Rhine-Westphalia and 55 in Hamburg).

Once again, this effect is easily demonstrated in a graph (Figure 3.6). When we compare the city-state of Hamburg with North Rhine-Westphalia, we discover a substantial deviation of the slope parameter (with similar β: 8.6

Figure 3.6: The cube rule function for Hamburg and North Rhine-Westphalia for the sixteen Bundestag *elections from 1953–2009*

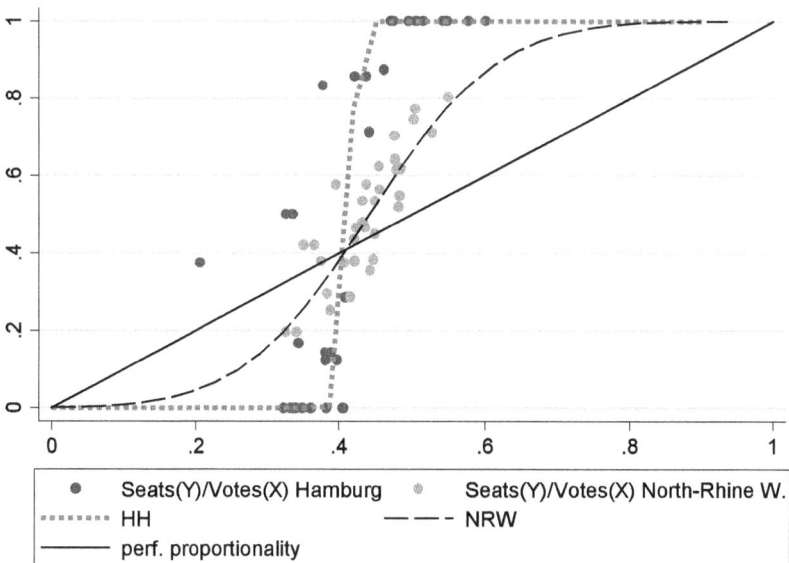

[Hamburg] and 5.8 [NW]). This difference is caused primarily by the number of electoral districts, for which the results of the first and second votes have to be calculated.

When considering the two parameters ρ and β together, my findings can be succinctly summarised by stating that the high number of constituency parties undoubtedly exerts the strongest influence on the disproportionality in the plurality components of the German mixed member electoral system. In particular, this factor has an effect on the left shift of the cube rule function, but not on its slope. In the following section, I address several of the consequences of disproportionality with regard to aspects such as the internal composition of the parliamentary parties or the creation of surplus seats.

Consequences of Disproportionality: Turning Compensation into Cannibalism

As already briefly argued above, one important consequence of a disproportionate translation of votes into seats in the plurality tier has remained largely unaddressed in the literature to date. It regards the make-up of the parliamentary parties in terms of directly elected and party-list candidates in those parties in which district mandates play a role at all, namely, the SPD and the CDU/CSU. If one of the two major parties wins (relative to the others), this vote gain leads to an even greater gain in district mandates (winner's bonus). Since the major party with vote gains has a greater chance of forming the government than the party suffering vote losses, a pattern emerges in which roughly 3/5–2/3 of the members of the major ruling party in parliament are directly elected representatives. On the contrary, the ratio in the major opposition party is exactly the opposite with party-list representatives making up the majority (Manow and Nistor 2009). Figure 3.7 illustrates this development.[3]

The composition of parliamentary parties, in which, on a regular basis, 3/5–2/3 of the seats in the largest governing party are district mandates, has one implication that is rarely noted. It is related to theories of democratic representation. From time to time, authors express sharp criticism about the institution of party-list candidatures, arguing that party-control over list composition minimises voters' influence on who will enter parliament (cf. Armin 2002, 2004). Yet, the leading parliamentary party regularly consists primarily of district MPs. These representatives are, in a very direct sense, responsible to the voters in their constituencies. Complaints about MPs being completely obedient to the party leadership, and generally about politics being out of touch with voters, therefore seem to be exaggerated.

If the largest government party is mainly represented by district candidates, a complementary effect holds for the largest opposition party, which again is rarely noted: In a pure majoritarian system, the party that was defeated in the last election

---

3. The period of the Great Coalition from 2005–2009 has not been included as government participation in the calculation for either party.

Figure 3.7: Percentage of directly elected Bundestag members in each of the respective parliamentary parties for the CDU/CSU and SPD, 2nd–17th legislative periods

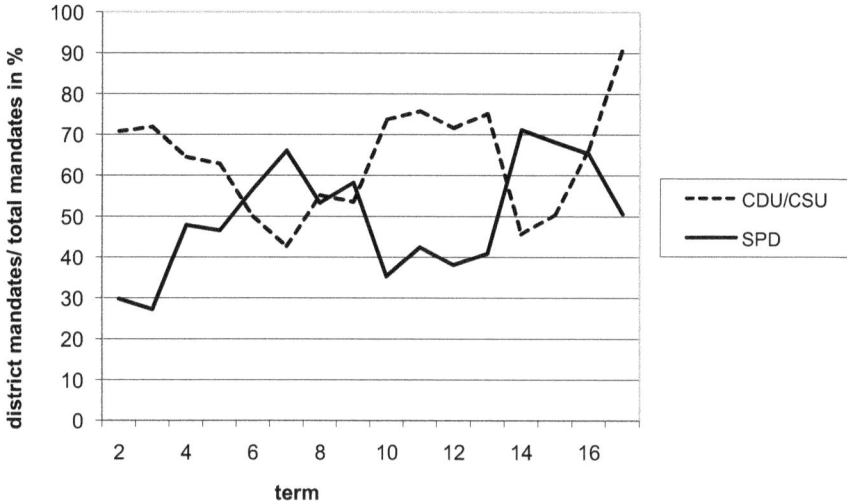

will lose many marginal seats and will only retain its absolute strongholds. As a consequence, the opposition's ideological position will move *away* from the centre and become more extreme – the parliamentary party will consist mainly of the party's ideological die-hards. Jonathan Rodden has described this effect for labour parties as the intra-party conflict between 'suburban moderates' and 'urban radicals' (Rodden 2010, 2011). Take, for example, the British Labour Party. After losing power in 1979, it experienced a longer period of internal strife, a period in which the orthodox party wing, which had been less affected by the lost election than their moderate colleagues, tried to commit the party to a more radical platform. Only after a longer period in opposition, when the party desperately desired to return to government, were the moderates able to gain predominance.

In Germany's mixed-electoral system, this effect is moderated. While the very same logic applies in its plurality tier – the defeated party will only be able to defend its absolute strongholds and will, therefore, *move further away* from the political centre after losing an election – this effect is countered by the change in the overall composition of the largest opposition party: its composition will shift in favour of a considerably larger number of list MPs. Their interests are, however, more closely aligned to those of the party leadership – which wants to regain the median voter it has lost. We therefore would expect that the left needs shorter periods of ideological or programmatic regeneration in opposition in mixed-electoral systems, than it does in majoritarian systems. With respect to the ideological positions of the government's and the opposition's main party, the

Figure 3.8: The polarity of the constituency-vote percentages for the CDU/CSU and SPD, sixteen Bundestag elections (1953–2009), 9–16 German states

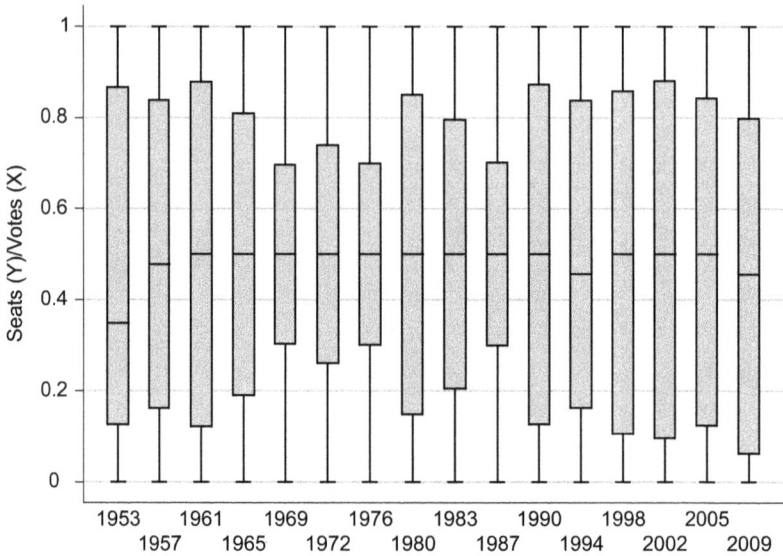

two electoral components in the German mixed election system *do*, in fact, also moderate each other in an ideological sense (Shugart and Wattenberg 2001b).

Another development involves the polarisation in the distribution of district mandates. In cases in which one party can win all the electoral districts, leaving other parties without a single district mandate, it becomes more probable that the percentage of district mandates is more than twice as high as the party-list percentage – a prerequisite for the emergence of surplus seats (Behnke 2007). As the box plot graph in Figure 3.8 shows, this polarisation was quite pronounced in early *Bundestag* elections and appears again in the most recent ones.[4]

An important consequence of the increase in the polarised distribution of district mandates is that it affects parties' nomination strategies. Not only do they have to protect the candidates campaigning for a district mandate against poor election results by also assigning them a promising ranking on the party list, but parties also have to safeguard their party-list candidates against the contingency of good

---

4. In this context it can also be seen that surplus seats usually act as a bonus for the election winner. They enhance the general electoral trend, reward the victor, and offer, thereby, a thoroughly welcome concentration effect. Time and again, such a concentration effect of the electoral results is placed in a favourable light in the discussion on reforming the German electoral system (Linhart 2009: 650, n.47). But it is rarely mentioned in the discussion of surplus seats that they, too, have these effects. Surplus seats are quite exclusively seen as a deplorable breach with the principle of proportionality.

results and the disproportionate success of the parties' own district candidates, by assigning them good districts. With electoral success, compensation turns into cannibalism: a high number of successful district candidates reduce the number of promising list positions. As we have seen, this danger has increased over time, and surplus seats are an indicator of exactly this phenomenon. Therefore, in the light of a possible election victory, parties have to protect their candidates holding top party-list rankings from their own constituency candidates, at best by giving them a double candidature, that is, a party-list candidature *and* a candidature for a district mandate in a relatively 'safe' electoral district. In other words, key party candidates have to be protected against threats from two different scenarios – victory and defeat. Thus, we should expect to see a trend toward an increasing number of double candidatures, an expectation that indeed is verified empirically (Manow and Nistor 2009; *see* Chapter Seven). The importance of the instrument of the double candidacy may be demonstrated by a thought experiment. Imagine its absence – in this case, list-candidates would have an interest in their own party's rather mediocre electoral success, whereas district candidates would want a very strong electoral performance. It is clear that this would put party unity under stress.

Finally, I find it important to establish the connection between the increasing disproportionality in the plurality component of the German mixed member electoral system over time and the appearance of surplus seats. Among the various possible causal factors for surplus seats (Grotz 2000; Behnke 2003c, 2009), the effective number of constituency parties, and thus the β-parameter, are the main focus of interest here. The effect of β is illustrated well in Figure 3.9. In this graph, the German states where that surplus (or overhang) seats occurred are marked with 'Ov'. As can be seen, surplus seats were produced in the 2005 *Bundestag* election especially in places where parties won around 40 per cent of the constituency vote but gained 80 per cent or more of all district mandates. Since, due to vote splitting, the constituency-vote share of the CDU/CSU and the SPD, (the two major parties and the only ones to regularly win district mandates), is higher than their percentage of party-list votes, the discrepancy between the percentage of district mandates and party-list votes (second votes) becomes even larger than the discrepancy between district mandates and constituency votes (first votes) shown in Figure 3.8. Figure 3.9 verifies the rule of thumb that 'surplus seats are produced when a party's share of district mandates among all district mandates is more than twice as great as the party's share of second votes in this German state' (Behnke 2007: 187).

Surplus seats are especially a result of the different vote-seat allocation rules in the German mixed member electoral system, meaning the greater disproportionality in the plurality tier in comparison to proportional representation. However, the difference in the electoral formulas alone does not make surplus seats probable; a further condition that also has to be fulfilled is the presence of a strong third party with a good number of constituency votes. This can help one Party, Party A, to

> win many district mandates over the second-place Party B with only relatively small majorities of the vote. Thus, a surplus mandate for Party A becomes [...] quite possible (Grotz 2000: 713).

Figure 3.9: Percentage of the constituency vote, percentage of district mandates, and surplus seats for the CDU/CSU and the SPD in the 2005 Bundestag elections

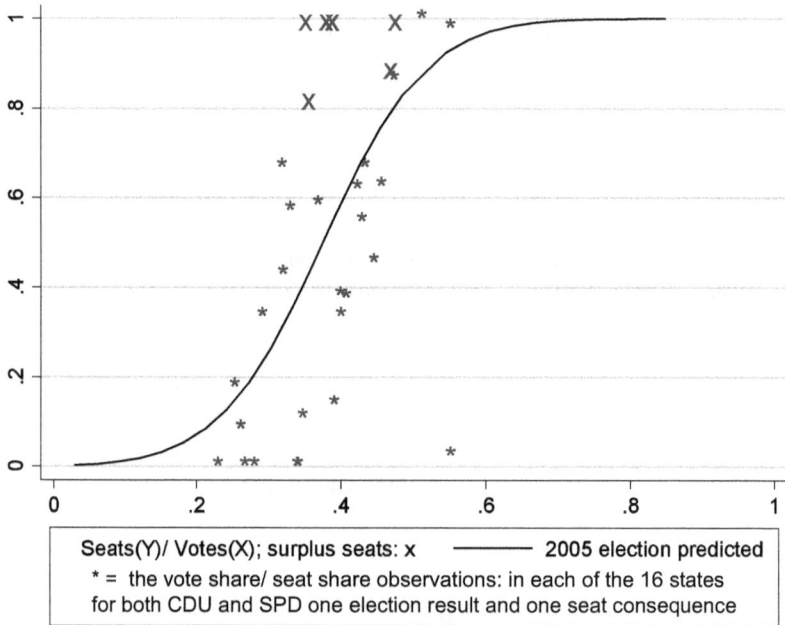

Seats(Y)/ Votes(X); surplus seats: x ——— 2005 election predicted
* = the vote share/ seat share observations: in each of the 16 states
for both CDU and SPD one election result and one seat consequence

The degree of the left shift of the cube rule function, indicating the increase in the effective number of constituency parties, should therefore be a good explanatory factor for the appearance of surplus seats, for the opposite of the above also holds true: if a party wins more than 50 per cent of the party-list vote, then the share of directly elected seats *cannot* lead to surplus seats (Behnke 2003c; Grotz 2000: 713).

In turn, it shows the advantage of measuring disproportionality in the plurality components of the German mixed member electoral system with the parameters of the cube rule function. These parameters are able to determine, precisely, the divergence between the representation in different electoral rules – meaning between proportional representation and majoritarian rule – which Grotz considers to be 'more difficult to operationalize' (Grotz 2000: 719) because, in the case of proportional representation, $\rho = 1$ and $\beta = 0$.

We therefore should consider the β-parameter of the modified cube rule function to be a good predictor for surplus seats. To what degree does this expectation hold true? Before answering this question, we need to keep a methodological point in mind: the dependent variable is a counting variable. It is therefore a discrete, non-continuous, non-negative variable. Moreover, its distribution is characterised by over-dispersion (with variance larger than the mean) (Gelman and Hill 2007: 20–21, 114–118). I therefore cannot estimate the influence of β on the probability of the appearance of surplus seats with a normal

Table 3.1: β as explanatory factor for surplus seats (negative binomial regression)

	Model 1	Model 2
β-German state	**18.389**	**16.804**
	(0.000)*	**(0.010)***
β-*Bundestag* election	**23.082**	**16.905**
	(0.000)*	**(0.028)**
District size		−0.000
		(0.001)***
Voter Turnout		−10.494
		(0.063)*
Vote Splitting		0.000
		(0.067)*
Constants	−5.833	8.554
	(0.000)***	(0.183)
Observations	390	390

p-values in parentheses; * significant at the 10%-level; ** significant at the 5%-level; *** significant at the 1%-level. Pseudo-R^2: = 0.12; Prob > χ^2 = 0.000

OLS regression. Instead, I use a negative binomial regression (*see* Table 3.1).[5] First I look only at the influence of β (Model 1) and then, in a second model specification, I control for other determinants causing the appearance of surplus seats as they are named in the literature: the degree of vote splitting, the differences in election turnout, and the size of the electoral districts, measured by the average number of eligible voters per electoral district (Model 2, see Grotz 2000; Behnke 2003c). The degree of vote splitting is operationalised here as the sum of the absolute values from the differences of the first and second votes for the CDU/CSU, SPD, FDP, *Grüne* and PDS/*die Linke*, divided by the number of parties.

The regression verifies the strong and stable influence of the β-parameter on the occurrence of surplus seats (*see* Table 3.1). When other explanatory factors are included, these two variables still maintain their significance – even though the strength of the coefficients (slightly) decreases. At the same time, all of the assumptions mentioned in the literature on other determinants causing surplus seats (e.g., Grotz 2000) are verified: the probability of surplus seats is increased by a low level of voter turnout, by a high level of vote splitting, and is inversely related to the size of the electoral district as measured by the number of eligible voters. The regression also shows that the common perception that surplus seats are a 'highly unpredictable phenomenon' (Roberts 2000: 196), or

---

5.   A zero-inflated negative binomial comes essentially to the same results.

that 'the exact mechanisms leading to surplus seats are non-predictable due to their multi-factorial causation' (Ministry of the Interior, quoted from BVerfG (95, 335 [1997])[6] is misleading.

Disproportionality in composition and size

Let us now sum up: How are votes translated into seats in the plurality component of the German mixed member electoral system? First (*see* Figure 2.1), regarding constituency votes and district mandates, the pattern of disproportionality of the well-known cube rule is also evident in the German electoral system. However, a closer examination allows the uncovering of considerable deviations from this pattern at the level of the so-called sub-distribution (*Unterverteilung*), that is, at the level of German states where the compensation between first and second votes actually takes place. These deviations are especially pronounced in two ways: first, through the slope of the cube rule function, which is considerably steeper at the state level than at the national level and varies with 'secondary district magnitude', meaning with the number of electoral districts in each state. Second, the increasing left shift of the curve mirrors the development of the German party system from a three-party to a five-party system, particularly since German unification. Since all parties represented in the *Bundestag* usually have their own candidate running for office in each electoral district (*see* Chapters Four and Seven), this increase in the number of parties translates also into a greater number of constituency parties, that is, in parties competing for a district mandate. This raises the disproportionality of the plurality components: a large number of electoral districts can consequently be won with a share of the constituency votes barely over 30 per cent. The comparisons between pre- and post-unification elections (*see* Figure 3.1), between German states with many, and those with few, electoral districts (*see* Figure 3.6), and between the *Bundestag* election results in the East German and West German states after 1990 (*see* Figure 3.3) illustrate the effect of the two parameters influencing disproportionality: the number of electoral districts and the effective number of constituency parties. However, I could not detect any partisan bias in the process of translating votes into seats. Disproportionality is very pronounced in the plurality components of the German electoral system, but it is a 'fair' disproportionality in advantaging neither the Social nor the Christian Democrats (*see* Figure 3.4).

This chapter's second part looked at the consequences of disproportionality, focusing on three key effects: first, the effect on the internal composition of the two major parliamentary parties in the *Bundestag*, that of the SPD and the CDU/CSU, in respect to the type of mandate each representative held (district or party list) and to the status of the parliamentary parties (government or opposition).

---

6. 'Die exakten Wirkungszusammenhänge bei der Entstehung von Überhangmandaten seien angesichts ihrer, multifaktoriellen Ursachen' nicht im Einzelnen vorhersehbar' (quoted from BVerfG 95, 335, III).

The second focus lay on the effect on the nomination strategies used by those parties that regularly win district mandates, namely, the SPD and the CDU/CSU. As was shown, when nominating candidates and anticipating the possibility of electoral defeat, the parties have to protect constituency candidates by giving them also promising party-list rankings. At the same time, however, anticipating the possibility of victory they have to protect their party-list candidates against the success of the party's own constituency candidates. Parties in their nomination strategies need to take into account two scenarios, compensating losers and stopping (district) victors from cannibalising other (list) candidates. I will come back to this in Chapter Seven. Finally, the third focus was on the determinants of surplus seats. As was shown, the larger effective number of constituency parties, as mirrored in a high β of the cube rule function, has a very strong and very robust influence on the probability that surplus seats occur. This influence remains significant when other explanatory factors are taken into consideration (*see* Table 3.1).

In conclusion, I would like to address some implications of this chapter's findings. First, as should have become clear, the German system *is* indeed a mixed member electoral system – even if it has been claimed otherwise from time to time.[7] All told, the effect of the electoral system on the *numerical* composition of the parties at the national level may have largely corresponded with that of proportional representation in its purest form – although the strongly growing number of surplus seats stands for the increasing deviation from proportionality. The way in which each of the electoral components, proportional representation and plurality voting function, however, strongly deviates from the way they work in a system that is strictly proportionally representational or strictly majoritarian. Furthermore, in cases in which the distribution of seats deviates from a purely numerical proportionality – through surplus seats – such deviations are essentially caused by the interaction of the electoral components, namely the difference of the vote-seat allocation formulas in the German mixed member electoral system.

In addition, the chapter's findings also have implications for our understanding of the dominating logic of representation in the German electoral system. In the controversy over the supposed role differences between representatives who are elected directly and those holding party-list mandates (among others, Stratmann and Baur 2002; Lancaster and Patterson 1990; Patzelt 2007; Klingemann and Wessels 2001b) the empirical data reported here tends to support the position that there will be *no* pronounced difference in the roles of these two types of representatives. The importance of double candidatures, the great danger faced by constituency candidates of losing their district mandate even in cases of low vote fluctuation – all this must motivate representatives to keep an eye on the interests of the electoral district *as well as* on the party program. A more direct test of the

---

7.   'The electoral system in West Germany is not – contrary to widespread opinion – a 'mixed system' but proportional representation' (Jesse 1990: 71).

mandate-divide thesis, holding that members of parliament elected in the district should apply different parliamentary and electoral strategies than those elected via the party-list, however, will be postponed for the moment (*see* Chapter Eight). Rather, I will ask, next, why small parties contest districts even if they have no chance of winning them. It is to this question that I would like to turn now.

Chapter Four

Contesting Districts: Why small parties enter (hopeless) district races

The two preceding chapters have linked the increasing disproportionality in the plurality component of the German electoral system to the increasing number of district parties. A high effective number of parties is a feature that indicates a 'contamination' effect of the majoritarian tier and the PR tier in a mixed member electoral system (Cox and Schoppa 2002; Ferrara, Herron, and Nishikawa 2005b). In mixed member electoral systems, small parties enter majoritarian district races although they usually have no chance of winning them. The contamination literature argues that small parties contest districts, rather, with the expectation to improve their PR-vote share:

> By running a candidate in SMD, particularly if the candidate is experienced, popular, telegenic, or charismatic, the party can advertise its platform more widely, enhance voter awareness of its program, increase its visibility, attract greater attention to its policy objectives, and potentially gain more votes in the PR component of the election by drawing the support of voters who would not have voted for the party otherwise (Ferrara et al. 2005b: 37).

Duvergerian tendencies within the plurality tier are trumped by vote-maximising objectives in the PR-tier.

However, as of yet, we lack robust empirical evidence that small parties' district candidates do indeed help boost the party's PR-vote share. This has at least been true for the prototype and oldest example of a mixed member electoral system, the German one. Our lack of direct evidence for a positive impact of a party's candidature for a district on the PR-vote share, is largely due to the fact that German small parties almost always nominate own candidates for every district. This renders it impossible to compare small parties' vote shares in districts with and without own candidates. Without variance in the independent variable, i.e. district candidatures, we cannot measure effects on the dependent variable, i.e. small parties' PR-vote share at the district level.

In this chapter I propose to circumvent this problem by measuring the effects of what I would like to call 'quasi-incumbency'. With quasi-incumbency, I refer to one specific feature of the German electoral system, namely the possibility to run in a district and on a party list simultaneously (so called dual candidacies; *Doppelkandidaturen*). Given that almost all MPs of small parties are elected into parliament via the PR-tier of the electoral system but simultaneously contest a district, I claim that we should expect quasi-incumbency advantages to become visible and measurable in those districts in which small parties were represented by a *member of parliament*, as compared to those districts in which they were represented with just a 'simple' candidate. In accordance with the incumbency-advantage literature, I assume that quasi-incumbents, as compared to 'simple' candidates, can serve their district better and build up a reputation in the local constituency, have higher media-presence and political visibility and, therefore, enjoy better chances of making themselves known among their electorate. I therefore propose to compare small parties' PR-vote shares in districts in which these parties were represented by a member of parliament, to those districts in which they were not. I claim that if we should find systematic evidence that quasi-incumbency matters, we can infer that the simple presence of a candidate should also have an effect on the party's district PR-vote share, since in both cases the causal mechanism is identical: with district candidates, voters can link a face to the party and its program, and district campaigns and constituency services of various kinds should positively influence a party's PR-vote share at the district level.

The chapter proceeds as follows. First, I briefly rehearse some of the arguments about contamination effects in mixed member electoral systems. I will also briefly describe the candidature nomination procedure in the German electoral system with a special emphasis on the possibility of double candidatures, i.e. on the possibility to run both as a district and as a list candidate (second section). In the third section, I describe my data, which covers the time period from 2002–2009 for the small liberal party (*Freie Demokratische Partei*, FDP) and the small Green party (*Die Grünen*), with around 600 observations for each. The restriction to the last three elections is due to the major re-districting process that took place in 2002 and that makes comparisons between the 1990s and 2000s problematic. I concentrate on those two parties since they have not managed to win more than four districts over the last forty years (one district for the FDP in 1990 and one for the Green party in 2002, 2005 and 2009). In other words: although these parties have an only negligible chance of winning a plurality of votes in one of the – currently – 299 electoral districts of Germany, they, nevertheless, nominate own candidates for each district in every election. In the fourth section, I analyse the PR-vote effect of SMD candidatures of members of parliament in the case of the liberal and the Green party. I control for the potential endogeneity of my results with a Regression Discontinuity Design (cf. Hainmülller and Kern 2008; Lee 2008) and by running a fixed effects model.

Contamination and quasi-incumbency

Recent literature has begun to address the so-called 'contamination effects' in mixed member electoral systems, i.e. effects of the PR-tier of the electoral system on the majoritarian tier and vice versa (Ferrara and Herron 2005: 39; Ferrara, Herron, and Nishikawa 2005b; Cox and Schoppa 2002; Shugart 2001b, 2001a; Shugart and Wattenberg 2001c; Herron and Nishikawa 2001). A prominent argument in this literature runs as follows: in electoral systems which combine list-PR and plurality in single-member districts, the *Duvergerian* tendency toward a two-party contest under majoritarian rules is muted by the fact that small parties enter district races even though they have no chance of winning them. Why do small parties enter hopeless district races? They enter with the intention 'to give their party a human face they can use to boost the party's vote totals' (Cox and Schoppa 2002: 1031). Ferrara, Herron and Nishikawa (2005b) concur:

> By nominating a candidate in SMD, a party can attract greater attention to its policy objectives and hence receive a substantial vote bonus in the PR component of the election by drawing the support of voters who would have otherwise voted for the other list. In turn, the boost that parties can expect to receive by running their own SMD candidate provides them with an incentive to participate in majoritarian races regardless of their chances of winning a district (Ferrara, Herron, and Nishikawa 2005b: 13; Ferrara and Herron 2005: 20).

As a consequence, the number of parties participating in majoritarian electoral competitions at the district level tends to be higher in mixed member electoral systems. This is the case because competition does not seem to be constrained by 'the logic of Duverger's law to the same extent that it is in pure first-past-the-post elections' (Ferrara, Herron, and Nishikawa 2005b: 13; cf. Herron and Nishikawa 2001). In fact, the higher number of district parties in mixed member electoral systems has itself been taken as evidence for the existence of contamination effects (Herron and Nishikawa 2001; Cox and Schoppa 2002).

The behaviour of small parties would hence represent a prototypical case of contamination: in a mixed member electoral system, small parties behave differently in the plurality tier compared to how they would *otherwise*, in a pure plurality system, behave because small parties anticipate the effects that their behaviour has for their performance in the PR-tier of the electoral system (see Ferrara, Herron, and Nishikawa 2005b: 9). Yet to date, the literature has mainly come up with indirect evidence for contamination effects at the aggregate level only (higher effective number of district parties) without empirically proving at the micro level that joining a district race does indeed pay off for the entering (small) party.

Empirical evidence at the micro-level is hard to provide, exactly because it is very rare for small parties in mixed member electoral systems *not* to enter district races (*see* Table 4.1) – presumably because they anticipate that SMD candidates might improve their PR vote (Cox and Schoppa 2002). This, however, is an unsatisfactory response to the question since it takes the lack of evidence for the nexus between entry and vote boost as proof of its existence. Yet, estimating 'contamination effects caused by the presence of district candidates is only possible if parties run candidates in some but not all districts. [...] the identification of treatment effects becomes impossible without variation in the treatment variable'

(Hainmüller and Kern 2008: 215). Studies therefore have often rather claimed, than actually demonstrated, that district races affect the PR vote share, since it proved impossible to compare small parties' PR-vote share in districts with and without candidates.

For instance, Cox and Schoppa state in their study of contamination that they would have preferred to estimate the candidature effects at the district level in Germany, yet 'this was not possible [...] because of the way parties [...] have responded to the incentives by interaction effects. Exactly as we anticipated [...] German parties have consistently run SMD candidates everywhere, even when their candidates have had no chances of winning' (Cox and Schoppa 2002: 1035). Similarly, Ferrara, Herron and Nishikawa state that they could not measure district effects on the PR-tier because parties 'placed candidates in most SMD races, precluding an effective comparison between their PR performance in the presence and absence of affiliated candidates' (Ferrara, Herron, and Nishikawa 2005b: 41).

As a solution to this problem, Ferrara *et al.* went back as far as to the German elections in 1953 and evaluated the effects of district candidatures on the PR-vote for such small and marginal parties as the *Bayern Partei* (BP), the *Deutsche Partei* (DP), the *Deutsche Reichspartei* (DRP) or the *Zentrum* – parties, which in this early election did not run candidates in every electoral district (Ferrara, Herron, and Nishikawa 2005b: 152, note 17). Ferrara *et al.* claim to have found micro-level evidence for contamination – at least in this single election – in three of their four cases (2005b: 45, Table 3.2; but see below). Hainmüller and Kern (2008) show, in their important analysis of incumbency effects on parties' PR-vote share at the district level, that these effects do indeed exist. Yet, this fails to solve our problem since – as Hainmüller and Kern concede – they 'cannot estimate incumbency effects for small parties such as the Greens and Liberals, because these parties never win districts seats' (2008: 221). Therefore they only show that district incumbency affects the PR-vote share for the two major German parties, the Christian Democrats and the Social Democrats. However, it is the small parties for which the contamination literature predicts the non-*Duvergerian* behaviour to enter district races without much hope of winning them (cf. Moser and Scheiner 2012: 55). That small parties almost never have district incumbents is the very reason why this chapter proposes to measure quasi-incumbency effects in order to identify small parties' PR-tier electoral payoff from their participation in the competition for district seats.

As this brief literature review shows, apart from the weak evidence provided by Ferrara *et al.*, we still lack conclusive evidence for exactly the type of party which – according to the contamination literature – should show different 'district behaviour' in a mixed member electoral system as compared to a purely majoritarian one, namely small parties. Cox and Schoppa simply take the impossibility of measuring such an effect as proof of its existence. Ferrara, Herron and Nishikawa detect such effects only for some marginal parties in the very first election in which German voters could cast two votes, a plurality vote at the district level and a PR-vote for one of the party lists.[1] Yet, we have strong reasons to suspect that their study mainly measures differences in parties' regional strength and *not* contamination effects (see below, third section). Finally, Hainmüller and Kern, in their important study on incumbency effects on PR votes, restrict their analysis to parties that succeed in winning districts, whereas I want to find out whether we can verify that *small* parties gain in the PR-tier of the electoral system when they enter hopeless SMD-races. Much of the empirical evidence for the presence of candidature-contamination effects is, therefore, still based on findings from rather young, and rather unstable, party systems like the Russian or like the post-1992 Italian one (Herron and Nishikawa 2001; Ferrara, Herron, and Nishikawa 2005b).

I therefore propose to test the contamination thesis for the German electoral system in an indirect way. I will examine particularly those districts in which small parties were represented by candidates who (via the party list) had already been elected into parliament in the previous term. In other words, I use one distinctive feature of the German electoral system, namely the possibility of double mandates, to assess how the SMD race might affect PR-vote shares for small parties. As stated above, although candidates of small parties almost never win district races,[2] almost all small parties' list candidates also run in a district. Parties expect candidates to campaign in their district and – after having been elected into the *Bundestag* – they expect MPs to engage in constituency service and to 'shadow' the directly elected district representative. In Germany 'all parliamentary parties […] see to it that deputies are assigned to constituency service regardless of which tier they are elected from' (Klingemann and Wessels 2001b: 291; Patzelt 2007: 83; Lundberg 2007; Saalfeld 2005: 219). This introduces an element of district competition between constituency- and list-representatives (Lundberg 2007: 49; Patzelt 2007). Candidates have strong incentives to meet their party's expectations, since being placed on a promising list position depends on a proven record of campaigning at the district level and of devoting a substantial amount of time to constituency work. This explains the fact that the time that double listed MPs declare to spend on constituency work does not differ substantially between directly elected candidates and those who entered parliament via the party list (cf. Patzelt 2007: 55, Table 3).

All this enables us to compare small parties' PR-vote shares in two types of districts: districts in which a small party is represented by a 'simple' candidate and districts in which the small party's candidate actually has been a member of parliament during the previous term, since he or she had been elected into parliament via the party's list vote. In districts, in which small parties have

---

1.   In the first *Bundestag* election in 1949 voters had only one vote, which simultaneously determined the district candidate and parliament's partisan complexion.

2.   It was in 1990 that the Liberals won their last district seat under the rather unusual circumstance of German unification. In the three decades before the 1990 elections, the FDP had never won a single seat, yet placed candidates in each and every district at each and every election. The Greens managed to win a district seat in Berlin in the 2002 election, and the candidate (Hans-Christian Ströbele) was re-elected in 2005 and 2009.

been represented by a MP, that member of parliament had comparatively more opportunities and resources for making herself widely known – i.e. to connect the party and its policies 'with a human face'. Hence, I hypothesise that if the simple placement of candidates in Single Member Districts allows parties to improve their performance in the PR-tier due to the publicity of the candidate, this 'human face'-effect should be even more pronounced in those districts where this candidate is a MP and thus more prominent. Members of parliament have more resources, enjoy better media presence, and better opportunities to deliver goodies to their home- or in this case 'quasi-home'-district (cf. Lancaster 1986; Stratmann and Baur 2002). In brief, 'if the mere presence of a district candidate has a positive effect on her party's PR vote share in her district, it seems plausible to expect incumbency to have an even bigger effect' (Hainmülller and Kern 2008: 214).

Previous work has already confirmed that district incumbents in Germany's mixed member electoral system enjoy electoral advantages. Bawn showed incumbency status to matter for candidates' nominal votes in Germany's mixed member electoral system (Bawn 1999). As she demonstrated, the candidate vote gap, i.e. the difference between the party's and the candidate's vote share at the district level, is larger when the candidate had been a member of the previous parliament and when she belonged to one of the governing parties (Bawn 1999: 494, 498; Gschwend 2007). Hainmüller and Kern demonstrate, for both the Social and the Christian Democratic party, (usually the sole German parties that can realistically hope to win district races), that incumbency status also affects these (German) parties' PR-vote shares (Hainmülller and Kern 2008). In the following section I present empirical evidence that quasi-incumbency matters for small parties' PR-vote share as well.

Candidate selection and the incentives for double candidatures in Germany's mixed member electoral system

Table 4.1 demonstrates why we cannot simply compare districts with and without small parties' candidates in order to identify candidate effects: the number of districts in which small parties like the Liberals or the Green party were *not* present with own candidates is simply much too small. In fact, focusing on the period from 1965–2009, the Liberals failed to present district candidates in only five out of the potential 3,617 districts over all 13 elections falling into this period. In per cent, they did not run own candidates in only 0.14 per cent of all cases. Whereas the number for the Green party is considerably higher (N = 128 uncontested districts since 1980 out of a total of 2,625 potential districts, which roughly equals ≈ five per cent of all 'contestable' districts), almost two thirds (N = 74) of these cases were due to the exceptional circumstances of German unification when the Green party – in contrast to the Liberals – had no established partner party in former East-Germany to merge with. The Green party, therefore, could not present candidates for all of the East-German districts in the German elections after

Table 4.1: Share of contested districts, Liberals and Green Party

	I	II	III	IV	V
Election	Total number of districts	Number of districts with FDP candidates	Number of districts with Green candidates	Coverage FDP in % (II/I)	Coverage Green party in % (III/I)
1965	248	248		100.0	
1969	248	248		100.0	
1972	248	248		100.0	
1976	248	248		100.0	
1980	248	248	228	100.0	91.9
1983	248	248	244	100.0	98.4
1987	248	248	247	100.0	99.6
1990	328	328	254	100.0	77.4
1994	328	324	309	98.8	94.2
1998	328	327	325	99.7	99.1
2002	299	299	297	100.0	99.3
2005	299	299	297	100.0	99.3
2009	299	299	296	100.0	99.0
2013	299	298	299	99.6	100.0

Source: Bundeswahlleiter 2013, Table 1.3.

unification in 1990 (*see* Table 4.1). A poor representation of the Green party in the east, however, largely reflects differences in regional party strength and in the Green's organisational entrenchment in the early years after German unification. Therefore we can draw only very limited inferences from these 74 cases of uncontested districts for the research question of interest here.

Exactly the same problem of regional differences in party strength complicates the analysis of early federal elections in Germany (see Ferrara *et al.* 2005b). To circumvent the problem of 'no variance in the independent variable', Federico Ferrara and his co-authors went back to the 1953 *Bundestag* election in order to study the electoral performance of small parties which were present in some, but not in all, of the 242 electoral districts in this election. They analyse the electoral performance of four parties, the *Bayernpartei* (BP), the *Deutsche Partei* (DP), the *Deutsche Reichspartei* (DRP) and the *Zentrum* (Ferrara, Herron, and Nishikawa 2005b: 152, endnote 17) and claim to have found evidence for a positive effect of a party's district presence on the PR-tier votes in three of their four cases. Closer inspection reveals, however, that Ferrara *et al.* mainly measure differences in regional party strength, rather than small parties' district candidature effects.

Whereas the authors are well aware of the problem of endogeneity caused by the tendency of party leaders to 'nominate candidates in districts where they know that their party enjoys a high level of popularity, rendering candidate placement at least partially endogenous to the model' (Ferrara, Herron, and Nishikawa 2005b: 39; see Moser and Scheiner 2012: 54–55), they – unfortunately – do not control for endogeneity in their German case study. Yet, regional disparities in electoral support affect their German data heavily. As already indicated by its name, the *Bayernpartei* ran own district candidates only in its regional strongholds, in the thirty-four Bavarian districts, while not fielding candidates in the rest of Germany. Nomination strategies therefore were clearly *not* 'characterised by enough variation in the placement of SMD candidates to yield meaningful results' (Ferrara, Herron, and Nishikawa 2005b): 41) and, according to the authors' own criteria, this party should not have been included in the analysis. Even more surprising is the inclusion of the *Zentrum*, given that the Center Party in the 1953 election contested only one single district in the whole of Germany (district nb. 87, *Oberhausen*). Needless to say, it is simply impossible to draw any inference by comparing the *Zentrum's* electoral performance in this single district with the party's performance in the other 241 where it had not been present.[3] This holds true even more when taking into account that the one candidature of a *Zentrum* candidate was the result of pre-electoral coordination with the Christian Democrats, who agreed to field no own candidate in this district (*see* for more on this the next chapter, Chapter Five). This points to yet another problem that renders Ferrara *et al.*'s identification of candidacy effects in the German 1953 election: we know about forty-seven cases of pre-electoral coordination at the district level in the election in 1953, i.e. in about 20 per cent of all districts. In almost all of them, parties of the centre-right (*Zentrum*, DP, DRP and CDU) formed alliances against the Social Democrats. Failing to control for parties' pre-electoral coordination, risks getting severely biased results (cf. Chapter Five).

Discarding the *Zentrum* and the *Bayernpartei* because of the reasons displayed above, leaves us with only two out of Ferrara *et al.*'s original four cases, the *Deutsche Partei* and the *Deutsche Reichspartei*, which in 1953 ran own candidates in 189 and sixty-one (of the 242) districts, respectively. But the evidence in these cases points to a regionally highly uneven followership. The *Deutsche Reichspartei* (DRP) and its predecessor, the *Deutsche Konservative Partei*, for instance, were parties established in the British occupation zone only. Not surprisingly, we can identify clear geographical clusters when looking at the districts in which the DRP ran own candidates (*see* Figure 4.1; black districts are those with DRP-candidates). The same holds true for the *Deutsche Partei* (DP), given that this party, 'despite its ambitious name, was mostly a remnant of the old *Deutsche Hannoverische Partei* that had long embodied Hanoverian resentment against the forced incorporation of their kingdom into Prussia' (Massicotte forthcoming, ch. 3: 14).

---

3. The inclusion of the *Zentrum* party in their study is hard to reconcile with the authors' claim that they excluded parties that 'did not run candidates in enough districts' (Ferrara, Herron and Nishikawa 2005b: 41).

Figure 4.1: 1953 federal elections, districts with DRP candidates

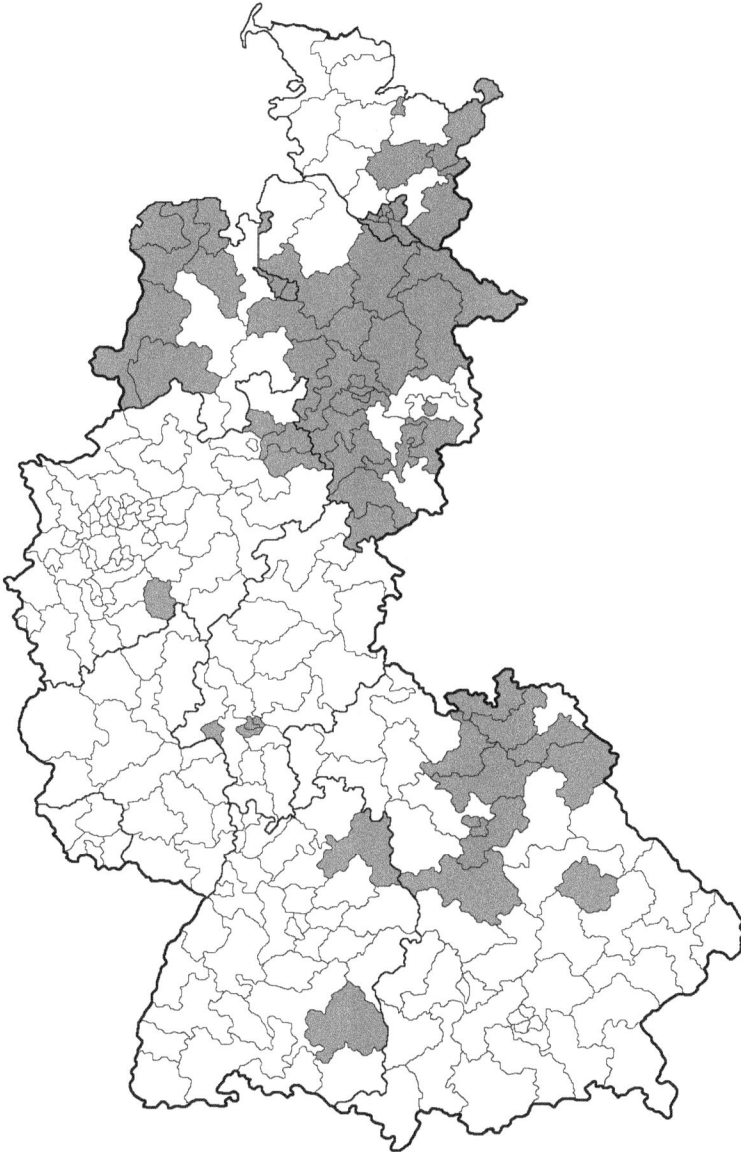

As can be seen from Figures 4.1–4.4, at least for the DRP, we have very strong evidence for potential endogeneity: electoral strength and the regional pattern of candidatures correlate highly.

Figure 4.2: 1953 federal elections, districts with DP candidates

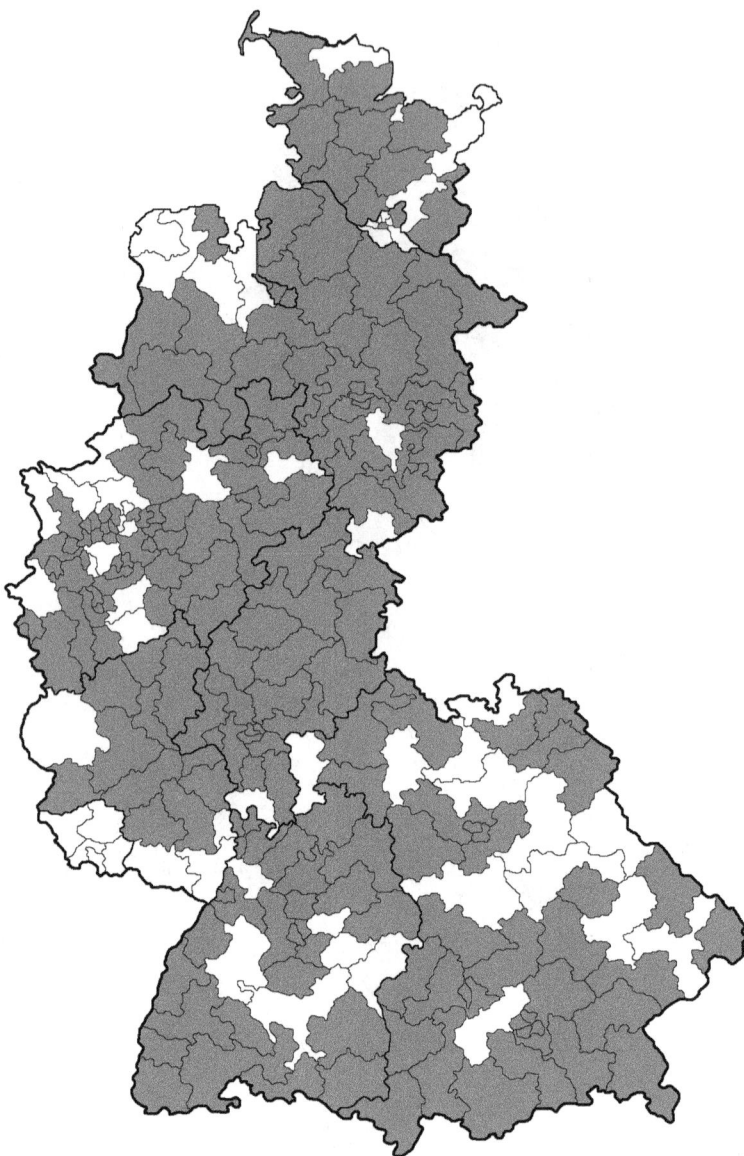

Figure 4.3: 1953 federal elections, elections results of the DRP

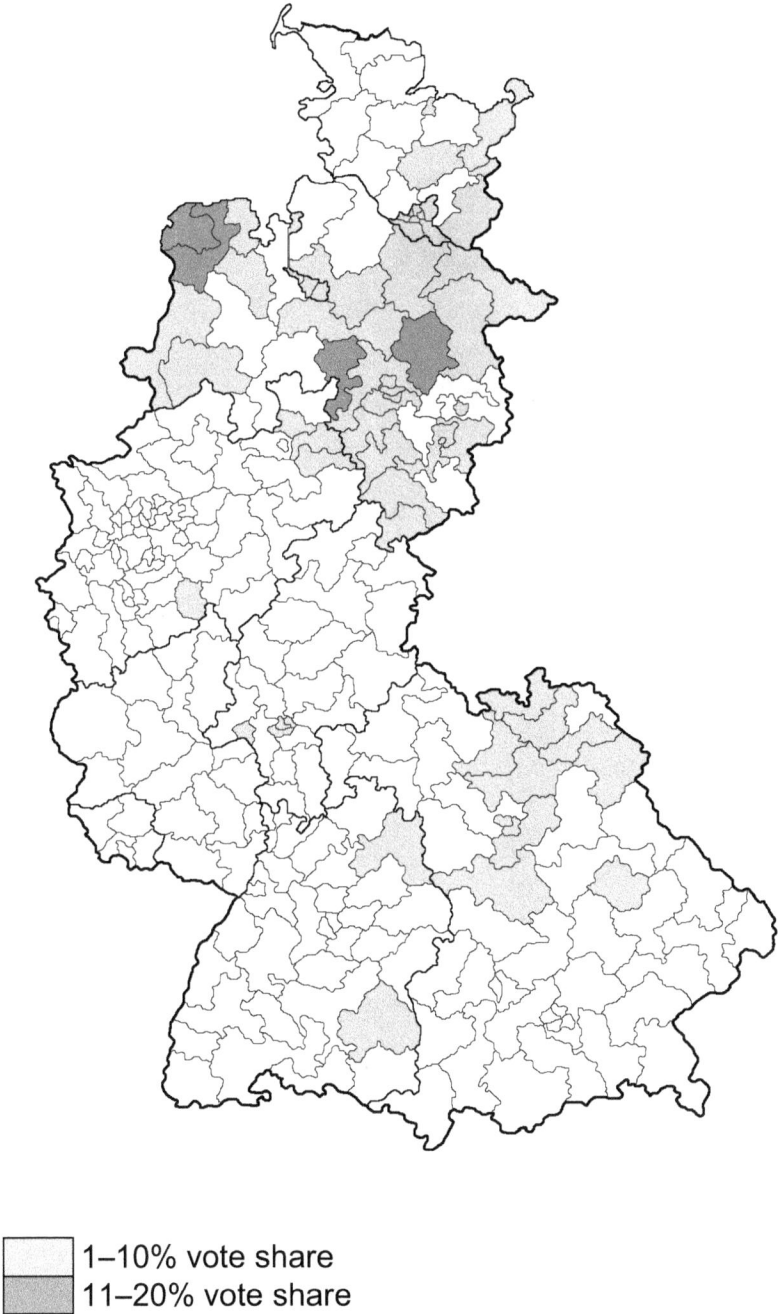

1–10% vote share
11–20% vote share

Figure 4.4: 1953 federal elections, elections results of the DP

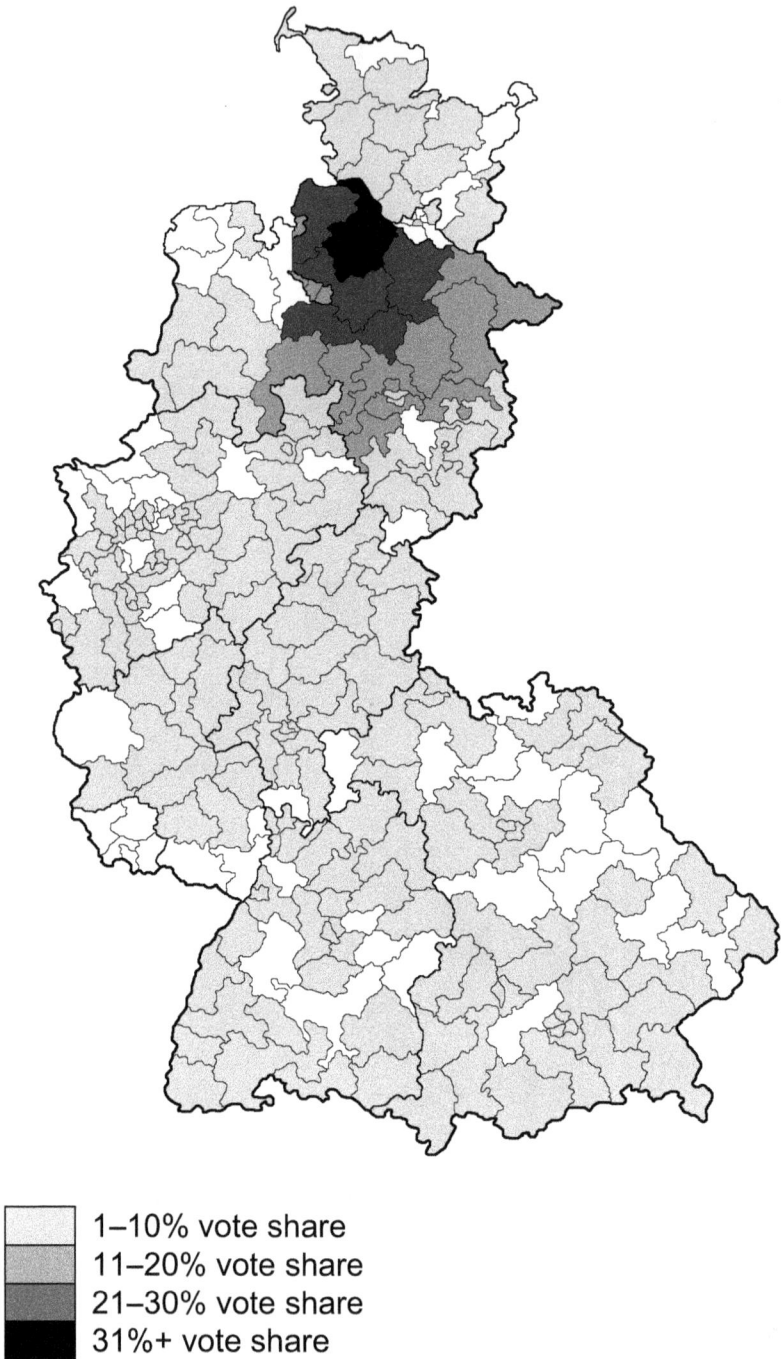

1–10% vote share
11–20% vote share
21–30% vote share
31%+ vote share

In the following, I replicate the Ferrara *et al.* study for the *Deutsche Partei* and the *Deutsche Reichspartei*. I include both the 1953 and the 1957 elections, since in both elections the two parties contested some, but not all districts.[4] I also code all cases of electoral coordination in which the DP and DRP were involved – twenty-five in the 1953 election and twelve in 1957 (Schindler 1984: 108–109). Including the 1957 election increases the number of observations from 242–489 and also allows me to run a fixed effects model that controls for district characteristics. Table 4.2a replicates the study by Ferrara *et al.* with, and without controlling for the cases of pre-electoral coordination. Table 4.2b reports the findings of the fixed-effects regression.

Table 4.2a demonstrates how crucial it is to control for pre-electoral coordination. Especially in the case of the *Deutsche Partei*, the results change drastically and the overall model fit improves significantly once we account for those cases in which the DP (and DRP) agreed on district alliances – predominantly – with the Christian Democrats, but also with other parties of the centre-right. The simple OLS results seem to strongly confirm contamination effects, but once I control for district characteristics in a fixed-effects model (Table 4.2b), we see that most of the variation is explained by the parties' different regional strongholds. Although the candidacy-variable remains significant, the measured effects – especially in the case of the *Deutsche Reichspartei* – are quite weak with only half a percentage point.

To sum up these findings: in one, maybe in two of the four cases analysed by Ferrara, Herron and Nishikawa, we find some evidence in support of the contamination hypotheses – regarding elections more than fifty years ago and two marginal parties that have long vanished from the German party system. The question is whether we can provide more conclusive and contemporary evidence for the existence of contamination? For this I propose to study the effects of 'quasi-incumbency'. It is one specific feature of the German electoral system that makes this analysis possible: the dual candidature. I will briefly explain what is meant by this.

As Tables 4.3 and 4.4 reveal, in Germany a very high percentage of candidates, and an even higher percentage of actually elected members of parliament, ran both in a district and on a list. The share of those actually elected to the parliament who ran a double candidacy is almost 100 per cent in the case of the Liberal Party. After a somewhat lesser coverage in the early years, the same now holds true for the Green party. This allows us to compare district level PR-vote shares in those districts in which small parties' (list) candidates had been members of parliament in the previous term with those district level PR-vote shares where the district candidates had not. This is exactly the variance we need to test the contamination hypothesis without using a more direct measurement, i.e. the comparison of vote shares in districts with and without own candidates. For both cases, small parties'

---

4. The *DP* was, in 1953, present in 189 of 242 districts and in 1957, in 229 of 247 districts. The *DRP* was present in sixty-one of 242 districts in 1953 and in 228 of 247 districts in 1957.

Table 4.2a: Candidate effects for the Deutsche Reichspartei and the Deutsche Partei in the 1953 elections

	PR-vote at the district level for the *DRP*	PR-vote at the district level for the *DP*	PR-vote at the district level for the *DRP*	PR-vote at the district level for the *DP*
DISTRICT CANDIDACY	2.167	1.920	1.870	4.419
	(0.000)***	(0.018)**	(0.000)***	(0.000)***
PRE-ELECTORAL COORDINATION			1.158	9.827
			(0.000)***	(0.000)***
Constant	0.547	1.780	0.503	−1.186
	(0.000)***	(0.013)**	(0.000)***	(0.077)*
Observations	242	242	242	242
Adjusted R-squared	0.305	0.019	0.340	0.306

p-values in parentheses; * significant at the 10%-level; ** significant at the 5%-level; *** significant at the 1%-level.

Table 4.2b: Candidate effects for the Deutsche Reichspartei and the Deutsche Partei in the 1953 and 1957 elections, a fixed-effects model

	PR-vote at the district level for the DRP	PR-vote at the district level for the DP
DISTRICT CANDIDACY	0.556	1.290
	(0.000)***	(0.000)***
PRE-ELECTORAL COORDINATION	1.322	1.882
	(0.000)***	(0.000)***
Constant	0.639	2.127
	(0.000)***	(0.000)***
Observations	489	489
Number of districts/ units	247	247

p-values in parentheses; * significant at the 10%-level; ** significant at the 5%-level; *** significant at the 1%-level.

vote shares in districts represented by a list-MP and the vote share in districts not represented, I calculate the difference between the district level- and the regional level-PR vote shares. A positive coefficient would indicate that quasi-incumbency has an electoral payoff.

Table 4.3: Share of Liberal (FDP) and Green district candidates with a dual mandate

Election year	Number of FDP district candidates	Number of those with a dual mandate	Number of Green district candidates	Number of those with a dual mandate	dual mandates FDP in %	dual mandates Greens in %
1949	236	114			48.3	
1953	224	151			67.4	
1957	247	179			72.5	
1961	247	190			76.9	
1965	248	177			71.4	
1969	248	199			80.2	
1972	248	202			81.5	
1976	248	193			77.8	
1980	248	204	228	92	82.3	40.4
1983	248	213	244	130	85.9	53.3
1987	248	221	247	106	89.1	42.9
1990	328	286	254	97	87.2	38.2
1994	324	257	309	146	79.3	47.2
1998	327	250	325	180	76.5	55.4
2002	299	247	297	150	82.6	50.5
2005	299	264	297	169	88.3	56.9
2009	299	267	296	155	89.3	52.4

Source: Own calculations from (Vierhaus and Herbst 2003), (Manow and Flemming 2011b) and (Bundeswahlleiter 2009)

This research design allows me to avoid a couple of methodological problems that studies in this field regularly face. Most importantly, strategic entry or exit does not affect my results. In the case of small parties, the probability of entry into or withdrawal from a district does not depend on the expected chances of winning that district. Both the Liberals and the Greens almost always entered district races although their candidates almost never had even a remote chance of winning them. This study's research design is also not haunted by problems caused by the interdependence of multiparty election results (Tomz, Tucker, and Wittenberg 2002; Katz and King 1999), since I compare vote share *differentials* of one and the same party between different types of districts, those with a MP as candidate and those with 'normal' candidates. Differentials are calculated with respect to the party's average district vote share (at the regional level).[5] Moreover, I focus on

---

5. Taking average vote shares at the state level already accounts for regional differences in party strength and therefore gives a more prudent estimate for quasi-incumbency effects than the national average vote share would.

Table 4.4: Liberal (FDP) and Green MPs with a dual candidacy

Election year	Number of FDP MPs (+ substitutes)	Number of those with a dual mandate	Number of Green MPs (+ substitutes)	Number of those with a dual mandate	FDP MPs with dual mandates in %	Green MPs with dual mandates in %
1949	62	49			79	
1953	55	48			87	
1957	46	45			98	
1961	71	67			94	
1965	54	54			100	
1969	36	36			100	
1972	48	47			98	
1976	43	43			100	
1980	58	57			98	
1983	35	35	53	39	100	74
1987	48	48	47	42	100	89
1990	83	82			99	
1994	48	47	50	49	98	98
1998	45	45	50	49	100	98
2002	47	46	55	53	98	96
2005	61	57	50	48	93	96
2009	95	93	71	69	98	97

Source: Own calculations from (Vierhaus and Herbst 2003) and (Manow and Flemming 2011b)

two parties only, the Liberals and the Green party, and only very rarely do MPs of the Liberals and the Greens run for the same district. It is the data for these two parties that I would like to turn to now.

Data and empirical evidence

The following analysis is based on almost 600 observations for each of the Green party (*Die Grünen*) and the FDP (*Freie Demokratische Partei*),[6] comprising the elections of 2002, 2005 and 2009. Due to a major re-districting process in 2002, we cannot compare terms before and after 1998. Election data at the district level were provided by the German statistical office, information about list- and

---

6.   In the case of the Green party, incumbency effects can first be measured for the 1987 election, since the party entered the *Bundestag* for the first time in 1983.

Table 4.5: 'Quasi-incumbents' as district candidates and the party's district PR-vote share, Liberal Party (2002–2009) – OLS regression

Liberal Party	District PR-vote share		District PR-vote share
Candidate incumbency	0.040	Party incumbency	0.010
	(0.000)***		(0.018)**
Constant	0.119	Constant	0.120
	(0.000)***		(0.000)***
Observations	598	Observations	598
Adjusted R^2	0.067	Adjusted R^2	0.008

p-values in parentheses; * significant at the 10%-level; ** significant at the 5%-level; *** significant at the 1%-level.

Table 4.6: 'Quasi-incumbents' as district candidates and the party's district PR-vote share, the Green party (2002-2009) – OLS regression

Green Party	District PR-vote share		District PR-vote share
Candidate incumbency	0.046	Party incumbency	0.013
	(0.000)***		(0.003)***
Constant	0.090	Constant	0.091
	(0.000)***		(0.000)***
Observations	594	Observations	594
Adjusted R^2	0.076	Adjusted R^2	0.013

p-values in parentheses; * significant at the 10%-level; ** significant at the 5%-level; *** significant at the 1%-level

district-candidatures comes from the biographical handbook of the Members of Parliament and from an own data-source (Vierhaus and Herbst 2003; Flemming and Manow 2011b). To capture the effects of candidates who had already been elected to the German *Bundestag* in the preceding election, I coded dummy variables for quasi-incumbency for those districts in which green and liberal MPs ran (also) as district candidates (incumbent). I coded both party- and candidate-incumbency. I ran a conventional OLS-regression. Tables 4.5 and 4.6 display the impact of party- and candidate incumbency for the Liberal and the Green party, respectively.

The results for both parties in Table 4.5 and 4.6 are very similar. All coefficients are positive and significant. Substantially, candidate incumbency has an average vote share effect of around four to five per cent, while party-incumbency has a significantly weaker effect, around 1 per cent. As we can see from Tables 4.5 and 4.6, it does indeed make a systematic difference which type of candidate runs in a district. This is first *direct* evidence for systematic contamination effects between the plurality and the PR tier in the German mixed member electoral system *for small parties*. It is advantageous for small parties to be present with an incumbent or quasi-incumbent because it does help to boost their PR-vote shares. Given that these effects of quasi-incumbency have to be added to the already existent effect of 'mere presence' when small parties enter district races (which we cannot measure), the effect size can be considered substantial.

Concerning the strength of the effect, we also have to keep in mind how enormously important each percentage point is for a small party with which it can move away from the five per cent electoral PR tier threshold. Any percentage point above this threshold secures parliamentary survival and dilutes voters' worries about possibly wasting their vote. Since the quasi-incumbency effect has to be attributed to the same mechanisms that also make a small party candidate's sheer presence in a district electorally profitable, we can infer from these findings that entering district contests has generally a positive impact on the PR-vote share of small parties.

However, these regression results also suffer from the endogeneity-problem that haunts all studies in this field: do parties garner particular support where they nominate candidates [MPs] or do they nominate candidates [MPs] where they enjoy particular support? I cannot completely rule out that a party might want to 'reward' districts in which it is strong by nominating MPs as candidates in them, thereby allowing a more prominent and possibly more efficient representation of district interests in national politics. But with a regression discontinuity design (RDD) I can test whether this problem of endogeneity affects my findings (Lee 2008; Imbens and Lemieux 2008; Hainmülller and Kern 2008). RDD allows us to compare 'marginal districts' that should resemble each other in all dimensions that might affect a party's relative electoral strength except in that one dimension of theoretical interest, i.e. incumbency.

The logic of a regression discontinuity design for our context is straightforward:

> Based on the assumption that parties do not exert perfect control over their observed vote shares, incumbents that barely won a race should be similar in their distribution of observed and unobserved confounders to non-incumbents that barely lost. This provides us with a naturally occurring counterfactual exploitable for causal inference under a weaker set of assumptions than conventional regression designs commonly used in the incumbency literature (Hainmülller and Kern 2005: 1).

Very much like in a natural experiment, the assignment of the treatment, here a successful race for a seat in parliament, is almost random. RDD's basic methodological consideration is that if actors have no *precise* control over 'the assignment variable' – in our case over the election of a candidate – then comparing districts just below the cut-off and just above the cut-off, i.e. districts with candidates on the last successful and on the first unsuccessful list rank, comes very close to local randomisation (Lee and Lemieux 2010). A party may want to 'reward' districts in which it enjoys particular electoral support by running candidates in them on promising list positions, so that voters can expect to be represented with an 'own' MP in the next parliament. But given that a party has no perfect control over electoral outcomes, districts in which the candidate of a small party narrowly made it into parliament, and districts in which he or she narrowly failed to make it, should be very 'similar in their distribution of observed and unobserved confounders'. In particular, it seems safe to assume that they are similar with respect to the extent of political support enjoyed by that particular party, the variable potentially causing endogeneity in our context. Any remaining differences in PR-vote shares *in the subsequent election* between those two types of marginal districts should, then, be attributable to the difference in the treatment variable only, namely whether an MP as a shadow incumbent could, or could not, have helped to increase the party's district PR-vote share through active constituency service, higher media presence and the like.

To address the endogeneity problem, I apply a RDD framework in the analysis of district PR-vote shares for liberal and green candidates since 2002. The sample comprises all candidates of these two small parties with dual candidacies over three terms, which translates into 270–510 observations. Restricting my analysis to the post-2002 elections is due to the major redistricting that took place after 1998, which renders district comparisons beyond this time period problematic.[7] The RDD framework asks for a variable that allows identifying marginal districts. I computed a 'margin of victory'-variable by taking the last list rank on which candidates were still elected into parliament as my cut-off. My margin-of-victory variable is a transformed list position-variable, generated by subtracting from each list rank the last list position that brought a candidate of this party into parliament and multiplying it with -1. This creates a 'margin of victory'-variable with all successful list positions in the positive, all unsuccessful in the negative and the last successful list rank equalling zero. My treatment variable again is incumbent, coded as party incumbency. It reports whether an MP had represented the liberal party in the district in the term prior to the election analysed.

But before reporting the results of the local regression, I start with some graphical presentations. They help to visualise the relation between the outcome and the treatment variable, in particular helping to identify a jump in the outcome variable around the cut-off point. The graphical presentation also helps to understand the basic logic of RDD, by pointing to the importance of the functional form that we assume for the relation between the dependent and the independent variable (here the party's PR-vote share in the district is reported on the y-axis and

---

7. For the Greens a pre-1998 analysis is further complicated by the party's unstable record of *Bundestag* membership. 1983 saw the party's first *Bundestag* appearance, so the first election for which we could possibly detect (quasi-)incumbency effects is the one in 1987. However, the party failed to return to the *Bundestag* in the following elections by missing the five per cent electoral threshold (with a 4.4 per cent share of the national PR-vote). Only eight delegates from *Bündnis 90* from the new eastern states were elected due to the temporary lifting of the five per cent hurdle for the new Eastern German states in the 'unification elections' of 1990.

Figure 4.5: Regression discontinuity for candidates of the Green party, below the cut-off districts with candidates on unsuccessful list ranks, above the cut-off districts with candidates on successful list ranks, Bundestag elections from 2002–2009

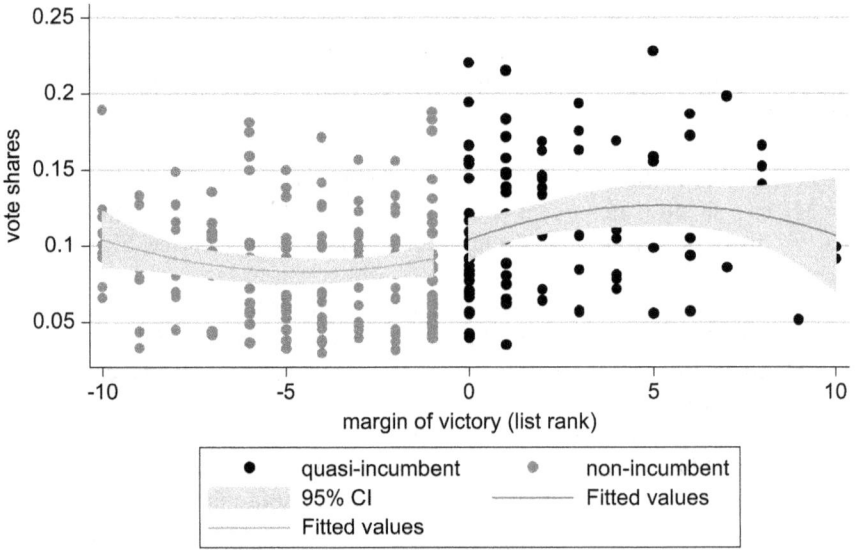

the list rank of small parties' candidates with a cut-off at the last successful list rank, is reported on the x-axis).

Both graphs suggest a possible jump at the cut-off point. I will investigate this jump more closely in the following.

To be very flexible with respect to the functional form of the MoV-variable, I consider 2nd, 3rd and 4th order polynomials, plus the interaction terms with the incumbency dummy (Imbens and Lemieux 2008; Lee 2008; Hainmüller and Kern 2008) without and with a bandwidth of ten observations. A regression equation (as a 4th order polynomial) therefore would look like this:

$District\ PR\text{-}vote\ share_t = Margin\text{-}of\text{-}Victory_{t-1} + MoV^2_{t-1} + MoV^3_{t-1} + MoV^4_{t-1} + Quasi\text{-}Incumbent_{t-1} + QI*MoV_{t-1} + QI*MoV^2_{t-1} + QI*MoV^3_{t-1} + QI*MoV^4_{t-1}$

The QI = quasi-incumbency could be either party- or candidate-incumbency. The coefficient of the incumbent-variable gives us the pure marginal vote effect of (quasi-)incumbency in a district, since the 'margin-of-victory'- variable turns to zero in marginal districts, so all interaction terms turn to zero, too. Table 4.7 displays the results of the RDD-estimation for liberal candidates, Table 4.8 provides the results of the identical RDD-analysis for the Green party, again, for the 2002–2009 time span. For both parties, I ran 16 different specifications, from a simple linear regression to the 4th polynomial for both party- and

Figure 4.6: Regression discontinuity for candidates of the Liberal party, below the cut-off districts with candidates on unsuccessful list ranks, above the cut-off districts with candidates on successful list ranks, Bundestag elections from 2002–2009

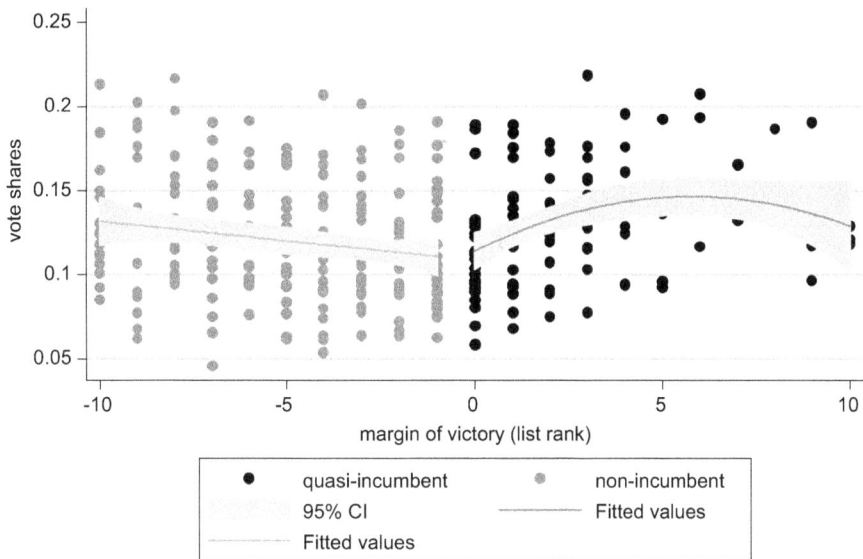

candidate-incumbency with and without a bandwidth of ten observations on both sides of the cut-off point. Results are very robust under all specifications. The incumbency coefficient is always positive and, with only a few exceptions, also significant. The effects vary – for the FDP between 1.4 and 4.3 per cent, for the Greens between 0.5 and 3.6 per cent. Coefficients are therefore in the same range as in the simple OLS. The RDD also confirms the difference between party- and candidate-incumbency, with the latter having a stronger effect throughout. These results point to 'personalisation': the effect on a party's district vote does indeed seem to be largely caused by the person running in it.

In other words, a comparison also of the 'last successful' with the 'first unsuccessful' district in terms of their parliamentary representation, i.e. a comparison of districts that in all other relevant dimensions should resemble each other, produces evidence for the existence of quasi-incumbency effects. In fact, given that incumbency should affect the PR-vote share only in addition to the 'mere-presence'-effect, incumbency appears astoundingly strong in its electoral impact of between three and four percentage points for the candidate effect (*see* Table 4.7 and 4.8).

A comparison between the findings in Table 4.7 and 4.8 also confirms the OLS analysis above in that all regressions find a stronger effect for the FDP than for the Green party. This might have to do with the fact that the Greens are particularly strong in those city-states like Berlin, Hamburg or Bremen where the notion of a

Table 4.7: A regression-discontinuity analysis of quasi-incumbency effects, Liberal candidates, 2002–2009 (15th, 16th, and 17th term)

#/Nb.	Model	sample N	Coefficient at cut-off	p-value
	Party Incumbency/ no bandwidth			
1	Regression	511	.0156	.001
2	Regression 2nd polynomial	511	.0137	.008
3	Regression 3rd polynomial	511	.0151	.010
4	Regression 4th polynomial	511	.0173	.005
	Party incumbency/ bandwidth +/−10			
5	Regression	312	.0149	.006
6	Regression 2nd polynomial	312	.0103	
7	Regression 3rd polynomial	312	.0058	
8	Regression 4th polynomial	312	.006	
	Candidate incumbency / no bandwidth			
9	Regression	511	.0399	.000
10	Regression 2nd polynomial	511	.0381	.020
11	Regression 3rd polynomial	511	.0359	.003
12	Regression 4th polynomial	511	.0403	.001
	Candidate incumbency / bandwidth +/−10			
13	Regression	312	.0406	.000
14	Regression 2nd polynomial	312	.0429	.000
15	Regression 3rd polynomial	312	.0323	.022
16	Regression 4th polynomial	312	.0414	.040

'district' and constituency service for a particular neighbourhood within the city might become elusive. The weaker results in the case of the Green party might also have something to do with the Greens' 'social movement'-background, with their strong aversion against a 'personalisation' and professionalisation of politics and their 'direct democracy'-leanings. According to a party decision in the early 1980s, the entire parliamentary party was supposed to change in the middle of their first term (so-called '*Rotationsprinzip*') with members of parliament resigning and list-candidates substituting them at mid-term. This limited the maximum period of constituency service during the 1983–1987 terms to two years only and may, alone, have made incumbency effects in the subsequent elections unlikely. With the failure to re-enter parliament in 1990 and a landslide victory in 1998, the party's presence in many districts might simply have been too unstable to allow for long-term investments into reputation or pork-barrel politics. Even though, I do find positive effects, both for MPs being present and having been present in a district also for the Green party's PR-vote share.

Table 4.8: A regression-discontinuity analysis of quasi-incumbency effects, Green candidates, 2002–2009 (15th, 16th, and 17th term)

#/ Nb.	Model	sample N	Coefficient at cut-off	p-value
	Party incumbency without bandwidth			
1	Regression	319	.0138	.014
2	Regression 2nd polynomial	319	.0145	.02
3	Regression 3rd polynomial	319	.0160	.022
4	Regression 4th polynomial	319	.0136	.051
	Party incumbency with bandwidth +/−10			
5	Regression	273	.0141	.023
6	Regression 2nd polynomial	273	.0137	.064
7	Regression 3rd polynomial	273	.0082	
8	Regression 4th polynomial	273	.0054	
	Candidate incumbency without bandwidth			
9	Regression	319	.0324	.000
10	Regression 2nd polynomial	319	.0326	.000
11	Regression 3rd polynomial	319	.0322	.003
12	Regression 4th polynomial	319	.0297	.006
	Candidate incumbency with bandwidth +/−10			
13	Regression	273	.0325	.001
14	Regression 2nd polynomial	273	.0355	.000
15	Regression 3rd polynomial	273	.0286	.01
16	Regression 4th polynomial	273	.0292	.01

A final objection may be raised against the analysis above. While the RDD-design is crucial in ruling out endogeneity, one could object that the results above are only based on a relatively small number of observations, i.e. marginal districts. I finally rerun the OLS-regression that identified quasi-incumbency effects both for the Liberal and the Green party (Tables 4.5 and 4.6) as a fixed-effects model, which controls for district characteristics. As Tables 4.9a and 4.9b show, the coefficients remain robust and are mainly in the same range as found previously (with the exception of party-effects for the Greens).

Contamination between the PR- and the plurality-tier

This chapter has provided robust empirical evidence that small parties do receive direct electoral payoff from entering district races with own candidates. To my knowledge it is the first study to provide such evidence. The contamination literature's plausible assumption that small parties enter district races to boost their

Table 4.9a: Quasi-incumbency effects for the Liberal party, 2002–2009, a fixed-effects model

	District PR-vote share		District PR-vote share
Candidate incumbency	0.047	Party incumbency	0.010
	(0.000)***		(0.076)*
Constant	0.118	Constant	0.119
	(0.000)***		(0.000)***
Observations	598	Observations	598
Units/ districts	299	Units/ districts	299
Adjusted R-squared	−0.794	Adjusted R-squared	−0.982

p-values in parentheses; * significant at the 10%-level; ** significant at the 5%-level; *** significant at the 1%-level.

Table 4.9b: Quasi-incumbency effects for the Green Party, 2002–2009, a fixed-effects model

	District PR-vote share		District PR-vote share
Candidate incumbency	0.017	Party incumbency	0.001
	(0.004)***		(0.897)
Constant	0.092	Constant	0.093
	(0.000)***		(0.000)***
Observations	594	Observations	594
Units/ districts	299	Units/ districts	299
Adjusted R^2	−0.960	Adjusted R^2	−1.017

p-values in parentheses; * significant at the 10%-level; ** significant at the 5%-level; *** significant at the 1%-level.

PR-vote share had not been substantiated before. Germany can be considered as a critical case, since it represents the longest established mixed member electoral system. Hence, parties, candidates and voters have had a long time to learn and strategically adapt to its complex electoral rules (Bawn 1999). If not here, it is hard to imagine where else one could find conclusive evidence in support of the contamination hypothesis.

This chapter proposed to circumvent the notorious 'no measurement of the dependent variable with no variance on the independent variable'-problem – caused by the fact that small parties tend to contest every district in every election – by looking at what I have called 'quasi-incumbency'. Quasi-incumbency refers to those double listed MPs who entered parliament through the party list but at the same time ran a candidature in a district. I have argued that the basic 'linking a party to a face'-argument of the contamination literature should *a fortiori* apply to those quasi-incumbents, members of parliament from which their parties expect active district-level campaigning and constituency service, and who have more resources and more opportunities than the non-MP to engage in this kind of local activity. Given that parties look at their members' district performance (in terms of nominal- and PR-votes at the district level) when they decide upon the party list for the upcoming elections, small parties' members of parliament have every incentive to meet their party's expectation. This local activity component appeared in all regressions as a substantial addendum to the party's district PR-vote share. Since the quasi-incumbency effect is caused by the very same mechanisms that also make a small party candidate's sheer presence in a district electorally beneficial – constituency service, visibility, connections to the local 'civil society' etc. – we can infer from these findings that entering district contests generally has a positive impact on the PR-vote share of small parties.

With respect to the debate on whether the components of a mixed member electoral system mutually moderate each other or lead to role differentiation with extremely party oriented politicians in the PR-tier on the one hand, and extremely district-oriented politicians in the majoritarian tier on the other (Bawn and Thies 2003), the findings of this chapter again speak rather in favour of the moderation-conjecture (Shugart and Wattenberg 2001c; Shugart 2001b, 2001a). At least, the dual candidacy-feature of the German electoral system secures that even members of parliament who will never have a chance of winning a district will engage in serious constituency service, since a good electoral performance in the district is a precondition for being re-nominated and placed on a promising list position. The schematic contrasting of list- versus district candidates does not seem to capture how the micro-incentives in the German electoral system really work. But again, I would like to postpone the more detailed discussion of the mandate-divide hypothesis (Sieberer 2010) to a later chapter (*see* Chapter Nine). In the next chapter, I turn to a different consequence of the preceding analysis. If small parties face incentives to enter district races, this reduces the vote share with which districts are won. This, in turn, opens the opportunity to strike inter-party deals at the district level. Put differently, pre-electoral agreements at the district level should become more likely. We then need to ask why we have not seen more of them in the recent past. This is the question that the next chapter addresses.

Chapter Five

Coordinating: Locally or nationally? Or what if German parties suddenly behaved in a *Duvergerian* fashion?[1]

I would like to start by briefly summarising the main results of Chapters Two to Four. The preceding chapter demonstrated that it pays for small parties in the German mixed-electoral system to enter hopeless district races because they benefit from contamination effects. Being present with a district candidate positively affects the party's PR-vote share in that district. Not surprisingly, the small 'established' parties in Germany almost always named candidates for each and every district, in each and every election (Cox and Schoppa 2002; *see* Table 4.1). With the recent trend toward a higher number of parties due to the advent of, first, the Greens, and then after 1990, of the ex-communists [PDS/*die Linke*], parties have increasingly entered races in each and every district. Small parties and their voters likewise, should not care much about the electoral fate of their district candidates – given that these parties, of course, know that they have virtually no chance of winning a plurality of constituency votes. Thus, even when parties nominate own candidates for each district, voters may still bring about a *Duvergerian* outcome in the plurality tier by casting their nominal votes mainly for one of the two major candidates, candidates of either the SPD or the CDU/CSU – knowing that otherwise they would waste their vote (Cox 1997).

But German voters do not behave in a *fully Duvergerian* fashion – with an increasing number of parties that contend districts, the effective number of district parties (or the effective number of candidates) has increased, too (*see* Figure 5.1; Pappi *et al.* 2006). But German voters also do not behave *fully non-Duvergerian*: with the rising number of parties, voters are more likely to split their tickets. As a consequence, the difference between the effective number of parties and the effective number of candidates has increased over time as well (*see* Figure 5.1).

Lack of information might be one reason why we do not observe Duverger's Law on the district level in German parliamentary elections. Firstly, voters may not fully understand the electoral rules – which vote is for the district, which one is for the party. Secondly, voters may not be fully informed about parties' prospective vote shares (Herrmann 2012). Voters cannot always be perfectly sure about which party will end up second and which third – especially if parties have regional

---

1. This chapter is based on joint work with Valentin Schröder.

Figure 5.1: The effective number of parties and the effective number of candidates, Bundestag elections, 1949–2009

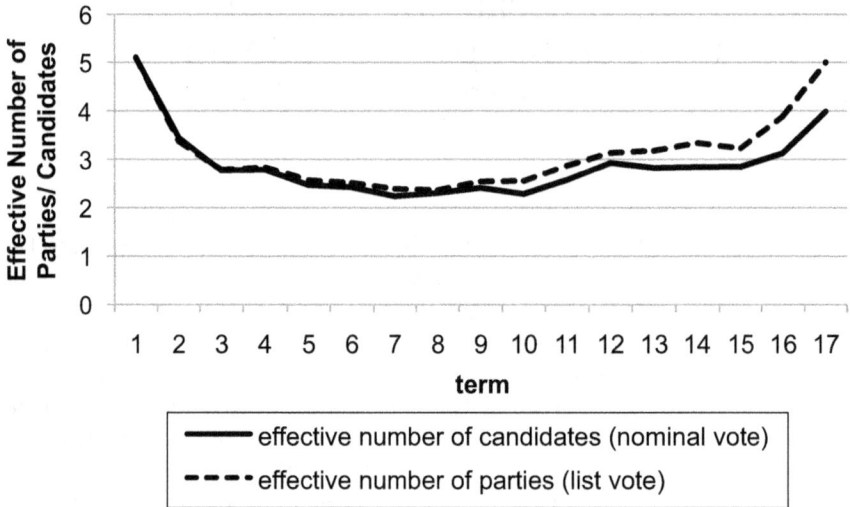

Source: Own calculations on the basis of Bundeswahlleiter, various years

strongholds, as the PDS/*die Linke* has in the east. But with imperfect information about parties' support in a constituency, strategic voting reaches limits:

> To vote for a candidate that is not one's first preference obviously makes sense only if one can be sure that the preferred candidate is out of the running. Without common knowledge of who is trailing in the electoral race, voter coordination on two candidates is unlikely to succeed (Herrmann 2012: 64).

Robert Moser and Ethan Scheiner have formulated the informational preconditions for strategic voting pointedly: 'Less Information, Less Strategic Defection, Less Duverger' (Moser and Scheiner 2012: 28). And with more parties competing in districts, the informational requirements that voters need usually increase, too. It is therefore no surprise to see a simultaneous increase in the (effective) number of parties and in the (effective) number of candidates (although concomitantly the inclination to split votes increases, too). This, in turn, has made the vote-seat translation in the plurality tier more disproportionate, and thereby surplus seats more likely.

We have now come full-circle: due to the increasingly disproportionate electoral outcomes in the plurality tier (leading to more surplus seats) caused by the lack of local coordination, parties might start to reconsider their strategies. In particular, at least some parties might consider whether pre-electoral coordination at the district-level, i.e. stand-down agreements or explicit district alliances, might not prove to be more advantageous, than each party pursuing a strategy of 'going alone'. In other words, if voters don't behave *Duvergerian*, parties might. And parties might, *because* voters do not behave fully *Duvergerian*: given high vote shares of third parties in many – especially eastern - districts,

> successful strategic coordination in districts could have made a difference in determining the winner. In each year, the average share of the vote for the third place finisher in the constituency was enough so that, had it been jointly given to the candidate in second place, the winner would have been defeated (Herrmann 2012: 70).

Electoral coordination in the plurality tier, i.e. locally, is not wholly unfamiliar to German parties. As was mentioned above already, for the early federal elections we *do* observe quite a considerable number of these district-level agreements (Schindler 1999): thirteen agreements in 1949, 47 in 1953 and 20 in 1957. In later elections, however, German parties decided to coordinate at the national level exclusively, i.e. only within the PR-tier.[2]

This, however, provokes a couple of questions: we may first ask why parties switched their strategies from local (plurality-tier) to national (PR-tier) coordination after the 1957 election. Secondly, we might wonder why parties did not return to district-level coalitions in the light of the recently increasing electoral costs of PR-tier coordination, i.e. the increasing number of surplus seats (*see* Chapter Two and Three). Finally, investigating the costs and benefits of decentralised vs. centralised coordination also appears warranted, given that one of the very few studies examining the incentives for district coalitions in mixed-electoral systems has identified rules in its majoritarian component as being conducive for local coordination. These features, like the dual ballot or the plurality rule, are shared by the German system, but *without* leading to district-level inter-party agreements (Ferrara and Herron 2005).[3] Accordingly, we may ask: why is there no district level coordination in the German case?

Obviously, these questions are again closely connected to surplus seats. With respect to perfect proportionality, parties' strategies to file own candidates for each district, irrespective of their chances to win, appear as perfectly rational. If a mixed system secures

> fully proportional outcomes, parties face little incentive to coordinate. Even those parties that have no hope of winning any single-member district [...] are not at all damaged by the electoral formula because the compensatory

---

2. See Kleinert, however: 'such a culture of district alliances and joint candidates has remained alien to the political system of the Federal Republic' (Kleinert 2012: 191).

3. Ferrara and Herron hypothesise 'that parties are more likely to coordinate in the single-member district races of dual ballot mixed systems than in single ballot mixed systems' and that 'more coordination is observed in single-member district races of mixed electoral systems if the majoritarian component of the election operates through plurality, rather than majority-runoff or majority-plurality' (Ferrara and Herron 2005: 19, 20).

mechanism guarantees that their total seat share will be proportional to their vote share. Hence, there is no reason for parties to form pre-electoral alliances in the single-member district elections of MMP systems, because the outcome is inconsequential for the maximisation of their seat total (Ferrara and Herron 2005: 20).

What is more, 'going alone' does not cause any damage, it – as we saw above (Chapter Four) – even can benefit a party's seat total. The same appears to be true for voters. Parties do not need incentives to arrange pre-electoral alliances at the district level, and also, voters have no need to behave *Duvergerian*:

> Because strategic defection from weaker to stronger parties in the SMD tier will typically have no effect on the total number of seats won by each party, voters in linked systems should have less reason to vote strategically in SMD balloting (Moser and Scheiner 2012: 55).

In contrast to this rationale, we also saw that (Chapters Two and Three) with surplus seats, seat totals increasingly deviate from vote totals. Put differently, recent German elections did *not* 'generate fully proportional outcomes' – in fact, this was less and less the case. But with an increasing number of surplus seats, the majoritarian component gains prevalence over the PR-component, which, in turn, should make district-level electoral coalitions appear more attractive for parties (Moser and Scheiner 2012: 21). Consequently, we might expect parties to have second thoughts about the actual advantages of national over local coordination. Put differently: how much disproportionality do we need to see before parties begin to re-estimate the advantages of centralised versus decentralised coordination, or coordination in the majoritarian- vs. the PR-tier? In the following, I will first discuss when and why German parties coordinated locally (second section). I will then assess a counterfactual: how would the seat shares appear, had German parties coordinated fully at the district level. In order to demonstrate this scenario, I will assess the effects of a couple of different coalition scenarios (third section). A short summary concludes.

Going alone or joining (local) electoral forces?

Obviously, there is a nexus between disproportionality and its consequence, surplus seats on the one hand, and electoral coordination on the other. Surprisingly, however, this nexus has not been an issue in the recent German electoral reform debate. In this debate, surplus seats were predominantly perceived as an inevitable consequence of a mixed electoral system. Among the factors contributing to their occurrence, the German literature highlights:

- regional differences in voter turnout
- differences in district size (relevant especially after unification and until the re-districting reform of 2002)

- a growing tendency to split votes
- the increasing fragmentation of the party system (Grotz 2000; Behnke 2003c; Behnke 2003a; Behnke 2009; Grotz 2009; Nohlen 2009; Strohmeier 2009; Behnke and Grotz 2011; Behnke 2012)

Even the *Bundesverfassungsgericht*, Germany's constitutional court, in one of its several rulings on surplus seats views them as a 'necessary consequence' of Germany's personalised PR- system (BVerfG 79/179 [1988], B, para 2, sentence 1; cf. BVerfGE 16/130) [1963]), in other words: as an inevitable effect of the electoral rules in place. That they became more frequent as of late, is predominately explained by recent changes in the contextual parameters listed above. None of those however, apart from the district size, can be changed by a simple legislative fiat. In fact, the redrawing of district boundaries in 2002 *did* address the one factor within the legislators' reach and was enacted with the intention of reducing the number of surplus seats – yet, their number continued to rise nonetheless. Consequently, it is electoral reform that is usually viewed as the only way to either finish with surplus seats altogether or, at least, help to reduce their numbers significantly.[4]

With the debate's almost exclusive focus on electoral reform, the influence the parties themselves may have on the frequency with which surplus seats occur has been ignored: namely the effects of electoral coordination in the district. Surplus seats are not randomly distributed over the various parties, but their allocation displays clear losers and winners. Obviously, since small parties almost never win districts, they also do not benefit from surplus seats. Moreover, since political geography puts the Christian Democrats at an advantage over their social democratic rivals (*see* Chapter Three), the CDU/CSU was the party that profited the most often from this feature of Germany's mixed electoral system. It is therefore anything but surprising that some parties had strong and others very little interest in the reform of the electoral system – electoral rules would probably not have changed were it not for the rulings of the constitutional court (cf. Rahat and Hazan 2011). Since the parties benefitting from the electoral rules showed severe reluctance to reform, it remains unclear why those parties disadvantaged by the status quo, did not contemplate arranging district coalitions in order to minimise the number of surplus seats of the political adversary. What exactly is meant by this? A brief example may clarify the point.

The federal elections in 2009 resulted in a record number of surplus seats, namely twenty-four. This high number did not take the parties by surprise – in fact a simulation had quite accurately predicted that the election would produce twenty-three of these additional seats and almost all of them would benefit the CDU/CSU (Behnke 2009). Social Democrats and Greens were therefore warned,

---

4. The most recent 2012 electoral reform, a response to two rulings of Germany's constitutional court that qualified key features of the electoral system as 'unconstitutional', will not eliminate surplus seats altogether, but will guarantee compensation seats, such that any initial deviation from proportionality due to surplus seats will be fully corrected (*see* Chapter Ten; see also Lang 2014).

and the fact that both parties had just started another initiative for electoral reform in the summer of 2009, proves that they were fully aware of what was going to happen. At that time, there was a very fair chance for the election to lead to a 'fabricated majority', one solely based on surplus seats. But could Social Democrats and Greens have done more than to appeal to the government to change the rules, a government in which the CDU benefitted from the existing rules and, therefore, remained particularly unenthusiastic about reform? Let's take Baden-Wurttemberg as our exemplary case. In this state, the Christian Democrats won thirty-seven out of thirty-eight districts in the 2009 federal election. Yet, they only gained 34.4 per cent of the list votes, qualifying them for not more than twenty-seven seats. Hence, the party gained ten surplus seats in Baden-Wurttemberg alone – almost half of the twenty-one surplus seats that were won by the CDU in 2009 (another three went to the Bavarian CSU). But how many districts would Social Democrats and Greens have been able to claim successfully, had they completely coordinated their district candidatures? If I simply add the nominal votes of the two parties, they would have been able to win eight more districts (i.e. a total of nine of the thirty-eight districts), the number of districts that went to the CDU reduced from 37 to 29. Put differently, *ceteris paribus* Social Democrats and Greens together could have reduced the number of CDU-surplus seats in Baden-Wurttemberg by 4/5 (from 10 to 2) – cutting their *overall*, nationwide number of these seats by a third from 24 to 16. This would have been a very substantial reduction indeed, and electoral coordination between the SPD and Greens in other states, besides Baden-Wurttemberg, might have helped to further reduce the CDU's surplus seats. This provokes the question: why actually did the Greens and Social Democrats decide *against* district-level coordination?

If not with respect to voters (Herrmann 2012), then, with respect to parties we can safely rule out 'ignorance' as a possible explanation – parties are rational and highly strategic actors, especially when it comes to seat maximisation. But what else might explain their non-coordination? Do small district parties insist on having 'their own' candidates? Do parties fear losing certain districts forever if they are not present with an own candidate in each and every election? Are the contamination effects from running own district candidates on party's list-votes really strong enough to render stand-down agreements wholly unattractive? Put differently: how much does the majoritarian have to dominate the proportional tier (Ferrara and Herron 2005: 21), before parties begin reconsidering the advantages of local coordination?

Interestingly, no such counterfactual played any role in the recent German debates about surplus seats. Only in passing did one contributor note: 'If Social Democrats and Greens could agree on joint candidates in the next elections, they would in the end be the ones benefitting from surplus seats' (Kleinert 2012: 190-191). Whereas the quick calculation above seems to support this assertion, it seems worthwhile to investigate in greater detail, and more systematically, whether this, in fact, holds true under various circumstances. This is what will be done in this chapter. Much depends, as we will see, on the interaction between parties and between parties and voters, which makes things far more complex than the simple Baden-Wurttemberg example above suggests. Therefore, this example alone cannot prove that district-level agreements would have resulted in better outcomes for the SPD and the Greens in the last federal election. Its simplicity immediately provokes a couple of objections. For instance: why should we assume that liberals and Christian Democrats remain passive bystanders when the left forms pre-electoral coalitions? And what will voters do? Can we really assume that they are at the full disposal of their party leadership and follow it blindly no matter which electoral coalition the leadership may choose? Moreover: how would district-level coalitions interact with the electoral 'three district'-rule, allowing a party that seizes at least three districts to enter parliament in a size proportionate to its party-votes? More specifically: what about the party-fragmentation on the left in the new eastern states, where the PDS/*die Linke* is a very strong third party, deeply at odds with the SPD? Would the picture alter substantially if the SPD and the PDS/*die Linke* succeeded in overcoming their deep hostility and formed district-level electoral coalitions? Was, after all, the 2009 election and the resulting high number of surplus seats perhaps just an exception, not likely to be repeated in the foreseeable future? At least the small number of surplus seats ($N = 3$) in the 2013 election suggests exactly this. Finally, how will parties manage to divide the additional district mandates among themselves? How would such a division interfere with the party-internal nomination procedures?

In the next section I will assess the effects of local electoral coalitions. In order to do this, I examine the outcomes of different local electoral alliances and work with varying assumptions regarding the seat distribution among the participating parties and the political camps that will form. I will then present the results of estimations for three different scenarios – **Scenario 1**: centre-left coordination only (SPD and the Greens); **Scenario 2**: centre-left *and* centre-right coordination (SPD with Greens on the one hand and CDU/CSU with the Liberals on the other); **Scenario 3**: a left block versus the bourgeois camp (SPD, Greens and *Linke* vs. CDU/CSU and the Liberals). All three scenarios share a basic naivety, namely the heroic assumption that voters will be completely loyal and follow their leaders fully and 'blindly'. This allows me to simply add the party vote shares of those parties assumed to belong to the same political camp (based on their public, national declaration of intent to form a joint government after the election). Obviously, these are heroic assumptions and they do not take into account voters either not turning out because they find the proposed coalition dreadful, or if turning out, abandoning their party in favour of a competing, to them more attractive, coalition. Heroic as this assumption about 100 per cent loyal voters may seem, in our context it helps to assess the coordination-scenario under the most favourable circumstances, favourable for district-level coordination, that is. Should I – even when making strong assumptions about the ease with which parties agree on joint candidates and about voters' willingness to support whatever joint candidate is presented to them – not find much alteration in the aggregate seat shares of the major party-political camps (or find even more unfavourable outcomes), I can safely conclude that PR-tier coordination is institutionally very robust in Germany's MMP-system.

In this case, the practical difficulties to coordinate the complicated and lengthy *internal* candidate nomination procedures *between* different parties – all this under conditions of high uncertainty and, in the plurality-tier, high electoral volatility – would only render district-level coordination even less attractive for parties.

However, I start by looking briefly at the district coalitions between 1949 and 1957 as well as at the subsequent practice of German parties to announce pre-electoral coalitions in the PR-tier combined with the sometimes explicit, sometimes implicit, appeal to voters to split their votes between the smaller and larger prospective coalition partner. According to these strategies, I will sketch two possible coordination equilibria: a decentralised one at the district level in which parties agree on joint candidates in all districts; and a centralised one with nation-wide campaigns for vote splitting and explicit declarations of a national electoral alliance. Subsequently, for the period in which electoral coordination at the district level ceased to matter and in which the advent of another left party (the Greens in 1983) opened new opportunities for electoral coordination, I calculate the number of surplus seats and their allocation had parties chosen to coordinate locally.

A *Duvergerian* counterfactual

As noted above, stand-down agreements were a quite regular phenomenon in Germany's first three federal elections (Schindler 1984) and appeared quite frequently in state elections in this period, too. Also, if we look at Germany's Imperial period with its majoritarian runoff elections (Reibel 2007; Reibel 2011; Schröder and Manow 2014), we see that German parties could look back on long tradition of local electoral coordination. For a party, the main promise of district-level arrangements lies in trading vote shares from a district in which it has only little chances of winning, for a vote share in a district where chances are much higher. Even if the link between the two components of Germany's mixed system are meant to secure full vote-seat proportionality, incentives for district-level coalitions remain, first because of surplus seats (see above), but, second, also due to electoral thresholds. Whenever small parties' entry into parliament proves to be easier via the plurality tier (because of the minimum of only three districts) as compared to the PR-tier (with its minimum of five per cent of the national votes), i.e. when the effective threshold is lower in the former than in the latter, parties should be expected to form electoral district alliances. In order to pass the electoral threshold, parties could hence focus on a small number of promising districts and would not have to entail the full, i.e. nationwide, coordination of candidates.

It is exactly this strategy that mainly explains the widespread practice of stand-down agreements in the early *Bundestag* elections. In 1949, the first federal election, parties had to pass a five-per cent threshold *in any state* in the PR-component, or had to meet a one-seat threshold in the plurality-component nationally. In 1953, the PR-threshold became more restrictive, since it was now applied to the federal level: to enter parliament, parties had to gain at least five per cent of all votes cast nationwide. The one-seat threshold, however, remained, and was only increased to three seats in the 1957 election (Klingemann and Wessels 2001b). These rules have stayed in place ever since.[5]

This confronted parties with clear-cut incentives. In 1949 under the single ballot, the CDU and FDP mutually withdrew candidates in five neighbouring pairs of districts.[6] After the introduction of the dual ballot and with the more restrictive *national* five per cent threshold, in 1953, parties in almost 20 per cent of all districts either unilaterally or reciprocally abstained from running own candidates. 20 district mandates, which would have gone to a different party or candidate without district agreements, were won in this way. All these mandates were seized by parties (CDU/CSU, FDP, *Zentrum* and DP) which before, as well as after, the election participated in government coalitions either at the federal level or in the state in question.[7] Both sides benefitted: smaller parties like the DP or the *Zentrum* managed to enter parliament, which they would have failed to do via the PR-component. The Christian Democrats gained two surplus seats, plus one seat via a CDU-candidate whom the Centre party agreed to put on its list in North Rhine-Westphalia (on a safe second list rank). As small as this gain may seem, in the second legislative term from 1953 onwards, it secured the CDU an own, if very narrow, majority in parliament with 244 of all 487 mandates.

In 1957, the Christian Democrats used district agreements successfully to help its coalition partner, the DP, to pass the (new) three-seat threshold. The CDU's landslide victory in that election again provided the party with an own parliamentary majority, making it independent from surplus seats or the placement of own candidates at high list-positions of coalition partners. But why did this apparently quite successful practice completely disappear in later elections? The situation remained the same, since small parties with vote shares close to the five per cent PR-threshold and, if left to their own devices, without a realistic chance of winning even one district (or, in fact, three of them), while at the same time being helpful in securing a parliamentary majority, continued to be present as potential coalition or coordination partners.

Seeking an explanation, we need to take account of the following: of course, the advantages of mutual stand-down agreements must be weighed against the electoral (PR-tier) payoff gained by running a candidate in each and every district (*see* Chapter Four). Moreover, district coalitions are not the sole instrument for maximising chances of participating in a coalition government after the election. The opposite strategy, centralised instead of decentralised coordination, might be just as, or even more, beneficial for the parties forming an electoral alliance.

---

5.   Apart from one exception in 1990, the year of unification, when the 5 per cent threshold was applied to the old western and the new eastern *Länder* separately.

6.   All eight districts in Hamburg, which were divided equally between the CDU and the FDP, and the two districts in Wuppertal (again, one for the CDU, the other for the FDP).

7.   The BHE/GB, a further coalition partner, supported candidates of other parties by abstaining from nominating own candidates.

If this coalition consists of a smaller and a larger party – as was the case in the Federal Republic of Germany since the 1960s (see Pappi *et al.* 2006) – central coordination might be the superior strategy: not the division of districts among prospective coalition partners, but a nationwide campaign of the smaller partner with an appeal to voters (of the prospective coalition partner) to cast their list-vote for it by emphasising how indispensable it is or will be for the formation of a legislative majority. The larger party – tacitly – tolerates this strategy directed at wooing away its voters (at least with their list- or party-vote). As a consequence, it might even be rewarded with surplus seats due to the increasing gap between nominal- and party-votes that is caused by strategic vote splitting. Accordingly, this would represent the *central equilibrium*: announcing the intention to enter a coalition after the election and asking voters to support this coalition by splitting their votes between the smaller and larger coalition partner. A *decentralised equilibrium*, in contrast, would comprise district-level party agreements and mutual stand-down agreements for all districts or for as many as the threshold requires.

The central equilibrium has dominated since the 1970s, with two parties clearly and explicitly announcing their coalition intentions – sometimes unilaterally, often bilaterally. Since the federal election in 1972 at the latest, the Liberals (FDP) were the first to benefit from the so-called 'borrowed votes' (*Leihstimmen*) of its prospective coalition partner (see for the elections from 1972 to 1980, Falter and Rattinger 1983; for 1983, Gibowski and Kaase 1986; and for 1987 and 1990, Forschungsgruppe Wahlen 1990, 1994). In the late 1990s a similar agreement could be observed on the left, between Social Democrats and the Greens. These arrangements do not only promise legislative majorities and surplus seats for the larger partner. The bigger party has an additional rationale for opting for the central strategy since central coordination does not require its leadership to accommodate the interests of its local and regional sections, which it would have to do if pursuing decentral arrangements. For individual candidates, the type of candidacy is of central importance for his or her election chances (*see* Chapter Six and Eight) – being directly elected in a district is the most attractive path into the *Bundestag*. An election in the district situates the candidate in a less dependent, and therefore, more autonomous position vis-à-vis the party (Patzelt 1997; Patzelt 1999; Schüttemeyer and Sturm 2005; Patzelt 2007; Zittel and Gschwend 2007). From a party's point of view, balancing local and regional interests as well as the representation of the different party wings (plus taking account of gender and denominational quotas) is of utmost importance. This makes the nomination procedure highly complex. For the larger parties, i.e. those with realistic chances to win district mandates (namely the SPD and the CDU/CSU), it often lasts one and a half year. The process starts with the nomination of the district candidates. Subsequently, and against the background of this nomination, party delegates decide upon the party's state lists (Peters 1956; Kaack 1969; Zeuner 1970; Schröder 1971; Schüttemeyer and Sturm 2005). Given its length and complexity, one can hardly imagine how parties could manage to synchronise the intra- and the inter-party nomination process. Should they, *after* having settled on a complex internal balance of candidates, start the process of exchanging districts among each other? And would this force them to re-open the internal processes afterwards – once the interparty exchange has taken place? Or should they start with mutual agreements? In the first case, they would endanger the previous deals, in the second they would need to settle on agreements very early – already shortly after midterm. Even if we ignore contingencies, for instance if elections are called early (as had been the case in Germany 1972, 1983, 1990 and 2005, that is in four out of eighteen cases), this would certainly overstrain parties' strategic and adaptive capacities. It would also spell disaster in case of sudden major shifts in the political landscape immediately before elections – for instance if one party faces a dramatic decline in popularity due to a major political scandal. Such a major shift in popular support would then also render many district coalitions obsolete. In short, even within a relatively stable political environment, the decentralised equilibrium presupposes extremely demanding strategic capacities and entails a very time –consuming inter-party coordination process. Any major changes in important political parameters like sudden shifts of party popularity are likely to overthrow the strategic calculations of the participating parties completely.

In the following I will ignore these complications and will make the most heroic assumptions in favour of parties' foresight and strategic capabilities: parties exchange votes in a most beneficial way, they never miscalculate and voters will be at their complete disposal. We also ignore the possibility of sudden changes in popular support. If under these ideal circumstances decentralised coordination leads to a significantly different (and more attractive) distribution of seats among the parties involved, we would need to explain the absence of district coalitions since 1957 with the political transaction costs discussed above (and ignored in the following). In this case, our explanation would need to resort to these practical problems of implementing the local equilibrium. If, however, even under these most ideal circumstances the decentralised arrangements lead to outcomes not much different from those produced by central coordination, the strategic shift of German parties after 1957 towards nation-wide coalitions would be easy to explain.

I examine the fourteen federal elections since 1961, simulating alternative outcomes under different assumptions about the electoral coalitions that will form. The simulations are based on three assumptions: The first assumption presumes that the nominal votes would have been cast analogous to the party-votes that actually had been cast in the elections. The second assumes voters to be indifferent with respect to the district candidates of their preferred coalition. Finally, the third assumption supposes parties to face no problems in dividing candidatures and districts among each other. The division is optimal ex-post: parties always choose the distribution that proves to be the most beneficial for them after the fact. The division will also maximise the number of surplus seats that parties will be able to claim. Needless to say, these are not very realistic assumptions. Even so, they help us to design a hard test for the attractiveness of the central equilibrium.

I start my counterfactual with the scenario mentioned above (Kleinert 2012) that has been the declared intent of both parties in all elections since 1994: a left coalition between Social Democrats and the Green party (**Scenario 1**). I start by assuming (unrealistically) that those two parties fully and efficiently coordinate their district candidatures, while the parties of the centre-right – CDU/CSU and FDP – prefer 'going it alone'. I will then, in a second and more realistic scenario, assume that both camps form blocks: a left block with the SPD and the Green party (but without the ex-communists, *die Linke*), and a 'bourgeois' centre-right block with the Liberal party and the Christian Democrats (**Scenario 2**). In fact, the coalition between FDP and CDU/CSU has been the declared will of both parties since 1983. In a third scenario, I assume that the left succeeds in overcoming inter-party hostility and proves capable to form one left block with Social Democrats, ex-Communists and the ecological Green party (**Scenario 3**).

Additional variation results from the assumption of how coalition parties distribute the seats among each other. One plausible conjecture is that the parties, as a rule of thumb, take the vote shares gained in the last election for dividing up the seats – a kind of Gamson-law for district-level coordination (Gamson 1961). One could also employ two other, more extreme scenarios: *all* district seats are either going to the bigger or the smaller party. Again, these rather extreme assumptions should simply help us to devise the most favourable conditions for district-level coordination. Below, I treat only the cases where parties apply a Gamson-like division rule oriented at the (party) vote shares in the last election.

The red-green coalition became an option only after the advent of the Green party in parliament, in 1980. I restrict **Scenario 1,** therefore, to all elections since 1983. In a second scenario, I analyse all elections since 1961 under the assumption that all members of a (prospective) coalition pooled their votes in favour of joint

Figure 5.2: Scenario 1 – Seat share of SPD and Green Party in a case of complete local coordination, with CDU/CSU, FDP and PDS/die Linke running separately (proportional division of districts)

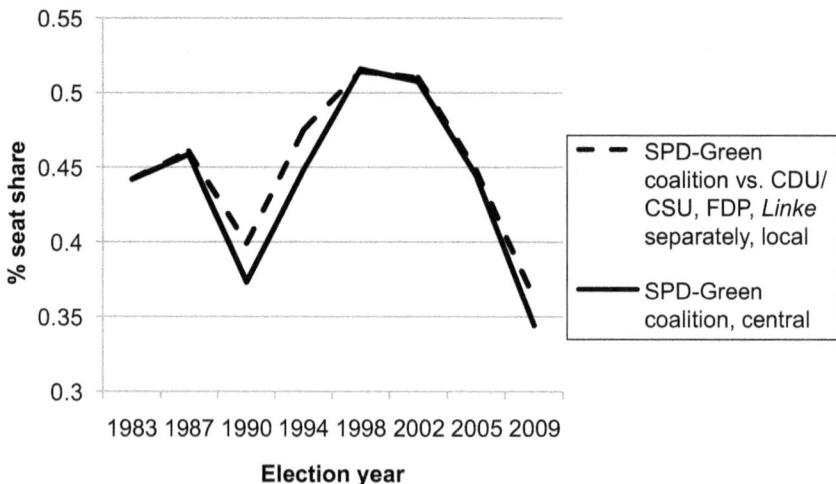

district candidates. Which parties favoured what coalition is coded according to Pappi *et al.* (2006). He and his co-authors based their coding decision on newspaper analysis, i.e. on either unilateral or bilateral public declarations of a party's intent to enter a coalition with another party. For the 2009 election, which is not covered by the Pappi *et al.* study, I assume, again, that the two *Lager* or camps situating the SPD-the Greens are on the one side and the CDU/CSU-FDP on the other. Finally, I investigate the effects of a hypothetical left-block of SPD, Greens and PDS/*die Linke* against a coalition of the centre-right consisting of the CDU/CSU and FDP starting with the 1990 election. Let's start with **Scenario 1**, complete local coordination between the Social Democrats and the Green party.

The following figures always compare the actual seat share of both parties with the one they would have obtained under a decentralised (plurality tier) instead of the actual central coordination (PR-tier; *see* Figure 5.2).

As can be seen easily from Figure 5.2, in no election would local coordination have changed the basic majorities and it only sometimes would have brought both parties a slightly advantageous distribution of seats. In other words, even under highly favourable (and unrealistic) assumptions, i.e. with only the left but nobody else coordinating, the district-level coordination outcome would not have differed much from the one actually obtained by national electoral alliances. Additionally, it would never have differed decisively, i.e. it would never have changed majorities. It seems as if local coordination simply does not pay off sufficiently for the participants, even if we do not take into account the veritable transaction costs that local coordination would entail.

Not much changes if I assume – more realistically – that not only the left coordinated their candidatures, but the centre-right did likewise (*see* Figure 5.3; **Scenario 2**). I am left with pretty much the same outcome. For all terms since (and including) 1998 the outcome is almost indistinguishable from the seat shares actually obtained under central, national electoral coordination.

A slightly different picture results if I assume that the fragmented left overcomes its mutual aversion. **Scenario 3**, depicted in Figure 5.4, relies on the assumption that a unified centre-right stands against a unified left, composed of Social Democrats, ex-Communists (PDS/*die Linke*) and the Greens. Again, this would never have changed parliamentary majorities, but viewed from the perspective of the CDU/CSU-FDP coalition, electoral outcomes would clearly have been more unfavourable as they were under central coordination. In this context one might want to stress a basic point: already a reduction in the government's margin of victory, say a reduction of its majority from twenty to five seats, would be a major achievement for the opposition parties.[8] Hence, our benchmark for assessing the benefits of local coordination should not focus exclusively on cases where it would have altered majorities. Even in these cases, however, the scenarios do not produce much of a difference.

---

8. This is not so much the case because the government's majority might be perceived as being shakier with narrow majorities (to the contrary, usually dissenting votes are *less* likely when majorities are narrow). It is rather that a narrow margin might shift the entire party-political centre of gravity much more toward the opposition.

Figure 5.3: Scenario 2 – Seat share of SPD and Green Party in a case of complete local coordination, with full coordination on the centre-right (proportional division of districts)

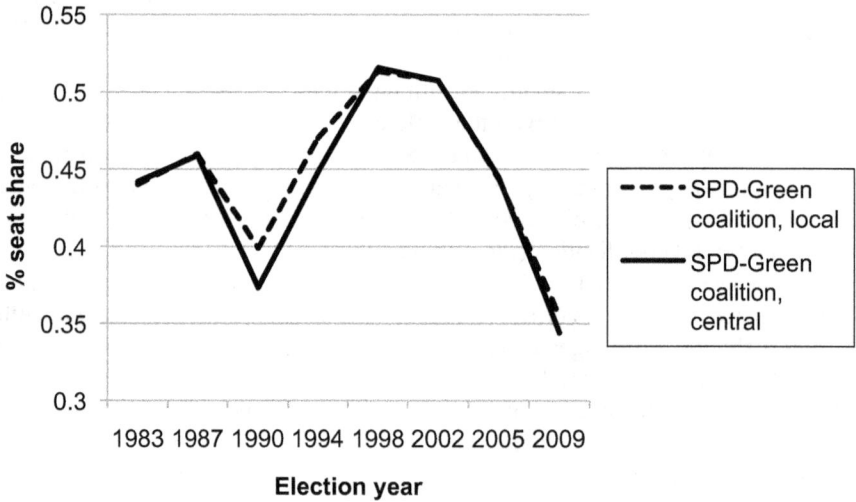

Figure 5.4: Scenario 3 – Seat share of CDU/CSU and FDP in a case of complete local coordination, with full coordination of a left block [SPD, Greens and die Linke] (proportional division of districts)

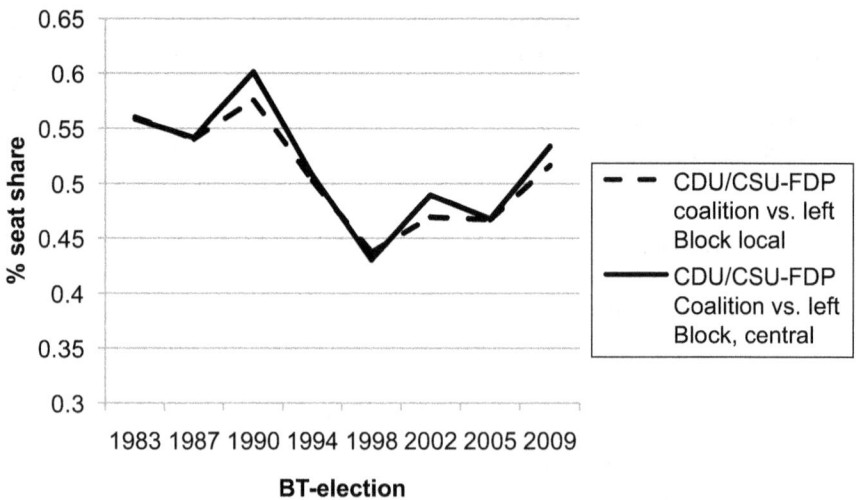

*Table 5.1: Seats per party under local coordination between CDU/CSU and FDP as well as between SPD and Greens (**Scenario 2**)*

Election year	*Linke*	Green	SPD	FDP	CDU/CSU	Total
1983	–	27	193	36	244	500
1987	–	42	186	46	222	496
1990	17	35	229	76	305	662
1994	0	53	260	57	296	666
1998	36	51	291	43	245	666
2002	0	55	249	47	248	599
2005	54	51	217	61	221	604
2009	76	68	146	93	221	604

It seems important to stress that in no single instance would any of the three coalition scenarios have led to different majorities. But one major difference between the centralised and the decentralised equilibrium has to be stressed, and this becomes apparent once I compare the seat shares for each party (*see* Table 5.1). Table 5.1 reports the seats per party in the scenario with coordination both between the bourgeois parties (CDU/CSU and FDP) and between the Greens with the Social Democrats. The important point is that a coalition on the left exclusive of the PDS/*die Linke*, would have barred this party from entering the *Bundestag* twice, in 1994 and in 2002. Consequently, local coordination is not an efficient instrument for changing political majorities, but it can be effective in holding down a rival within the own political sphere.

In 2002, *die Linke* missed the 5 per cent PR-threshold as well as the 3-districts plurality-threshold, but was represented with the two MPs that had won their constituencies. In 1994, the PDS/*die Linke* failed to meet the PR-threshold (with only 4.4 per cent of list votes), but since it seized four districts, it participated in the party-vote allocation and entered parliament with thirty MPs (four district-MPs plus twenty-six list-MPs). Local coordination, however, would have enabled the SPD and the Greens to prevent the PDS's entry in both instances. This again shows that local coordination in Germany's MMP can be, and has been, a rational partisan strategy with respect to the plurality-tier threshold rules. Regarding surplus seats or overall seat shares, in contrast, it is rather ineffective. The nomination of joint candidates in a district or in mutual stand-down agreements can be used in two ways: to help a smaller party to meet the former one district and later the three districts threshold (which explains local electoral alliances from 1949–1957) or to prevent a party from meeting it (which would have been possible in 1994 and 2002, had the SPD and the Greens formed an alliance against the PDS or *die Linke*). We can only speculate what would have happened in the case of *die Linke* being effectively prevented from entering the *Bundestag* in 1994, in the first post-unification election where the 5 per cent PR-threshold applied nation-wide.

If we compare that constellation – Social Democrats and Greens preventing *die Linke* from winning districts – with the constellation of *supportive* local alliances between the CDU and small bourgeois parties, we see that this electoral support is rather a double-edged sword, since the smaller party's survival depends on the larger party's goodwill. The several party mergers that took place between 1949 and 1957 on the fragmented right party spectrum show that this kind of local coordination is not in a long-term equilibrium. An *offensive* local alliance, however, in which two parties prevent the success of a third, seems feasible and would prove stable over the longer term – and with the same effect as the *supportive alliance*: a lower number of parties.

This points to the nexus between mixed electoral rules and the effective number of parties (Nishikawa and Herron 2004) and supports the expectation that the number of parties in a mixed member electoral system should be higher than in a pure plurality system but lower than in a pure PR-system (2004: 760). Again, a mixed system proves to combine the two components but unfold specific outcomes, different from the outcomes that either of the two components would have produced in isolation from each other.

Conclusion

It is now appropriate to summarise this chapter's findings. Germany had applied two rather antithetic electoral systems before it settled on the relatively stable and well-functioning mixed system in 1949. In the Imperial period, Germany had introduced universal male suffrage quite early – in 1871. It applied majoritarian rules with runoff elections, i.e. a 'two rounds, two ballots' or absolute majority system. Electoral coordination was purely local (Reibel 2007; Reibel 2011; Schröder and Manow 2014). In 1918, Germany switched to PR. Whereas politics during the Imperial period suffered from the fact that party elites lacked the capacity to control 'their' members of parliament since these were tied to local electoral alliances, the Weimar Republic rather suffered from the opposite extreme: high party fragmentation due to low legal thresholds made the formation of stable coalitions problematic (Abraham 1988). The two-rounds, two-ballots-system of the Imperial period forestalled intra-party cooperation, the pure PR-system of the interwar years hindered stable inter-party cooperation. Weimar's coalitions remained unstable since 'dissenting' MPs could easily break away from their party and found a new one.

After 1945, under the mixed electoral system of West Germany, local electoral alliances were quite frequent in the early *Bundestag* elections, but completely vanished after 1957. As of yet, they have not reappeared, although a higher degree of party fragmentation and the increasing importance of the plurality-tier for the seat distribution among parties could have made local alliances look more attractive.

As I demonstrated in this chapter, the reason for the lack of local arrangements lies mainly in the only marginal impact which decentralised coordination would have on the partisan distribution of seats. And what little impact there was, the latest electoral reform in 2012, which ensured that surplus seats will be fully compensated in order to guarantee exact proportionality, eliminated any remaining incentive for mutual stand-down agreements. With respect to the number of parties, however, local coordination *can* be an effective instrument to keep rivals at bay. This strategy, targeted at smaller parties with a geographically concentrated followership, would however, not require full-scale coordination, but could focus on a few critical districts only. With respect to the effective number of parliamentary parties and to the type of parties entering parliament (e.g. regional parties) I can therefore conclude, again, that mixed-member proportional systems like the German example do produce outcomes significantly different from both the PR and the plurality types.

PART II

CANDIDATES IN GERMANY'S MIXED ELECTORAL SYSTEM

Chapter Six

Candidatures: Turning candidates into MPs[1]

In order to address basic questions of political recruitment and democratic accountability we need to have information not only on who actually sat in parliament, but also on who ran for office (Cross 2008; Crisp 2007; Lundell 2004; Rahat 2007). Of whom did the pool of candidates actually consist out of which voters then chose their representatives? How often did Members of Parliament run for office before they were first successful? And how often did they run unsuccessfully subsequent to their last term in parliament? How exactly do they 'leave' parliament: by not being re-elected or already by not being re-nominated? These are simple, but as of yet largely unanswered questions[2] – questions of fundamental importance if we want to assess the effectiveness of 'elections as an instrument of democracy' (Powell 2000). They address basic democratic mechanisms: who sanctions – the voter or the party? How exactly does the selection process work and who actually selects – parties or voters (Rahat 2007, 2009; Rahat *et al.* 2008; Hazan and Rahat 2010)? To what extent does the nomination already provide the candidates with a quite secure prospect of actually being elected?

We hereby also touch basic questions of political representation: do deficits of 'descriptive representation' (Phillips 1995) have their origin in the nomination process or do they result from voters' behaviour – or do both combine? For instance, with respect to women's parliamentary representation we may ask where exactly selection-mechanisms work: already when parties nominate candidates or rather when voters select representatives out of the pool of candidates (Rule 1987; Wängnerud 2009; Diaz 2008)? And if the selection takes place already during the nomination process, we would like to know how women actually ran for office: as list- or as district- or as double-candidates, on which list-ranks and in which districts? Do parties differ in these respects?

Yet, despite the centrality of these questions for our understanding of elections and representation, information on candidates until today remains particularly poor for many electoral systems, including the German one (Porter 1995; Schüttemeyer and Sturm 2005). At the same time, mixed-electoral rules lend themselves particularly well to studying the relative impact on

---

1. This chapter is based on joint work with Peter Flemming.
2. For Germany, as a start, see Edinger and Schwarz (2009).

candidate selection of party-elites and voters, and their mutual interaction. In particular with respect to women's parliamentary representation, the German mixed-member system appears to be of specific interest, since the important role electoral rules play in this is undisputed in the literature (Matland 1998 [2002]). It is 'prevailing wisdom' that 'proportional representation (PR) systems are friendlier to successful female candidacy than district systems' (Iversen and Rosenbluth 2010b: 134). Often implied is that party-elites have more control over the composition of the party-list than over the nomination of candidates in the district (Carey and Shugart 1995). The extent to which women are represented in parliament can also be interpreted, then, as an indicator of how much party leaders manage to impose a general programmatic stance upon the micro-logics of candidate selection. Mixed electoral rules themselves seem to offer a compromise between leaders' programmatic interests and candidates' individual career strategies. Thus, the German electoral system provides an unique opportunity to test the established thesis that a PR system, as compared to majoritarian rules, is the more advantageous electoral system with respect to the representation of female politicians (Wängnerud 2009: 54) while holding a number of other potential explanatory variables constant. It also then lends itself perfectly to ask why exactly it is that both tiers of the electoral system have so different representational effects.

In the following, I look at career sequences of all candidates that ever ran for office in a federal election. I use a data set containing information on all candidates in German *Bundestag* elections since 1949 (implied: also on all *elected* candidates, i.e. all members of parliament since 1949). This gives us a complete overview over the personal side of sixty years of democratic representation in the Federal Republic.[3] Although the election is only the last step in a multi-stage-process of self- and external selection, the early steps in this process have rarely been addressed in the literature, primarily due to the lack of systematic data. Basic questions relating to these pre-electoral stages have, therefore, remained unanswered to date, but they can be addressed with the dataset at hand. I start with a general overview (in the second section) and will then highlight in particular how electoral rules impact female parliamentary representation (third section).

---

3. The dataset contains information on 53,760 candidatures and 35,211 different candidates. Among those, we observe 10,215 successful candidatures, based on 3,581 different persons, i.e. parliamentarians. Of all 35,211 candidates, 79.5 per cent were male and of all 3,581 *Bundestag* MPs, 81.0 per cent were male. The dataset contains information on the name, sex, party, the candidature (including information on the district, the list and the list-rank), on the district-vote. Moreover, it provides information on committee-membership in the *Bundestag* of those elected into parliament (information that will be used in Chapter Seven) and additional biographical information (academic title, date of birth and death, etc.).

Pre-selection and election: the path into parliament

A first important question is: do candidates and MPs constitute two different populations? Much indicates that they indeed do. Of all 3,581 Members of the *Bundestag*, 79.6 per cent had never run for a seat in parliament before their first entry. They succeeded in becoming an MP at their first attempt. If I take a look at the time after the first entry into the *Bundestag*, I furthermore see that 76.4 per cent of all MPs never ran subsequently for a seat *without* being elected. In other words, only about 20 per cent of MPs *before* their first entry, and only 24 per cent *after* entry, experienced electoral defeat, once or several times. Looking at the party-level, I see that these high numbers are especially due to the two main, large *Volksparteien*, the Social and the Christian Democrats. The smaller parties, as in the cases of the Liberals or the Greens, who almost never win district seats, have lower success rates but still lie above 50 per cent. For the SPD, 84.1 per cent had never been defeated in an election prior to their first term in the *Bundestag*. The numbers for the CDU and the CSU are 81.3 per cent and 83.3 per cent, respectively. Liberal MPs enter parliament at first attempt (64.6 per cent), candidates of the Greens are 68.4 per cent successful at first attempt. An interesting exception among the smaller parties is the PDS, or today, *die Linke*, the ex-communists. Its success rate is similar to those of the large parties, since 81.2 per cent of all their MPs had never run unsuccessfully prior to their first appearance in the federal parliament.

If I take a look at the career episodes *after* the first entry into the *Bundestag*, I see that here the PDS, or now *die Linke*, is at the same level as the FDP (Liberals) or the Greens. While 82.6 per cent of all Social Democratic MPs have never experienced electoral defeat, and while 79.9 per cent and 84.2 per cent CDU- and CSU-MPs never did so, the numbers for the smaller parties are significantly lower: decreasing to 64.6 per cent (FDP), or 65.1 per cent (Green Party) or to 67.1 per cent (PDS/*die Linke*). What seems most clear from the data is that, for a German MP, his or her *nomination* is the far more critical event than the *election* itself, the *selectorate* being more important than the *electorate* – which would provide a partial explanation for the strong role that parties continue to play in Germany's electoral system (cf. Shugart 2001b; Shugart and Wattenberg 2001c), and which more generally point to the crucial importance of ballot-control (Carey and Shugart 1995) for effective hierarchical control over MPs and for party-discipline in and outside parliament.

Above, we saw the distribution of the type of candidacy (list, district or double) for all MPs and how it developed from 1949 until today (*see* Figure 4.3). Figure 6.1 shows the type of candidacy for all candidates. With a much higher share of unsuccessful contenders in smaller parties, it is not surprising to find a higher share of pure list-candidates among the candidates as compared to the actually elected MPs. List- and double-candidates together account for almost 80 per cent of all candidatures, to roughly similar degrees. Of course, since all three types of candidatures have to add up to 100 per cent, they are not independent from each other, but it seems as if, in particular, the list-and the double-candidature are inversely related.

Figure 6.1: Type of candidature, all candidates 1949–2009 in per cent

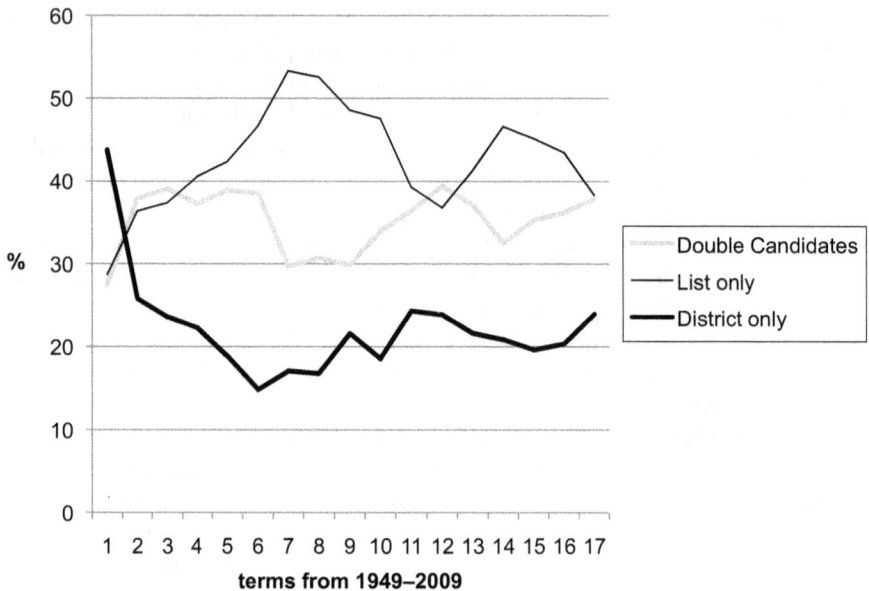

Source: Own calculations based on Bundeswahlleiter, various years

We can gain an overview over the typical career paths of German MPs when applying sequence analysis (Brüderl and Scherer 2006; Scherer and Brüderl 2010; Brzinsky-Fay and Kohler 2010).[4] Unlike in survival or event history analysis, the focus of interest in sequence analysis is not the length of time until the event occurs, but the pattern in which individual episodes or elements occur within a longer sequence. A sequence is an orderly succession of individual episodes or elements (Brzinsky-Fay, Kohler and Luniak 2006; Scherer and Brüderl 2010). Sequence analysis allows us to identify 'typical' career sequences, to calculate the 'closeness' or similarity of career patterns and to represent them visually.

I code seven different episodes and then look how they typically succeed each other, i.e. I look at career sequences (*see* Table 6.1). The episodes are: (unsuccessful) district candidature (1); (unsuccessful) list-candidature (2); (unsuccessful) double-candidature (3); district mandate after district candidature (4); list mandate after list-candidature (5); double-candidature with election in the district (6); double-candidature with election into parliament via the party-list (7).

---

4.   I apply the new Sequence-Analysis package for Stata (Brzinsky-Fay *et al.* 2006; Kohler *et al.* 2011).

Table 6.1: Sequence elements for analysing German MPs' political careers

Status	Coding
(unsuccessful) district candidature	1
(unsuccessful) list-candidature	2
(unsuccessful) double-candidature	3
district mandate after district candidature	4
list mandate after list-candidature	5
double-candidature with election in the district	6
double-candidature with election into parliament via the party-list	7

Table 6.2 reports the twenty most frequent sequences for all 35,211 persons, which in, up to now, seventeen national elections have competed for a parliamentary seat. Those twenty most frequent sequences apply to almost 31,000 of all candidates. Among these twenty, the eleven most frequent pertain to unsuccessful one-, two- or also three-time candidatures. Among the successful, the pure list-candidates (5) or the double-candidates (6 and 7) dominate (*see* Table 6.2).

Restricting the perspective to the order in which certain episodes appear within a longer sequence (i.e. coding a 337- and a 37-sequence as identical, like also a 6- and a 666-sequence), gives the following picture (*see* Table 6.2). In this perspective, we also see combinations of unsuccessful and successful episodes (like sequences 37, 73, 52). Their share, however, of the sequences of all 33,300 candidates amounts only to around one per cent (N = 380), and of the sequences of the 3,581 elected candidates, i.e. members of the *Bundestag*, somewhat more than 10 per cent.

Table 6.2: Sequence-frequencies, candidates and MPs, 1949–2009

Sequence	Number	%	cum. %
2 (unsuccessf. list candidature)	13,096	42.31	42.31
1 (unsuccessf. district candidature)	6,321	20.42	62.73
3 (unsuccessf. double candidature)	5,580	18.03	80.75
2 / 2	1,806	5.83	86.59
3 / 3	704	2.27	88.86
1 / 1	521	1.68	90.54
2 / 2 / 2	403	1.3	91.85
3 / 2	358	1.16	93
2 / 3	281	0.91	93.91
1 / 3	278	0.9	94.81

Table 6.2 (*continued*)

Sequence	Number	%	cum. %
3 / 1	246	0.79	95.6
7 (double candidature, elected via list)	221	0.71	96.32
1 / 2	208	0.67	96.99
2 / 1	197	0.64	97.63
5 (list mandate after list candidature)	183	0.59	98.22
3 / 3 / 3	135	0.44	98.65
6 (double candidature, elected in district)	113	0.37	99.02
7 / 7	110	0.36	99.37
2 / 2 / 2 / 2	105	0.34	99.71
7 / 7 / 7	89	0.29	100
Total	30,955	100	

Legend: (unsuccessful) district candidature: 1; (unsuccessful) list-candidature: 2; (unsuccessful) double-candidature: 3; district mandate after district candidature: 4; list mandate after list-candidature: 5; double-candidature with election in the district: 6; double-candidature with election into parliament via the party-list: 7.

Table 6.3: Sequence-frequencies with identical order of episodes, candidates and MPs, 1949–2009

Sequence	Number	%	cum. %
2	15,446	46.4	46.4
1	6,952	20.88	67.28
3	6,454	19.39	86.67
7	565	1.7	88.36
3 / 2	558	1.68	90.04
2 / 3	445	1.34	91.38
1 / 3	350	1.05	92.43
3 / 1	341	1.02	93.45
6	331	0.99	94.45
4	292	0.88	95.32
5	283	0.85	96.17
1 / 2	278	0.84	97.01
2 / 1	268	0.81	97.81
3 / 7 (unsuccessf. double cand., then list mandate)	150	0.45	98.26

Table 6.3 (*continued*)

Sequence	Number	%	cum. %
7 / 3 (double cand. elected via list, then unsuccessf. double cand.	147	0.44	98.71
7 / 6	105	0.32	99.02
6 / 7	90	0.27	99.29
5 / 2 (list mandate after list cand., then unsuccessf. list cand.)	83	0.25	99.54
4 / 6	79	0.24	99.78
2 / 3 / 2	74	0.22	100
Total	33,291	100	

Legend: (unsuccessful) district candidature: 1; (unsuccessful) list-candidature: 2; (unsuccessful) double-candidature: 3; district mandate after district candidature: 4; list mandate after list-candidature: 5; double-candidature with election in the district: 6; double-candidature with election into parliament via the party-list: 7.

My findings – quite surprising in their unambiguousness – show that the voter is only assigned a quite secondary, subordinate role when it comes to electing or sacking his or her representatives. We can observe here one of the basic mechanisms at work in a democratic system to secure discipline and loyalty among those elected into parliament vis-à-vis their party: since a very far-reaching decision about the election and re-election is taken at the point of the nomination already, the party appears as the most central point of reference for everybody who has made, or intends to make, politics his or her profession (Carey and Shugart 1995). The threat not to re-nominate is a credible threat, since such a refusal to support a candidate's further term in parliament, in most cases, would effectively put an end to a political career.

If for democratic accountability, as we have seen in the preceding paragraphs, the nomination process seems to be much more central than the actual election, then we can also assume that the pre-selection of candidates might be of greater importance for questions of 'descriptive representation' as well. I will investigate this question with respect to the chances of female candidates being elected into the *Bundestag*, in the next section.

Pre-selection and election: women as candidates and as MPs

As mentioned above, it is 'prevailing wisdom' that proportional rules 'are friendlier to successful female candidacy than district systems' (Iversen and Rosenbluth 2010b: 134). And Germany seems to strongly confirm this prevailed wisdom, given that 'women are still far more likely to get elected via the *Länder* lists than in the Single-Member Districts' (Saalfeld 2005: 219). 'From 1949 to 1983 inclusive, almost four-fifths of women elected owed their election to a party list. Since then, the figure has been two-thirds' (Massicotte forthcoming ch. 3: 12). By comparing the political fate of women in both tiers of the mixed electoral system, we can hope to converge to an answer to the question, *why* exactly does PR have this effect: if it is true that people cast a *party vote* in the proportional tier which is different from the *personal vote* in the plurality tier, one would need to know why exactly the personal vote discriminates against female candidates. Information on the share of female candidates, differentiated by party, also promises to give insights with respect to the question, whether the increase in the number of female candidates is due to a 'contagion effect', with some parties being the *avant-garde* and others following suit (Matland and Studlar 1996).

But what really explains why women might have more difficulties in winning districts (Hoecker 1994)? Are parties more progressive than their voters? Variants of Germany's election law at the state level, which allow for a personalised vote, show the 'disturbing feature' that 'women candidates traditionally tended to suffer more than others from the changes brought by preferences' (Massicotte 2011: 110). Is it therefore beneficial and of 'pedagogical' value when parties leave voters little choice over the gender composition of the parliamentary party by putting most of the female candidates on the closed list? Do voters stereotype female candidates as less assertive and firm in championing the district's interests (Huddy and Terkildsen 1993; Koch 2002; McDermott 1997)? But why then, if voters hold more conservative values than parties, are party lists with their fair amount of female candidates apparently electorally attractive? Why have all German parties, except the Liberals, adopted gender quotas?

Frances Rosenbluth and Torben Iversen think that something else other than voters' gender discrimination explains the striking differences in women's electoral success under majoritarian and proportional rules. They point to different 'political labour markets' in PR- and majoritarian electoral systems – and by implication, also in the proportional and the plurality tier of Germany's mixed-member system (Iversen and Rosenbluth 2010a). Their central labour market-argument is: 'Markets for professional politicians [...] function in a manner that is not very different from markets in other professions, except that political institutions (and parties) rather than economic institutions (and firms) shape incentives and outcomes'. In particular, Iversen and Rosenbluth claim that

> even in the absence of discriminatory social norms and a voter preference for male politicians, personalistic electoral rules should hurt the electoral chances of female candidates by placing a premium on seniority, career continuity, and individual clout in a way centralised, party-centred systems do not. (Iversen and Rosenbluth 2010a: 135)

The labour market analogy to district candidatures would be to professions with 'promotion on the job', i.e. internal careers with a premium on seniority; jobs, which require being present for very long office-hours and avoiding any longer spells off the job ('this [...] is what is known to produce [gender] inequalities in private labor markets that rely heavily on specialised skills and long tenure';

Iversen and Rosenbluth 2010a: 139). In turn, the labour market analogy to the party list candidatures is to professions in which the career depends on certified qualifications (often university degrees) and in which hiring and promotions are not based on informal and internal job assessments by superiors, but rather on external, 'objective', third-party certificates like an MBA or a law degree (which, as we know, leads to high shares of female employment even in the upper echelons of management; (Estevez-Abe 2006)).

According to Iversen and Rosenbluth, candidate-centred (personalistic) electoral systems produce strong gender differences in political representation because they advantage those with 'uninterrupted political careers' and with enough time to 'build up reputation with constituencies, fellow politicians, and bureaucrats' (Iversen and Rosenbluth 2010a: 139), exactly like 'internal' private labour markets with firm-specific skills do. Party-centred electoral rules, in contrast, are more amenable to women's representation because here 'generalised' political skills are more valued than the constituency-specific political skills required in the former system.

Again, the German data provides ample evidence to test these hypotheses. I will start by providing some general information and some descriptive statistics on women's representation in the *Bundestag*. Figure 6.2 shows the development of the number of female candidates over time, from 1949 until today. Figure 6.3 shows the development of the percentage of female candidates as a share of all candidates as well as the percentage of female MPs as a share of all *female* candidates.

Figure 6.2: The number of female and male MPs, 1949–2009

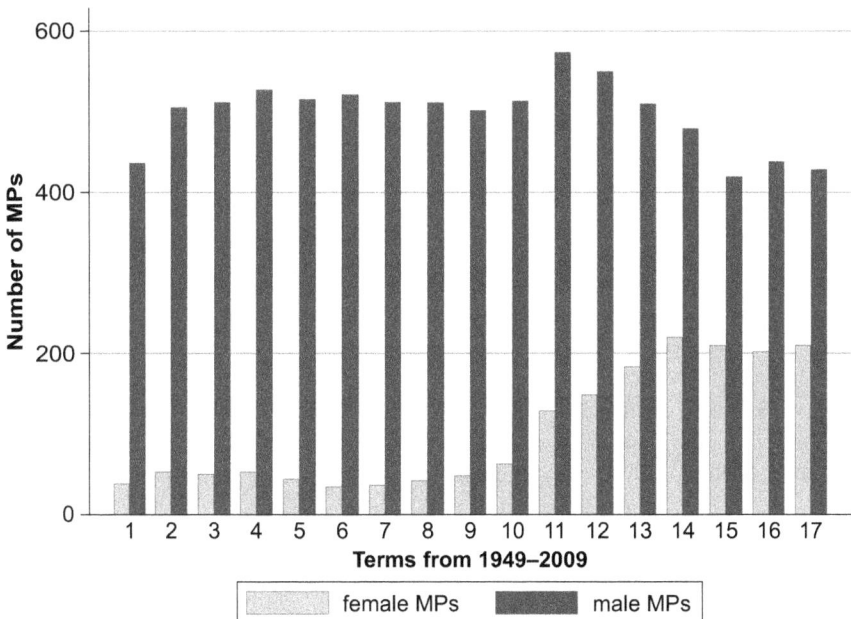

Figure 6.3: Share of female MPs of all female candidates, share of female candidates among the total number of candidates (both established and all parties), 1949–2009

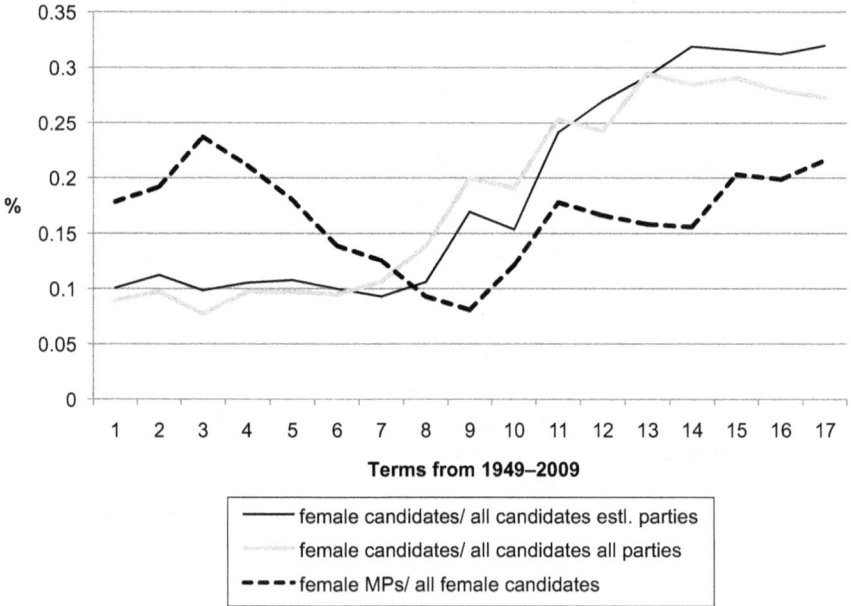

Source: Own calculations.

From Figure 6.3, three phases seem to emerge: first, a phase with very few, but then often successful female candidatures ('showcase-mandates'), subsequently a phase with more candidatures, but less success ('showcase-candidatures'), finally a phase with many successful female candidatures ('true integration'). As a general trend, the increasing share of women is clearly visible, both among the candidates as well as among those who were elected, with the increase among female MPs being higher than that among the female candidates since the 14th term. This points to the fact that especially the established parties a) have an over-proportionated share of female candidates and/or that b) they place those candidates in more promising positions, i.e. in better districts and on better list ranks.

We therefore need to know more about how exactly female candidates run for office. On which rank positions are they to be found? Figures 6.4 and 6.5 show the average list-position of women and men for the two major parties, SPD and CDU/CSU. The average list position is calculated by dividing the rank by the total length of the list (doing this for males and females, separately). This controls for the varying length of party lists due to the varying number of seats elected in each German state (from three in Bremen to around seventy in North-Rhine Westphalia).

Figure 6.4: Relative list position of male and female candidates, SPD, 1949–2009

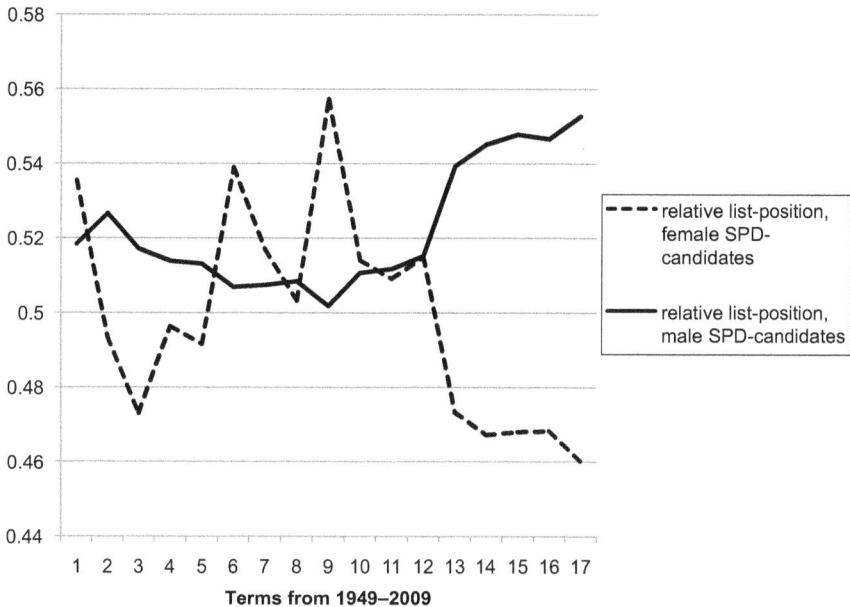

If list-positions were allocated in a fully gender-neutral way, both averages would not differ from each other and should oscillate around 0.5. As one can see in Figures 6.4 and 6.5, however, both parties do indeed pursue quite different nomination and placement strategies. Women's list positions, and thereby their electoral chances, differ considerably between the SPD and CDU/CSU: for the Social Democratic Party the significant increase in the number of female candidates goes together with systematically better list positions, whereas women in the CDU/CSU are placed less favourably than their male co-competitors on the party list (keep in mind that higher list places mean worse chances to get elected into parliament). This pattern is quite stable since the 8th term for the CDU/CSU, whereas SPD-women tend to have better chances of being elected into the *Bundestag* since the 12th term.

If we take a look at the numbers including the two small parties, the Liberals and the Greens since the 9th term (Figure 6.6), we do indeed see a pioneering role of the Social Democrats and the Greens. Starting from an almost identical share of female candidates in all parties of around 15 per cent in the election to the 9th German *Bundestag*, parties began to diverge from each other quite significantly in later terms. The Liberals have the highest share of men, and over time show almost no increase in female candidates. It is, of the four parties, the only one which has neither a binding nor an informal quota-rule for women's representation (Davidson-Schmich 2006; Caul 2001).

Figure 6.5: Relative list position of male and female candidates, CDU/CSU 1949–2009

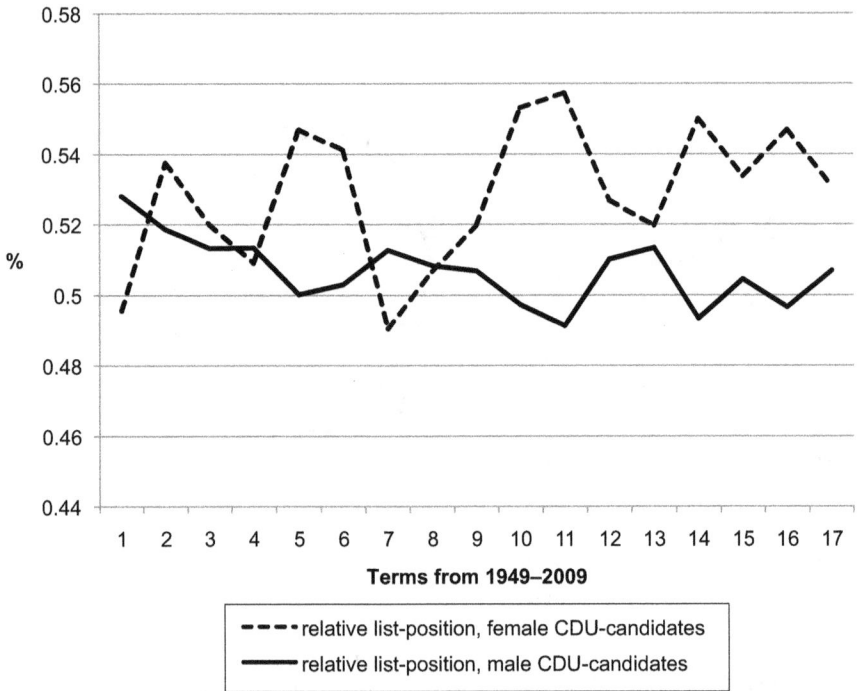

The Green Party was the first to introduce a gender quota in 1985, a quota that reserved each odd list rank for a female candidate. Other parties followed suit. *Die Linke* copied the 50 per cent quota of the Greens with female and male candidates alternating on the list. State party lists for the Social Democrats applied varying quota rules – between 40 and 50 per cent. Only recently, the SPD implemented the rule of alternating list positions between male and female candidates as practiced by the Greens and *die Linke*. Quota rules for the CDU and the CSU vary somewhat: the CDU aims at reaching a 30 per cent share of female candidates if there are enough qualified female candidates, the CSU, the Bavarian sister party, has only recently announced a similar rule. This leaves the Liberals as the only established party without a quota rule. Recent controversies concerning the disadvantages of female candidates in the FDP testify to the 'male' character of this party.

Asking which type of candidacy – list, district or double – prevailed under male and female candidates (analysis is restricted to the established parties since the 10th term), I find the hypothesis that PR, i.e. election through the party-list, is more favourable for women's parliamentary representation as compared to the two other paths into the German *Bundestag*, strongly confirmed. I find very few women among the district candidates – only the Greens send a significant number of women into district races (Figure 6.7).

Figure 6.6: Share of female candidates among all candidates, parties from the 9th to 17th term

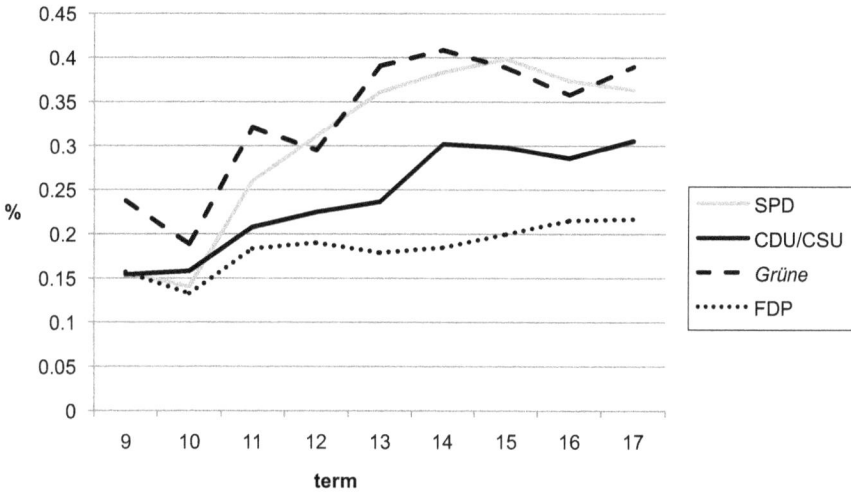

Figure 6.7: Type of candidacy for female and male candidates since the 10th term, established parties only (CDU/CSU, SPD, FDP, the Greens)

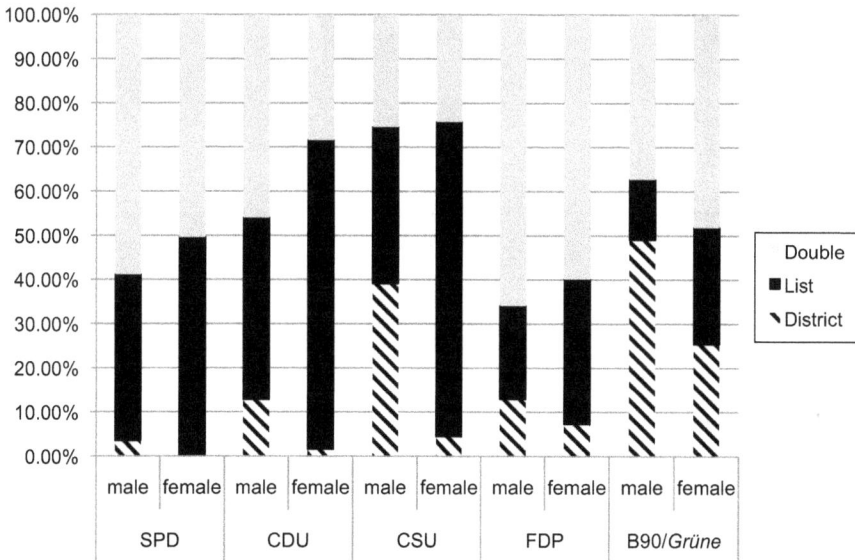

I can again apply sequence analysis in order to identify typical career patterns of male and female candidates. I present my findings as a Sequence Modal Plot. By way of calculating so-called Levenshtein-distances between sequences, I can identify a certain number of 'ideal-typical' careers (which do not necessarily have to have a complement in the real-word in exactly this form).[5] Levenshtein-distances provide a numerical expression of the similarity of two different sequences (Brzinsky-Fay et al. 2006; Scherer and Brüderl 2010). They are calculated by assigning costs to two basic operations ('insertion/ deletion' and 'substitution'), with which we can turn one sequence into another. The more operations we need to undertake, and the costlier these operations are,[6] the more dissimilar are the two sequences. A cluster-analysis of these distances helps in identifying typical career patterns (so-called Optimal Matching, OM). Figure 6.8 displays ideal-typical sequences by gender for all parties since 1949.

Figure 6.8: Sequence-Modal Plot, 'ideal-typical' career-sequences by sex and party, all terms

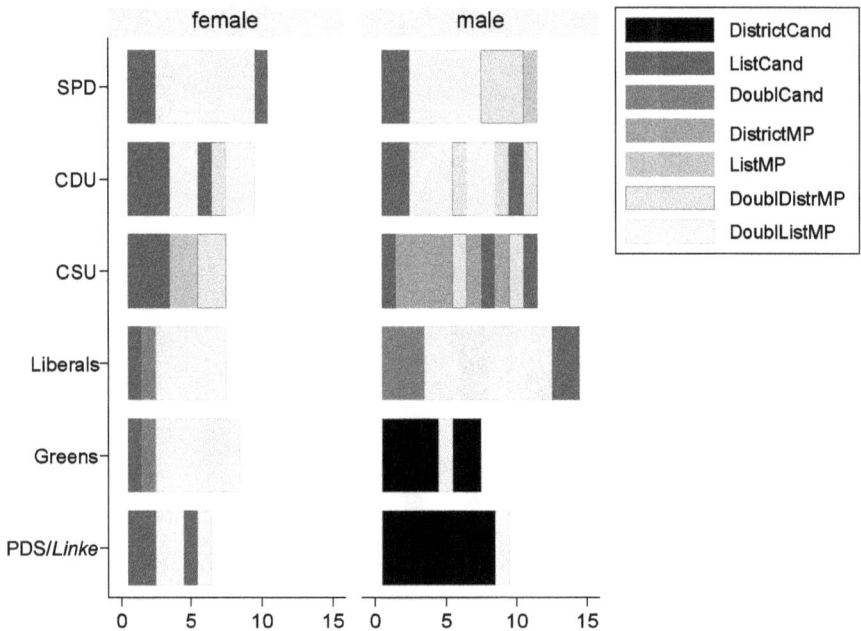

5. Stata-command: sqmodalplot, see (Kohler et al. 2011).

6. The default-costs assigned to the different operations in the Stata sequence analysis module are: 'Insertion or Deletion' [indelcost(1)] and 'Substitution' [subcost(2)]. I have used this Stata-default for our analysis.

Table 6.4: Political career sequences, male and female candidates, all parties and all legislative terms

	Women				Men		
Sequence-elements	Number	%	cum. %	Sequence-elements	N	%	cum. %
2	4,212	60.11	60.11	2	11,235	41.64	41.64
3	1,031	14.71	74.83	1	6,065	22.48	64.12
1	887	12.66	87.48	3	5,423	20.1	84.22
2/3	227	3.24	90.72	23	945	3.5	87.72
7	141	2.01	92.74	13	704	2.61	90.33
3/7	88	1.26	93.99	12	516	1.91	92.24
1/3	75	1.07	95.06	7	425	1.58	93.82
1/2	72	1.03	96.09	4	289	1.07	94.89
6	59	0.84	96.93	6	272	1.01	95.9
6/7	50	0.71	97.65	37	265	0.98	96.88
2/5	48	0.69	98.33	67	222	0.82	97.7
5	46	0.66	98.99	123	211	0.78	98.48
1/2/3	27	0.39	99.37	5	178	0.66	99.14
1/7	22	0.31	99.69	46	156	0.58	99.72
5/7	22	0.31	100	17	75	0.28	100
Total	7,007	100		Total	26,981	100	

Legend: (unsuccessful) district candidature: 1; (unsuccessful) list-candidature: 2; (unsuccessful) double-candidature: 3; district mandate after district candidature: 4; list mandate after list-candidature: 5; double-candidature with election in the district: 6; double-candidature with election into parliament via the party-list: 7.

Again, I observe clear differences in the career paths of men and women in Germany's political system. While the – successful or unsuccessful – candidature on a party-list or the double candidature with an election into parliament via the list is predominant among women, the role of the district candidature plays a much bigger role among male contenders for office. The successful exclusive district candidature – without a simultaneous place on the party list – can almost exclusively be found among CSU-candidates (who run in Bavarian strongholds). Restricting the analysis to sequences that contain the same episodes and comparing these again between men and women without further differentiation by party leads to the following results (*see* Table 6.4).

As Table 6.4 shows, female candidates are, on average, more successful than their male colleagues – the first successful sequence, sequence seven (double candidature with election via the list), appears 'earlier' in the table for female candidates, i.e. is more frequent among them. If female candidates are successful, they almost exclusively enter the *Bundestag* via the party list. Among the fifteen most frequent sequences with identical elements, I find none with a successful (exclusive) district candidature (sequence element four), even unsuccessful district candidatures are relatively rare among women as compared to men (sequence element 1; 12.7 as compared to 22.5 per cent).

We can now turn to the question why exactly women appear to have more difficulties in winning districts. As sketched above, we are confronted with basically two different explanations, one pointing to voters' conservatism, the other to different political 'labour markets' with very different career requirements (Iversen and Rosenbluth 2010a). In order to test Torben Iversen's and Frances Rosenbluth's political labour market thesis, the average age at first entry into the *Bundestag* as well as average tenure in parliament, evaluated by gender, might provide us with the first empirical evidence. It would also be of interest whether we do indeed see more career interruptions, earlier exit from the *Bundestag*, and more instances of 'interval truncation' (late entry combined with early exit) among female MPs.

Looking at the average age at first entry, the 679 female MPs of the total of 3.581 are substantially (and statistically significant) younger – by almost two years – than their 2,902 male colleagues (*see* Table 6.5) – first evidence that candidatures at the district level may in fact require much more time to build up a reputation and more long-term career investments. Supplementary evidence is provided by a recent study showing that female MPs more often have 'untypical' careers with late entry into a party (so-called *Quereinsteiger*, career changer), fewer cases of an extensive previous history of local party engagement or local office holding, etc. – fewer examples of the '*Ochsentour*', as the drawn-out process of working one's way up in the party is called in Germany (Bailer *et al*. 2011). So, women combine earlier entry into parliament with later entry into the party – which is in line with Iversen's and Rosenbluth's hypotheses.

But what about the time spent in parliament, once elected? Can we detect gender differences with respect to tenure, too? The argument of Iversen and Rosenbluth would lead us to expect shorter periods of *Bundestag* membership for

Table 6.5: Age at first entry into the Bundestag, *female and male MPs*

	Number	Mean	Std. Dev.	Min	Max
Age, Female MPs 1st entry	679	43.81885	8.780402	19	75
Age, Male MPs 1st entry	2,902	45.46864	9.373896	22	81

Table 6.6: Restricted mean, MPs of CDU/CSU, SPD, Liberals, Greens and the Left, by gender

Sex	Number	50%	Std. Err.	[95% Conf. Interval]
Female	648	4319	58.76	4019–4319
Male	2706	4033	64.47	3995–4268
Total	3354	4073	56.74	4019–4292

women. With a substantial number of right-censored records in our data set[7] and with a general increase in women's parliamentary representation over the most recent terms, I cannot simply calculate average tenures by gender (see Cleves *et al.* 2004: 91–93; Blossfeld *et al.* 2007; Box-Steffensmeier and Jones 2004: 16–19).[8] Instead, I need to apply survival analysis, for instance by calculating Kaplan-Meier estimates of the survivor function as an estimate of the probability to survive beyond a certain point in time (see Cleves *et al.* 2004: 93–107).[9] This then allows me to calculate the mean or the median as the point of time beyond which 50 per cent of all observed individuals are expected to survive. Alternatively, I can then compare the survival function by gender, for instance with a log-rank test (Cleves *et al.* 2004: 123–124). Given the right-skewed nature of survivor functions, one is better advised to calculate the median instead of

---

7. Since my observations end with the start of the 17th *Bundestag* term, 620 individuals are treated as having not yet 'failed', i.e. have not left parliament yet, or as having been substituted by someone who, in turn, has not 'failed' yet.

8. The averages reported in (Feldkamp 2005: 146–147) therefore seem problematic, as well as my own calculations (Manow 2007).

9. The Kaplan-Meier estimator of the survivor function $\hat{S}(t)$ as the probability to survive up to t_j

   is: $\hat{S}(t) = \prod_{j|t_j \leq t} \left(\frac{n_j - d_j}{n_j} \right)$ for a dataset that observes failures at times $t_1, t_2, t_3 \ldots t_k$ with n_j as

   the number of persons 'at risk' at time t_j, and d_j as the number of failures at that same time. I use the Stata commands sts list (for the Kaplan-Meier survivor function), sts graph (for graphing these functions), stci, rmeans (for calculating (restricted) mean survival time) and sts test (for comparing survivor functions) (Blossfeld *et al.* 2007, ch. 3; Cleves *et al.* 2004).

Table 6.7: Log-rank test for equality of survivor functions, all MPs by gender

Sex	Events observed	Events expected
Female	453	463.70
Male	2410	2399.30
Total	2863	2863.00
	chi2(1) = 0.30, Pr>chi2 = 0.5813	

the mean. But neither the median nor the comparison between survivor functions by gender reveal any differences in the survival functions of female and male members of the *Bundestag* (*see* Tables 6.6 and 6.7) – no matter if I restrict analysis to the 'established' parties (CDU/CSU, SPD, FDP, *Grüne* and *die Linke*), or if I include all parties.

But this overall picture changes once I take parties as my unit of comparison. Graphs of the Kaplan-Meier estimates reveal significant gender differences in tenure (or in the hazard of having to leave parliament, either during the term or at elections due to either non-nomination or non-election) for the Green party as well as in a comparison between Social and Christian Democrats (*see* Figures 6.9–6.11).

The Green party always has been a pace-setter when it comes to women's parliamentary representation, to female candidates and MPs and the introduction of gender quotas. It is therefore on the whole not surprising that this party has also used positive discrimination with respect to female politicians, as visible in their significantly better political survival chances (see above). Differences for the Christian and the Social Democrats are less obvious, but still observable (*see* Figures 6.10 and 6.11).

When restricting the comparison to the two only parties that regularly win district seats, the SPD and the CDU/CSU, we can observe differences in women's parliamentary representation that correspond to the differences in nomination strategies observed above, when comparing the 'relative list positions' of men and women (*see* Figures 6.4 and 6.5).

Given that the CDU/CSU and SPD

- assign women differently on attractive list positions, and
- differ with respect to their shares of list- and district candidates (and taking into account that district candidatures usually last longer than list candidatures (*see* Chapter Seven),

we see that the Christian Democrats provide female politicians with less attractive career prospects. Particularly in regard to longer periods of *Bundestag* membership, male CDU/CSU-parliamentarians clearly outdo their female colleagues. It seems reasonable to assume that the traditional family model – the married couple with kids – is more widespread among candidates of the Christian Democrats, as a visible personal commitment to a certain kind of family policy and

Figure 6.9: Survival estimates for the MPs of the Green Party, by gender

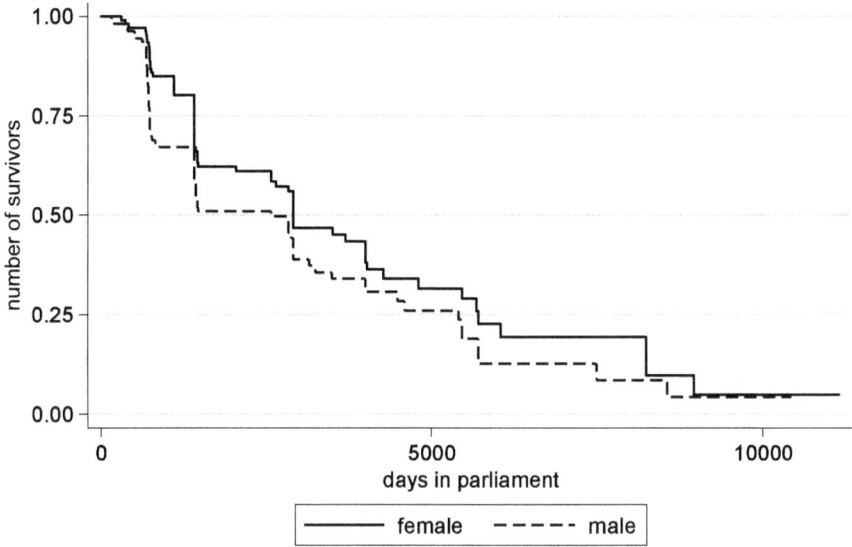

Figure 6.10: Survival estimates for CDU/CSU MPs, by gender

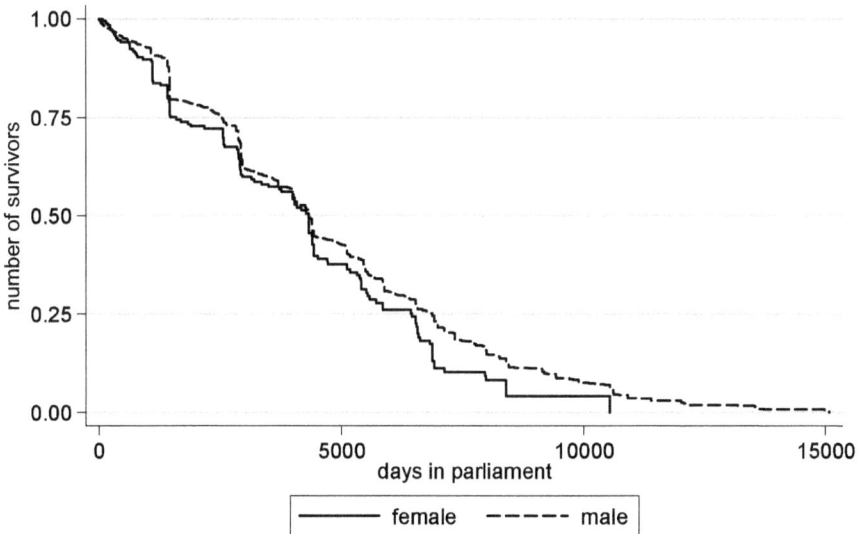

hence, a marker of political credibility.[10] But it is exactly this traditional family model which is particularly unfavourable to the political career pattern in which the Christian Democrat party has a comparative advantage: the district mandate. The observable party differences in women's parliamentary representation, and in their average tenure, can again be interpreted as support for the conjecture of Iversen and Rosenbluth. For the Social Democrats, however, the evidence proves a quite substantial capacity of the party leadership to orient the nomination process toward principal programmatic party interests (*see* Figure 6.11).

In the next chapter I will more closely analyse the political survival chances of German MPs and the effect of electoral rules on their re-election prospects.

Figure 6.11: Survival estimates for SPD MPs, by gender

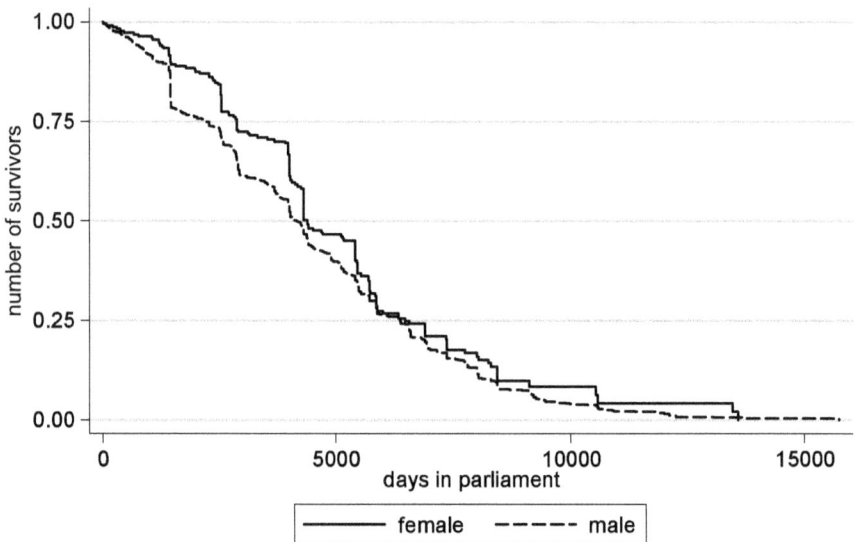

_____

10. Taking biographical information from *Kürschner's Volkskalender*, Hilke Brockmann has calculated the average number of children for female MPs for the period 1953–1965 and 2002–2009. In both periods, female CDU-MPs with kids reported the highest number of children (2.8 and 2.1, in the first and second period, respectively) among all female MPs with kids; see (Brockmann 2011: 16, Table 4).

Chapter Seven

Combining Candidatures: Hedging against electoral uncertainty[1]

As we have seen in the preceding chapters, the plurality tier in the German mixed member electoral system introduces an element of disproportionality and hence volatility. This rule-induced volatility has reinforced the secular trend of increased voter volatility in times of decreased party identification (Bartolini and Mair 1990). Volatility has further increased with the multiplication of parties since the 1980s. How have parties and candidates reacted?

According to the cartel party thesis, parties and candidates are faced with greater electoral volatility and, as a result, are increasingly turning away from the pursuit of electoral victory by, instead, concentrating on minimising the costs of electoral defeat (Katz and Mair 2009, 1995). Analysing parties' nomination strategies would be a promising way to test one central contention of the cartel party thesis – which, as of yet, has undergone only little empirical testing. Are the parties really sealing themselves off increasingly from voters, and are they immunising themselves vis-à-vis an ever more volatile 'verdict of the people'?

Hedging against electoral uncertainty can imply either assigning candidates safe districts or safe list positions, or both. As we have seen, disproportionality in the plurality tier of Germany's electoral system strongly affects its PR-tier: if the number of districts lost by the one party and won by the other increases from election to election, the number of compensatory list-mandates needed to secure overall vote-seat proportionality will fluctuate accordingly. But in order to understand parties' responses, we first have to clarify the question of what a safe list position is, or has been. And what qualifies a district as safe?

In this chapter I will focus on the first question, which at first sight may appear to be a simple one: when can a position on a party-list be considered as safe? By examining all *Bundestag* elections up until 2009 (excluding, as before, the first election in 1949), I want to discover which spots on a party list of a German state (*Land*) have guaranteed the candidate a good chance of being elected to the *Bundestag*. I study how such safe positions vary from party to party and state to state and how this has changed over time. Therefore, three dimensions will be analysed in the following, specifically that of party, state, and election year:

---

1.   This chapter is based on joint work with Martina Nistor (see Manow and Nistor 2009).

- I compare, first and foremost, the two major parties: CDU/CSU and SPD.
- I examine the differences among the sixteen German states.
- I throw a light on the changes from 1949–2009.

Once we are in a position to identify safe list positions, we can combine these insights with information about safe district in order to address how parties' nomination strategies might or might not have reacted to volatility: how are party-list and constituency mandates combined when it comes to double candidatures? Are safe constituencies combined with unpromising placing on the party list and safe party-list rankings with hopeless constituency candidatures, or are there privileged and disadvantaged groups of candidates who are given both promising (unpromising) spots on the party list as well as safe (or unsafe) constituencies? Does the double candidacy provide parties with the opportunity to guarantee its core personnel political survival no matter how voters cast their votes? Have parties successfully immunised themselves against the verdict of the democratic sovereign – in their increasing interest to minimise the consequences of losing elections rather than to maximise their chances of winning elections (Katz and Mair 1995, 2009)? Has therefore the German mixed-member system become *less* responsive towards elections, has it accordingly reduced the role of 'elections as an instrument of democracy' (Powell 2000)?[2]

Understanding how parties in the German electoral system protect their candidates from electoral uncertainty will also help us to better assess the relative attractiveness of party-list positions and district candidatures. In turn, this will also enable us to understand the incentive structure with which politicians are faced when running for office (*see* Chapter Eight), a pre-condition for answering the question whether we see a mandate-divide in the *Bundestag*, i.e. two different types of MPs depending on how they entered parliament, via the party list or with a district mandate (cf. Stratmann and Baur 2002; Lancaster and Patterson 1990; Bawn and Thies 2003; Klingemann and Wessels 2001a; Sieberer 2010).

Concerning the probability of being elected into parliament depending on the rank on the party list, I identify the last successful place on each of the party lists in each state that still secured a *Bundestag* mandate. This allows calculating the probabilities for a successful campaign for each ranking, by using the sum of the seventeen *Bundestag* elections so far.[3]

---

2. By studying the safety of list candidatures we also learn something about the opportunities available to voters to defeat candidates ('to throw the rascals out'; see Fearon 1999), and therefore, about the effectiveness of the basic democratic sanctioning mechanism in the German mixed member electoral system (Matland and Studlar 2004; Manow 2007) (*see* Chapter Nine).

3. We do not take substitutes into consideration in our analysis because the vacancy rate among *Bundestag* members during a legislative period is arguably not a systematic part of parties' nomination strategies.

My data are taken from the

- publications of the German Statistical Office (Veröffentlichungen des Statistischen Bundesamtes zu den Bundestagswahlen aus den Jahren 1965–2002 and the Sonderveröffentlichungen des Statistischen Bundesamtes zu den Wahlbewerbern 1953–2002),
- the data from the internet site of the Federal Returning Officer (www.bundeswahlleiter.de) for the elections of 1998, 2002, and 2005, as well as the
- biographical handbook of the *Bundestag* members (Biographisches Handbuch der Mitglieder des Deutschen Bundestages 1949–2002; Vierhaus and Herbst 2003).

I updated the data on the *Bundestag* MPs to include the last *Bundestag* elections.[4]

Before I turn to our analysis of the safety of the ranked positions on party lists, I would like to take a closer look at two questions: how large is the percentage of representatives who campaigned exclusively as either party-list candidates or in a constituency, as compared to those who competed for a parliamentary seat as both party-list and constituency candidates (i.e. a double candidature)? In the case of double candidatures, the question follows: which of the candidatures ended up gaining the representative a seat in parliament – the district vote or the place on the party list? Subsequently, I calculate a quotient from the number of list candidatures and the last place on the list that resulted in the candidate being elected – a quotient that will prove to be a good indicator of a party's general performance (third section). Finally, in the fourth section, I examine party-list rankings and investigate the nomination strategies of parties against the backdrop of identifying safe constituencies and safe rankings on the party list.

Types of mandates in each party

As already mentioned above, in the German electoral system half of the members of parliament represent constituencies, the other half are determined via the party lists in each of the (today 16) states. Should a representative resign, the highest placed candidate left on the state list is awarded the mandate, which is the third way to become a member of the *Bundestag*. By-elections determined the successor of vacant constituency seats until 1952 – since then replacement from the highest list-position has been the standard mechanism (cf. Massicotte forthcoming ch. 3: 4 and ch. 5: 16–17). Knowing this, we would like to inquire: are there differences in the way the parties assign mandates?

With regard to the small parties, usually 100 per cent of the seats in parliament won by the FDP (Liberals) and *Die Grünen* (Greens) are party-list mandates.

---

4. Since the state of Baden-Württemberg was created on 25 April 1952 by combining the states of Baden, Württemberg-Baden, and Württemberg-Hohenzollern, it is included in the analysis starting in the second legislative period.

Figure 7.1: Percentage of party-list mandates, SPD and CDU/CSU (legislative periods 1–17)

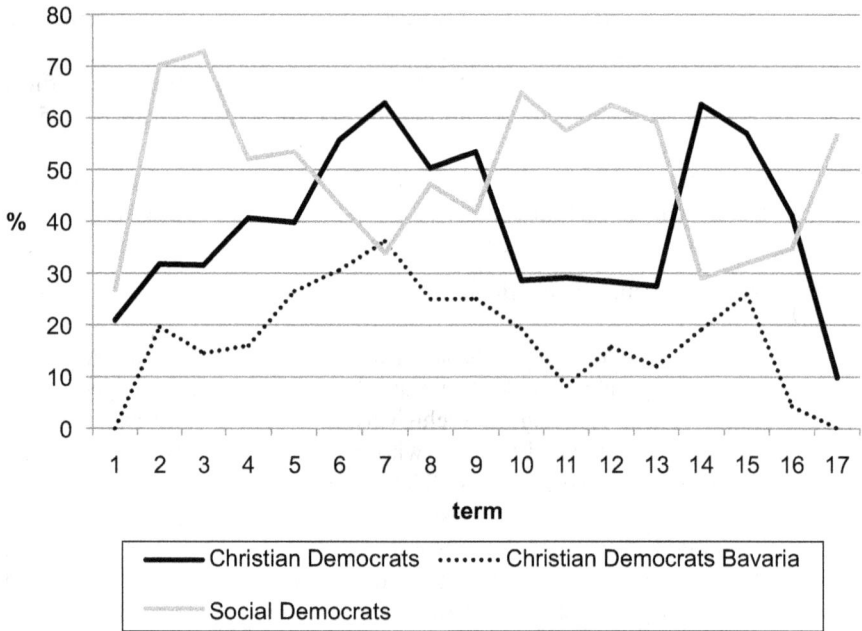

Exceptions, for the FDP, are a few district mandates in early *Bundestag* elections and a district mandate won in 1990 in Saxony-Anhalt (Halle). For the Greens, one district mandate was won in a single Berlin constituency in 2002, 2005 and 2009, all by Hans-Christian Ströbele. For the PDS/*die Linke*, the percentage of party-list representatives is less than 100 per cent due to a few constituencies that the party wins; yet in 2002 not a single party-list candidate gained a seat in the *Bundestag* because the party failed to gain the necessary five per cent of the general vote. Since the three small parties overwhelmingly receive their seats through their party lists, my focus in the following remains on the two major parties, the SPD and CDU/CSU, only.

Figure 7.1 charts each major party's percentage of list mandates out of all its elected candidates for all legislative periods. It shows that the values for the CDU and CSU run parallel, whereby the CDU generally receives more list mandates than the CSU, which is more successful in winning district mandates. The values of the Social Democrats are – not surprisingly – inversely related to those of the Union. When the Social Democrats attain a high percentage of list mandates among their elected representatives, the corresponding percentage for the Union is small, and vice versa.

We can see from Figure 7.1 that, on average, the Union wins more constituencies in all *Bundestag* elections than the SPD: calculated from all 17 legislative terms the CDU/CSU won 153, as compared to 110 districts by the SPD. One first presumption would be that the main reason for this may lie in electoral geography: the densely populated SPD constituencies in the (old) industrial centres might have resulted in victories by large leads, whereas the majorities secured in the constituencies won by the CDU were, on average, narrower (Rodden 2010; Gudgin and Taylor 2012 [1979]). However, as we saw in Chapter Three, the plurality tier does *not* generally disadvantage the Social Democrats – which is possibly explained by the (mostly rural) districts in which a high percentage of Catholics provide the Christian Democrats with very strong majorities, too. In fact, the vote margin by which districts are won is on average lower for the SPD than for the CDU (*see* above, Figure 3.6)

The overall finding of a stronger local basis for the Christian Democrats is modified by a fluctuation in the number of successful district mandates, explainable by the volatility of electoral success. This can be demonstrated when we compare the share of district candidates for the two major parties (*see* Figure 3.8, above).

Looking at the type of MPs' candidacies – list only, district only or double – we observe a drop in the number of single candidatures (both constituency and party-list) and a steady increase in the number of double candidatures (Figure 7.3). The minor exception to this trend is seen for the CSU, which maintains a high percentage of strictly direct-mandate candidatures throughout, the average

Figure 7.2: The percentages of strictly constituency candidatures, strictly party-list candidatures, and double candidatures among the members of the Bundestag *for the legislative periods 1–17*

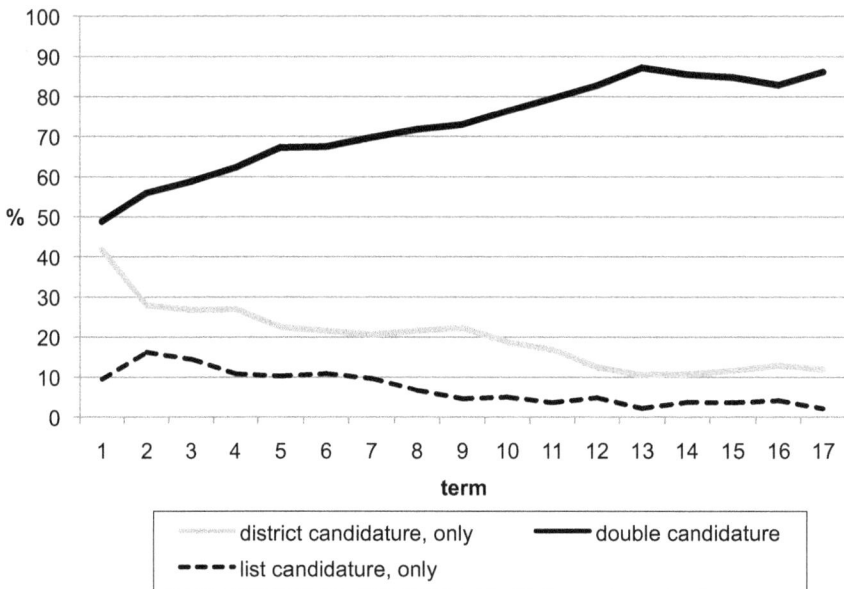

over the seventeen legislative periods equalling 55.8 per cent. The CDU follows with an average of 32.56 per cent, while the Social Democrats prove to have the lowest share of candidates campaigning solely for a district mandate. The SPD introduced the practice of double candidatures very early. For the smaller parties, it is not surprising to find them to be even more distinct. Already after the second legislative period, FDP candidates running solely for a district mandate no longer had a chance to win a seat in the *Bundestag*. For *Bündnis 90/Die Grünen*, only Hans-Christian Ströbele ran solely as a constituency candidate in 2002, 2005 and 2009; for the PDS the only person, as such, was Stefan Heym in 1994.

Among all the seats in the *Bundestag*, the percentage held by representatives who won solely by a party-list candidature, is less than that of those who ran solely as constituency candidates for all parties. This number, however, is dropping steadily (*see* Figure 7.2). As Chapter Four demonstrated, it pays for parties to have their candidates running both as list and constituency candidates, even when the latter race is a rather hopeless one. The exclusive list-candidature, therefore, has become a rare event. Accordingly, the percentage of double candidatures among elected representatives has increased steadily. The continual rise reached its peak in the thirteenth legislative period. Since then, the share of double candidatures has dropped again slightly. This is explained by the slight increase of those nominees running strictly as constituency candidates since 1994.

With regard to double candidatures, the numbers show that, on average (and excluding the first legislative period), 55.03 per cent of the elected CDU representatives with double candidatures owed their seats in the *Bundestag* to their place on the party list. For the CSU, this figure was only 18.21 per cent; for the SPD, 51.69 per cent; for the FDP, 98.32 per cent; for *Die Grünen*, 100 per cent; and for the PDS, 71.44 per cent.

Number of party-list mandates and the last successful party-list ranking

In the two major parties, the number of party-list candidates who win seats in the *Bundestag* does not usually correspond with the last successful spot on the party list in the respective states. For example, in the 2005 *Bundestag* election, nineteen list positions were awarded to the SPD for the electoral results in Baden-Württemberg. Due to the successful election of several double candidates, the last ranking on the party list to win a seat was number twenty-three.

This allows us to calculate the ratio of the number of all elected party-list candidates to the last elected spot on the party lists – the Number-Ranking Quotient (NRQ). It is calculated by using the following formula, with results calculated for every party, every state, and every election:

$$NRQ = \frac{\text{Number of all elected party-list candidates}}{\text{Last successfully elected party-list position (\textbf{R}anking)}}$$

This quotient can fluctuate between one and zero. For small parties, who very seldom win districts, this figure equals one always. In the urban strongholds of the SPD like Bremen, the figure often equals zero because not one of its party-list candidates makes it into the *Bundestag*. Empirically, the quotient fluctuates between 0.9 and 0.45 from election to election for both of the major parties CDU/CSU and SPD (*see* Figure 7.4). For the major parties, the quotient therefore mainly reflects regional strengths and weaknesses. For example, the coefficient for the CDU in Brandenburg is always at 1, as it is in Bremen (with the exception of the 1953 election). In Hamburg, the CDU result also displays a quotient at about 1. However, in Saxony, the CDU has not once had any successful party-list candidates to date. The complementary picture applies for the SPD, having its strongholds in city-states like Bremen or Hamburg, from which the party usually does not send list candidates to the *Bundestag* because it wins every district.

The value of the NRQ is linked to parties' nomination strategies. A higher NRQ means either that a party primarily assigned only 'pure' list mandates to the top ranks of its list or that only a few of the highly-placed double candidates were successfully elected via the district. Since the practice of allocating double candidatures has spread more and more over the course of time, a higher coefficient should point foremost to unsuccessful constituency candidatures, whereas a lower NRQ is to be interpreted as an indication of a high number of double candidates elected via the district. The quotient from the number of successful list candidates,

Figure 7.3: NR-Quotient for the SPD and CDU/CSU, 1st–17th term

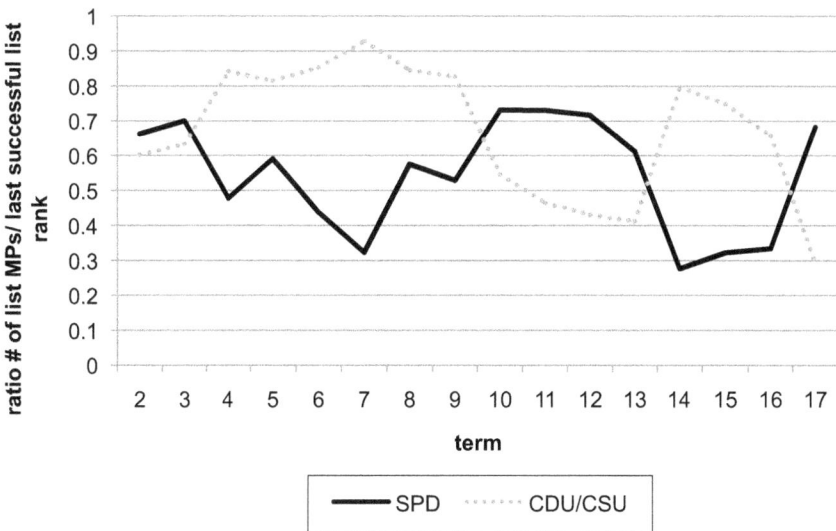

and the last elected rank on the party list, fluctuates considerably for both major parties and shows that statements about 'safe' placements on the party lists are specific to the respective time, state, and party. As far as changes over time are concerned, we see that the quotient can act as a good (inverse) indicator of the electoral success of the two major parties, the SPD and the CDU/CSU.

If the NRQ is high, a party's overall election results are poor. For example, the quotient for the CDU/CSU is quite high for the 4th through to the 9th legislative periods, rather low between the 10th and 13th legislative periods and increases again in the 14th legislative period (1998), only to drop afterwards – it therefore reflects the general electoral performance of the party (*see* Figure 7.3). From 1969 to 1983, the Union was in the opposition, had comparably few district mandates and, therefore, a high coefficient. The significant loss of votes for the CDU/CSU in the 1998 election also led to a high NRQ. However, during the Kohl era between 1983 and 1998, the Union had a very low coefficient displaying many successful constituency candidatures by people holding top ranks on the party lists, too. The development for the SPD inversely mirrors that of the CDU: starting in the third legislative period, what had been a very high quotient drops to its lowest point in the seventh legislative period, only to rise again between the eighth and thirteenth periods, in other words in the 1980s and 1990s. The 1998 election produces a significantly smaller quotient, after which a gradual increase occurs. Here, too, we see the connection to the SPD's electoral victories.

The comparison of the NRQs points to the important mechanism that influences the internal composition of the parliamentary groups in the German electoral system of personalised proportional representation: the parliamentary parties of each of the major *ruling* parties – be it the SPD or the CDU/CSU – prove to have an above-average share of district mandates, as already highlighted in the preceding chapter. The effect can be demonstrated well by a comparison of the fluctuation in constituency votes and district mandates. As became clear in Figure 4.5, even small vote changes lead sometimes to substantial changes in the number of district mandates for the SPD and CDU (*see* above, Chapter Two and Three). Whether the numbers are rising or falling, the fluctuation in the number of district mandates is appreciably greater than that of the constituency vote. Particularly visible are the two landslide victories of the Social Democrats in 1972 and 1998, where the Social Democrats' vote gains translated into an unprecedented high number of won districts.

Should a party gain a large number of constituency mandates because of a small gain of votes, this means fewer party-list candidates among the mandate-holders. As a result, the internal composition of each parliamentary group can also change significantly with a small shift in votes. It is certainly not a new observation that party-list candidates fare best, particularly 'when their party achieves only a mediocre or even a relatively poor result. Should the election results be surprisingly good, it is primarily the constituency candidates who benefit.'[5] But to the best

---

5. See (Kaack 1969: 24–25).

Figure 7.4a: Fluctuation of the share of district mandates and of the share of the constituency votes for the CDU, 1957–2009

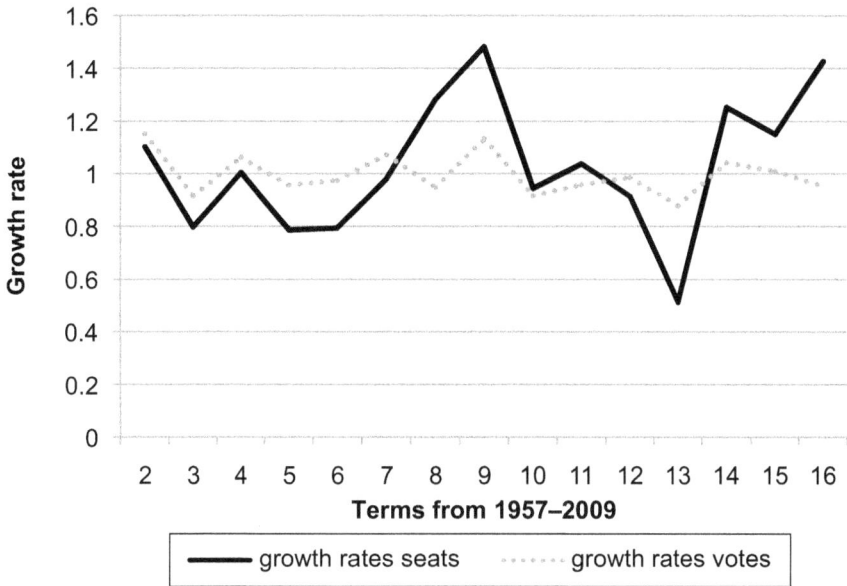

Figure 7.4b: Fluctuation of the share of district mandates and of the share of the constituency votes for the SPD, 1957–2009

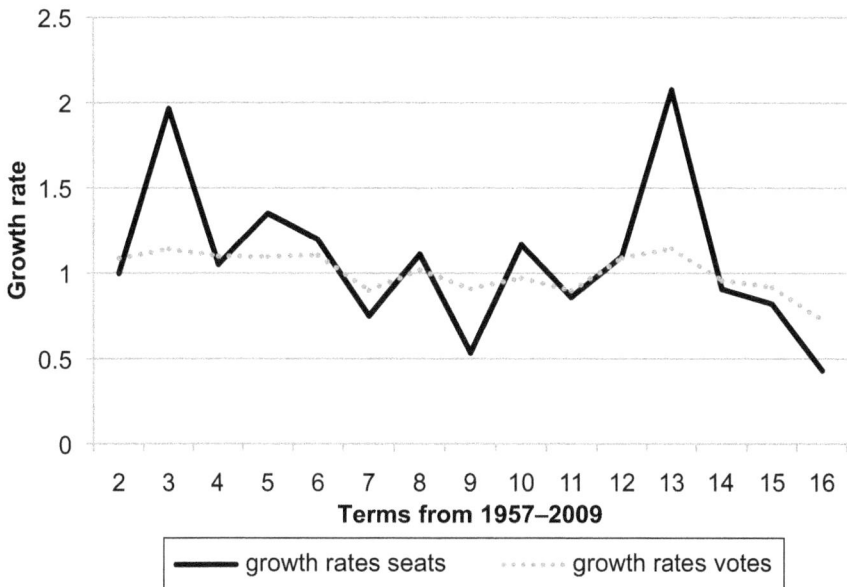

of my knowledge, this effect has, to date, been neither described nor explained systematically and empirically, let alone have its implications been discussed in the literature. However, there is one straightforward implication for the strategies that the party leadership uses to nominate their candidates: if the leadership wants to protect a certain core personnel against electoral volatility (including the volatility of the vote-seat translation in the plurality tier), it is insufficient to only use safe list-positions to protect its candidates running for district mandates against the contingency of *poor election results* in close constituency races. The party leadership must also protect its party-list candidates against the contingency of *good results* and the disproportionate success of their own district candidates.[6] I argue that this strategy can explain the obvious increase in the number of double candidatures. If party leaders want to protect the seats of a certain group of persons (who are important to the personnel planning of party politics, including a substantial number of female MPs, see preceding analysis) not only against the party's electoral defeat but also against its own electoral victory, one expectation would be that double candidatures usually (must) combine good list rankings with safe constituencies. Whether the data support this expectation is a question that will be addressed in the next section.

Safe party-list rankings, safe seats

In the literature, no clear criteria to determine the safety of party-list positions are stipulated. Kaack suggests that the 'top' two-thirds of the party-list rankings won in the preceding *Bundestag* election should be viewed as safe (Kaack 1969: 16). Yet, no reliable evaluation of the safety of list rankings can be based merely on the results of a single election, and the arbitrary removal of a set percentage of rankings would produce no more than a very rough and preliminary estimate of the promising rankings. Instead, I propose here to calculate the safety of list rankings by using the frequency with which, in the past, a certain ranking for a certain party in a particular state has led to a mandate in the *Bundestag*. In order to determine, more precisely, just how safe a list ranking for a party in one of the sixteen German states actually is, I calculate the probability to win a seat in parliament based on the results of past *Bundestag* elections for each of these list rankings. Again I look at all of the terms except the very first *Bundestag* election.[7]

Using this method, we can (restrictively) define a position on the list of a party in a state as being safe, when the candidates who held this position in the sixteen *Bundestag* elections studied had been elected into parliament each time.[8]

---

6. See Wüst *et al.* 2006.

7. Not included in the second and third *Bundestag* elections is also the Saarland, which did not join the FRG until 1957. The new German states are incorporated into the study for the last five legislative periods starting in 1990. For the party *Bündnis 90/Die Grünen*, there are seven legislative periods in the study, for the PDS/*die Linke* there are five.

8. As always, alternative operationalisations are conceivable. For example, from the candidate's perspective, the criterion of 'party-list ranking leading to a *Bundestag* mandate in the last five *Bundestag* elections' would perhaps be relevant. However, it is to be expected that these alternative specifications would affect levels, yet mirror the same general trend.

Figure 7.5: Average list rank that secured election to the Bundestag, *CDU/CSU and SPD 1953–2009*

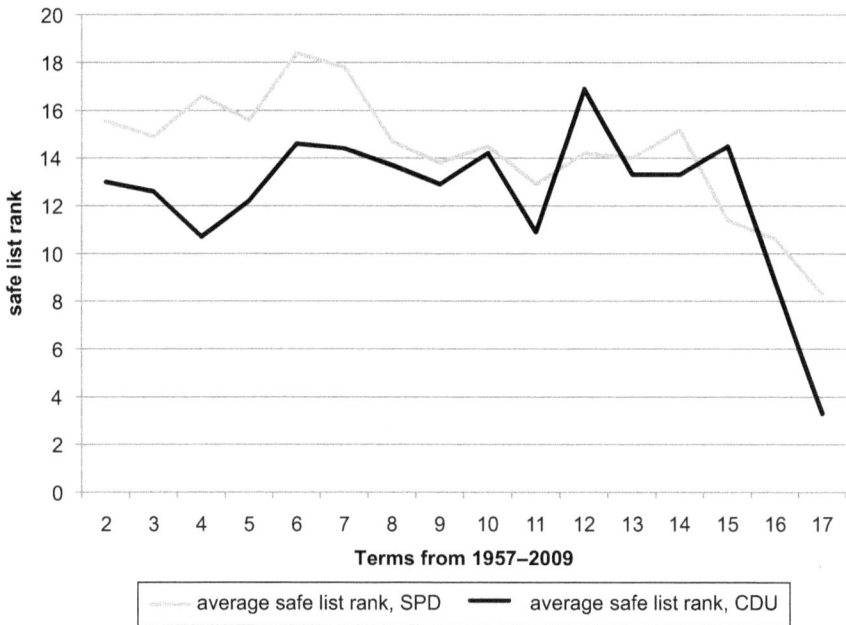

In calculating the average 'safe' list rank, that is the highest rank that in the past always secured entry into the *Bundestag*, I restrict my analysis to the group of 'old' states. With German unification and the addition of the five small new *Länder* from the east, a group of smaller states with fewer districts, and therefore also with shorter state party lists, entered the German electoral system. This by itself would have led to the reduction of safe list ranks, if averages are calculated across all state party lists.

Comparing the average of the last 'safe' list rank for SPD and CDU/CSU shows that over the period under investigation the average was cut by more than half in the case of the SPD (from about 16–8), and by more than two-thirds for the CDU/CSU (from around 13 to below 4; *see* Figure 7.5). While we would expect a declining trend to be – at least partially – a simple effect of the randomness of elections, cumulated over time, we do understand a lately accelerating erosion of parties' reservoir of safe list positions from Figure 7.5. If interested in the continuity of its parliamentary personnel and in securing its MPs' relatively secure career prospects, parties therefore face a much more challenging task today than they did in the first decades of the FRG.

We can now turn to the second critical question: what constitutes a safe district? To code constituencies as safe, I use two possible qualifications. For one qualification, we can apply the restrictive definition of a 'stronghold' (*Hochburg*)

Figure 7.6: Share of safe seats (won by at least a 10 per cent margin), by party, 1953–2009 in per cent of all constituency seats

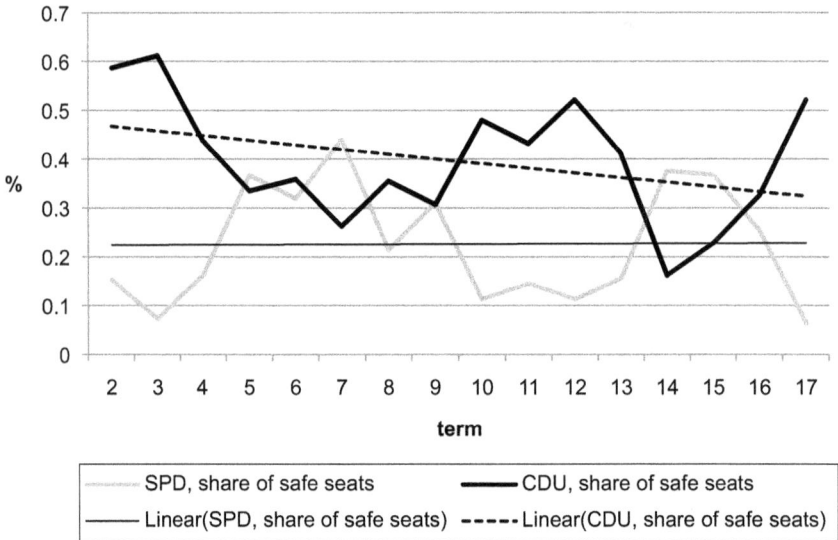

Figure 7.7: Share of party strongholds (won with at least 55 per cent of all constituency votes), by party, 1953–2009 in per cent of all constituency seats

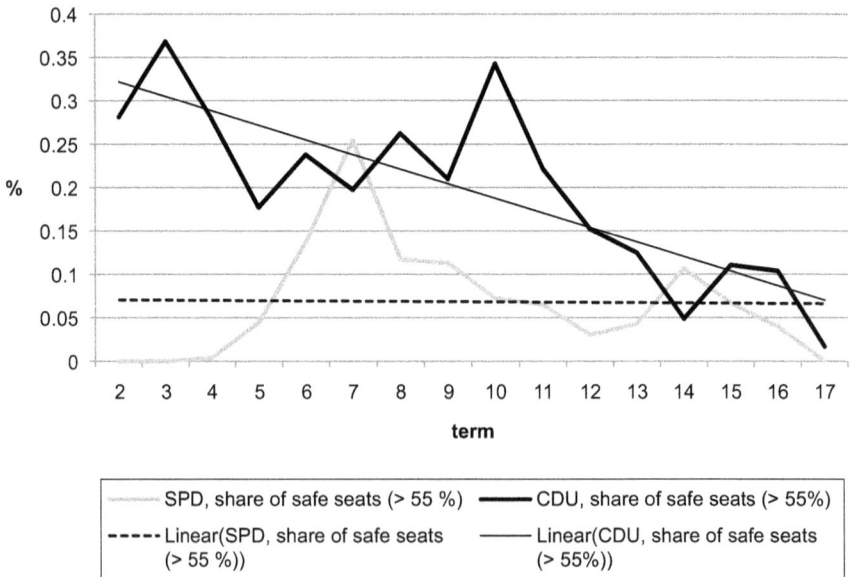

as found in Schindler (1999) and Feldkamp (2005, 2006): they label a district as a stronghold if a party receives more than 55 per cent of constituency, nominal votes. A less restrictive and more common criterion for a safe constituency defines it as safe when it is won with more than a ten per cent lead over the second-place candidate (Zittel and Gschwend 2007). Figures 7.6 and 7.7 show the share of safe districts as a percentage of all constituency seats, if we apply the stronghold or the ten per cent-margin criterion, respectively. Both figures show quite dramatically differing trends, but they add to a coherent picture. Whereas the increased volatility of vote shares has only slightly affected the number of districts, in which CDU/CSU-candidates won with at least a ten per cent- margin, the number of CDU-strongholds has declined dramatically (*see* Figure 7.7): party strongholds have become much fewer in number, as the dependency of candidates on general (but all in all more volatile) trends of party political popularity has become much higher, while specific socio-economic district characteristics have become much less decisive. This has altered the terms of competition dramatically, and parties and their candidates for office have to adjust their strategies to this new situation: with higher volatility and dependency on general trends, protection strategies have become more crucial, for parties as well as for candidates. The increase in the number of double candidatures (*see* above, Figure 7.3), has to be interpreted against the background of these trends.

Hedging against electoral uncertainty

The analysis of the nomination strategies used by party leaders has shown that the number of double candidatures has increased dramatically over the course of time. Simultaneously, the number of strictly party-list or constituency candidatures has greatly decreased. It is chiefly the three small parties and the SPD that prefer double candidatures, while the CDU and, especially the CSU, have fewer such candidatures. The reverse is true in the case of constituency-only mandates, despite a slight decrease in their number throughout the legislative periods. The percentage of representatives in parliament who won their seats strictly by way of a constituency candidature is small in all parties, and only for the CSU, of any appreciable size. The candidates of small parties are elected to the *Bundestag* nearly exclusively via party lists.

Usually the number of party-list candidates from one of the two major parties who are elected into the *Bundestag* in each German state, does not correspond with the last numerical ranking on the respective party list to which a seat is awarded (remember the example of the SPD in Baden-Württemberg). This is why I develop a measure to express this ratio (the number of elected party-list candidates / the last successful ranking). A high coefficient means that the double candidates of a party are rarely successful in winning a district mandate at the state level, and therefore, enter the *Bundestag* by way of their party lists. Conversely, a low figure indicates that many double candidates holding top rankings on their party lists are elected directly by their constituency. The measure fluctuates considerably for the CDU/CSU and the SPD, whereas the coefficient usually lies at one for the small parties. For the two major parties, the number/ranking-quotient systematically correlates (inversely) with their electoral success, because increases in the number of (constituency) votes lead to a disproportionate gain of constituency seats. Therefore, when a great share of the double candidates who held top places on their party lists are elected directly, the quotient drops. Overall, the NRQ identifies a regularity that has, as of yet, been rarely mentioned in the literature on the German mixed-member electoral system: since vote gains have a disproportionate impact on the success of constituency candidatures, the ratio of constituency mandates to party-list mandates *in the majority parliamentary party* of the German *Bundestag* is roughly two-to-one. For the largest oppositional party, the ratio is reverse. Both figures clearly diverge from a parliamentary-wide average of about 55 per cent of party-list representatives to 45 per cent constituency representatives.

In order to determine the safety of party-list rankings, I used the frequency distribution of each of the last successful rankings (according to party and state) to calculate the probability of success for each ranking. This way, we are able to report the exact probability for each ranking, each state, and each party to win a mandate with a specific ranking (in the specific state and party). 'Safe rankings' are defined as those that have guaranteed the candidate a parliamentary seat in every election. Having determined the number of safe rankings, we can study the candidate nomination strategies of the parties: how high is the percentage of safe constituencies, safe list rankings, and safe double candidatures, which result either in a safe constituency, a safe list ranking, or both for all representatives? Depending on the definition of 'safe constituencies', the percentage of safe candidatures has dropped considerably over time for the CDU/CSU and SPD: from over 40 per cent to about 30 per cent under a restrictive definition and from 65 to 54 per cent under a less restrictive definition in which the criterion is a vote lead (10 per cent) of the elected constituency candidate before the second best candidate. Moreover, safe candidatures today are almost exclusively double candidatures, because it has become the exception to find a constituency or ranking to be considered safe enough to seek office on the basis of the one alone.

Party leaders thus increase the number of safe double candidatures in reaction to the apparently increasing volatility of election results, which is by any account greater in the plurality component of the mixed member electoral system in Germany than in the proportional component. This way, leaders protect a large part of their MPs against election risks.

The cartel party thesis argued that parties or party leaders are increasingly putting more effort at minimising the costs of electoral defeat rather than maximising their prospects of electoral victory (Katz and Mair 2009, 1995). As I have shown in Chapters Two to Four, in Germany's mixed-member electoral system, parties additionally have to protect themselves against the costs of their own electoral success, because an over-proportionate gain of district mandates threatens to come at the cost of the party's own list candidates. This chapter showed, that double candidatures allow for exactly this double protection. So far, the cartel party thesis has not been empirically tested with regard to the nomination strategies of parties. Are the parties really sealing themselves off increasingly from voters, are they immunising themselves vis-à-vis an ever more volatile 'verdict of the people'?

Certainly, my finding that the combination of good rankings with promising constituencies is occurring more often can indeed be understood, as a confirmation of this shielding hypothesis. Still, it cannot be presumed that this group of elected representatives, those privileged with the insurance of a double candidature, gear themselves exclusively toward the party for this reason. Due to the contamination effects in the mixed member electoral system, active work in the constituency is one of the central criteria of a representative's performance that parties find relevant when deciding about re-nominating someone as a double candidate (*see* above, Chapter Four). In this respect, this chapter's findings would *not* support another assumption of the cartel party thesis, namely that the parties are also increasingly distancing themselves from society through their immunisation against electoral unpredictability.

PART III

MPS IN GERMANY'S MIXED ELECTORAL SYSTEM

Chapter Eight

Careers: Electoral rules and legislative turnover

This chapter addresses the question whether and how electoral rules affect legislative turnover, i.e. the re-election prospects of members of parliament. Recent research suggests that re-election prospects differ substantially between proportional and majoritarian electoral systems, with legislative turnover being much higher in the former than in the latter (Matland and Studlar 2004). Studying the likelihood of the re-election of German MPs also allows the effect of another feature of Germany's electoral system to be assessed, namely the possibility of double listing, which is also said to increase incumbency return rates (Matland and Studlar 2004: 102, 104).[1] The chapter analyses the legislative turnover of German district and list candidates for the seventeen federal elections held between 1949 and 2009. A study that analyses the effects of electoral rules in one mixed member electoral system has an important methodological advantage over a comparative research design: it allows for a number of intervening variables (e.g. district size, term length or other country or context specifics) to be kept constant. It therefore allows estimating the effects of single electoral rules more precisely. Moreover, analysing all the seventeen German post-war elections helps to avoid selection bias, which may alter results if we select particular and, perhaps, non-representative elections to calculate the German turnover rate (see more on this below). A potential disadvantage of a study of one mixed member electoral system, lies in the danger of possibly ignoring 'contaminated' effects (Cox and Schoppa 2002), i.e. the impact of one electoral tier on the other, so that the 'isolated' observation of electoral rules becomes impossible (cf. Ferrara, Herron, and Nishikawa 2005b).

Yet, mutual contamination of electoral rules should not seriously affect my findings since neither the specific incentives for ticket splitting (Bawn 1999) nor a party's interest in nominating candidates even in 'hopeless' districts (in the expectation that this will improve its performance in the PR ballot; *see* Chapter Four) – i.e. the two contamination effects in mixed-member electoral systems mentioned most often – should strongly bias the re-election probabilities for either district or list candidates. Of course, by analysing the effect of double

---

1. Given that the empirical evidence, on which this finding of the Matland and Studlar study is based, is rather small (only two of the twenty-five countries covered by the study allow for double listing (Malta and Germany) and the study covers only three elections in each country), it seems worthwhile to check, with additional data, whether double listing does indeed improve the prospects of being re-elected.

listing, my study already takes into account one important 'interaction effect' between the list and the nominal vote, which has no equivalent in either pure PR or pure Single-Member District Plurality systems.

The chapter is structured as follows. The subsequent section (second section) discusses two straightforward definitions of legislative turnover and reports turnover rates for all general elections to the German *Bundestag* since 1949. In the third section, I show how re-election prospects have differed between district and list candidates in Germany's mixed-member electoral system. I also inquire whether double-listed candidates have better chances of being re-elected than either district or list candidates. The fourth section concludes.

Legislative Turnover in Germany, 1949–2009

Before reporting turnover rates, we need to develop a precise definition as to what turnover is, and just how, exactly, we are to measure it. Turnover can be broadly defined as 'the proportion of membership that changes from one election to the next' (Matland and Studlar 2004: 92). For the exact calculation of turnover rates, however, we need a more precise definition. I propose to define turnover as the share of those who either do not return to the subsequent parliament or are not re-elected (cf. Moncrief *et al.* 2004: 361). This leads to a broad and a narrow definition of turnover. Legislative turnover is either defined broadly as comprising all who have been *members* of parliament$_t$ but are no longer members of parliament$_{t+1}$ (turnover rate = 1 – return rate), or it is defined more narrowly as comprising all who have been *elected* to parliament$_t$ but failed to be re-elected to parliament$_{t+1}$ (turnover rate = 1 – re-election rate). Whereas the first definition includes all those who were not elected but became members of parliament during the term (in Germany the so-called *Nachrücker*, i.e. substitutes who replace MPs who leave parliament during the term for whatever reason),[2] the second definition excludes them. The difference is non-trivial (*see* Table 8.1). For instance, during the 12th term of the *Bundestag* (1990–1994) ten members of parliament died and twenty-seven resigned and these vacancies were filled from party lists.[3]

Both definitions have straightforward counting rules (*see* Figure 8.1): the return rate ((1) in Figure 8.1) can be calculated by counting the number of MPs sitting in parliament on the *last* day of the previous parliament and the *first* day of the subsequent parliament, with the total number of seats in the previous parliament as the divisor. The re-election rate ((2) in Figure 8.1) reports the percentage of incumbents who have been elected at one general election and are re-elected at the next general election, i.e. who were members of parliament

2.   There are no by-elections in Germany. MPs leaving parliament are substituted from the party lists.
3.   I count a total of 739 substitutes or non-elected members for all seventeen terms (on average 43.5 MPs per term), including the 144 MPs sent to the *Bundestag* from the East German *Volkskammer* in September 1990.

Figure 8.1: Return rate, re-election rate and short spells in parliament

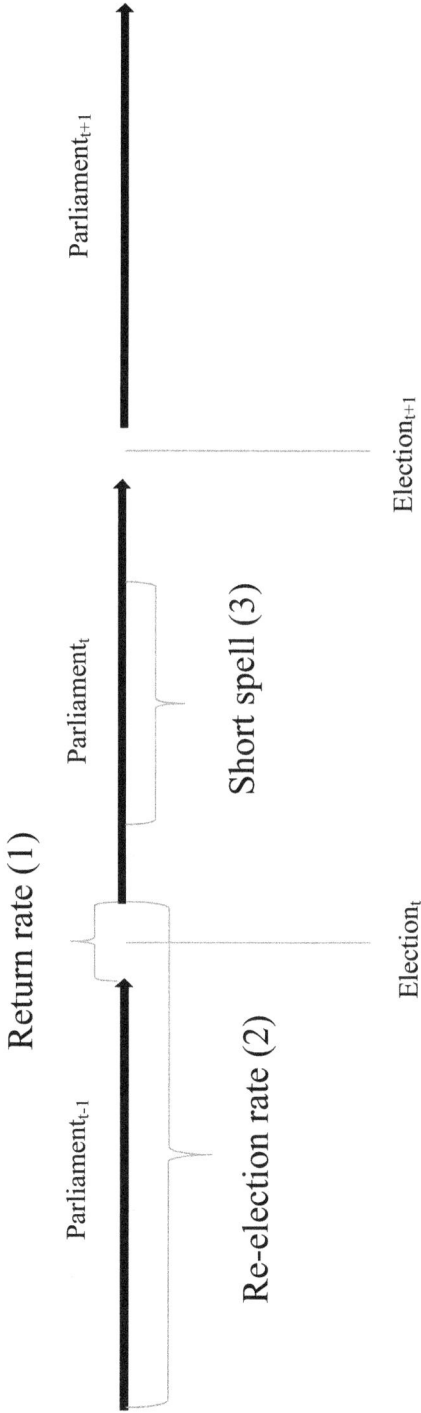

Return rate (1)

Re-election rate (2)

Short spell (3)

Parliament$_{t-1}$

Parliament$_t$

Parliament$_{t+1}$

Election$_t$

Election$_{t+1}$

Table 8.1: Restricted mean of German MPs, in days

No. of subjects	Restricted mean	Standard Error	[95% Confidence Interval]
3483	4392.503	55.39304	4283.93 – 4501.07

on the *first* day of the previous and on the *first* day of the next parliament.[4] These counting rules, however, would fail to account for those MPs, who entered late and exited early (short spell, (3) in Figure 8.1) – 'interval truncation' in the parlance of survival analysis.[5] Given that my data set provides day-data on entry and exit, I can also calculate precise numbers of those with such short spells by counting the members, who entered later than the day on which parliament constituted itself for the first time and who left before parliament dissolved at the end of the term.

The basis of my calculation is a data set with information on each of the 3,581 MPs who sat in the German *Bundestag* between 1949 and 2009 (Vierhaus and Herbst 2003; Wissenschaftliche Dienste 1998, together with additions for the 14th, 15th, 16th and 17th term). The data set contains the name and party affiliation of each MP, his or her date of entry and exit, and whether the MP was elected directly or via regional party lists – including the type of candidacy: district, list or double. I start with some descriptive statistics. The 3,581 MPs occupied a total of 10,215 seats in seventeen legislative terms;[6] 5,610 (54.9 per cent) seats were determined by party lists.[7]

---

4. One is confronted with a further subtlety when calculating return or re-election rates: how to treat those members of parliament whose career has been interrupted for one, two or even three terms? Since I calculate return or re-election rates by looking at two subsequent parliaments only, I treat MPs with an interrupted spell of membership as 'new'. The *Datenhandbuch zur Geschichte des Deutschen Bundestags* treats these MPs as 'returning' and therefore reports a slightly lower rate of legislative turnover (Schindler 1999). Again, differences are not that trivial: I count, over 16 terms, 129 MPs who returned to parliament after a spell of one, two or even three terms of absence.

5. I am grateful to Till Melchert, who pointed this out to me.

6. Average total number of seats in the *Bundestag* is 551. The higher figure that results from dividing 10,215 seats by seventeen terms (= 601) is explained by the fact that whenever an MP leaves parliament during the term and is replaced by a list candidate (a so-called *Nachrücker*) the seat is counted twice.

7. Why does the share of list candidates fail to equal the number of directly elected members of parliament? Three factors explain the – admittedly slight – deviation. First, the German electoral system does not have by-elections. If an MP resigns or dies during the term, he or she will be substituted by the highest-ranking candidate on the party list who failed to make it into parliament at the last election. Second, until 1990, Berlin's members of parliament were not elected by the citizens of Berlin, but instead were elected by the parties in the city parliament. I have coded these MPs as list candidates as well. Third, during the process of German unification, the East German parliament (*Volkskammer*) sent delegates to the *Bundestag* before general elections were held in unified Germany in October that year. Again, I coded these MPs as list candidates.

Table 8.2: Return and re-election rates in Germany's sixteen general elections

I.	II.	III.	IV.	V.	VI.
Term	Returned MPs	Re-elected MPs	Seats	Return rate $(II._t/IV._{t-1})$	Re-election rate $(III._t/IV._{t-1})$
1st (1949–1953)			410		
2nd (1953–1957)	262	234	509	63.90	57.07
3rd (1957–1961)	352	335	519	69.16	65.82
4th (1961–1965)	386	367	521	74.37	70.71
5th (1965–1969)	376	351	518	72.17	67.37
6th (1969–1972)	346	334	518	66.80	64.48
7th (1972–1976)	368	346	518	71.04	66.80
8th (1976–1980)	394	381	518	76.06	73.55
9th (1980–1983)	379	365	519	73.17	70.46
10th (1983–1987)	419	408	520	80.73	78.61
11th (1987–1990)	394	393	519	75.77	75.58
12th (1990–1994)	403	349	662	77.65	67.24
13th (1994–1998)	453	444	672	68.43	67.07
14th (1998–2002)	491	484	669	73.07	72.02
15th (2002–2005)	420	412	603	62.78	61.58
16th (2005–2009)	449	437	614	74.46	72.47
17th (2009–2013)	419	408	622	68.24	66.45
Average				71.74	68.58

Sources: (Schindler 1999; Wissenschaftliche Dienste 1998; Feldkamp 2005, and own calculations)

If we were to calculate average tenure, the data would tell us that an average German MP remains in parliament for 3,617 days, quite exactly ten years. Since the parliamentary term of the German *Bundestag* lasts four years, starting from the day the parliament constitutes itself for the first time (Article 39, Section 1 Basic Law [*Grundgesetz*]), this would mean that the average *Bundestagsabgeordneter* remains in parliament for about two-and-a-half terms. However, in the past, a term has not always lasted full four years, with early elections having been called three times (1972, 1983 and 2005). Therefore the average number of terms served would actually be higher, almost three. Furthermore, averages would also tell us that German district and list candidates differ considerably with respect to tenure. Comparing those 1,048 MPs, who have always entered parliament via the district, with those 1,340, who always were elected via the party list (the other 1,193 MPs used both tracks during their career), shows district candidates staying for 2.92 terms and list candidates for 2.46 terms.

But as already mentioned above, simply calculating the average tenure without taking into account censored data, risks leading to biased results. I therefore calculate the restricted mean of the survivor function for all (non-censored) MPs, which indicates, according to Table 8.1, a membership in parliament that is about two years or 775 days longer than simple average tenure (4,392 days, *see* Table 8.1). This translates into a total tenure of three full terms. As we see, mean tenure significantly underestimates the average period of membership in the *Bundestag*.

But how likely is it for a member of parliament to be re-elected, and what are the determinants of re-election? I start with general descriptive statistics and will, in the subsequent sections, investigate the question of the determinants more closely, in particular, the effect of electoral rules. Table 8.2 presents the return- and re-election rates for all German elections between 1949 and 2009.

At least two important pieces of information stand out in Table 8.2. First, legislative turnover varies quite a bit, being relatively high in the early years and then increasing again after the 1990s. Second, the average legislative turnover in Germany has been substantially lower than previously thought. In Matland's and Studlar's pioneering twenty-five-country study, in which Germany is included with three elections, Germany is ranked third with a return rate of 78.7 per cent. It clusters with countries like the US, Australia, Ireland and the UK, all countries with electoral systems that are more majoritarian in character. Based on my data and on the less strict definition of return rates, the German electoral system would now be ranked in 9th

Figure 8.2: Short termers, substitutes, returning and re-elected MPs, as a share of total seats, 1953–2009

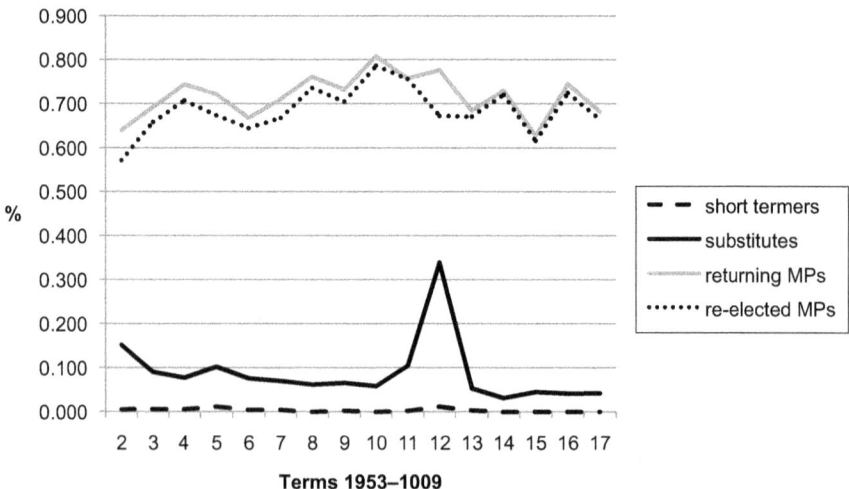

place instead, and it would cluster with a number of other countries with PR-electoral systems like Sweden, Malta, Belgium or Iceland (Matland and Studlar 2004: 93).

But additionally, Figure 8.1 allows us to report two other categories of MPs, those who substituted for an MP (*'Nachrücker'*) and those with only a short spell in parliament. The corresponding counting rules are: Firstly, late entry, meaning someone who was *not* a member of parliament at the first day when a new *Bundestag* was constituted, but who was a member at the last day of that parliament (1). Secondly, late entry and early exit, i.e. someone who was *not* a member of parliament at the first day when a new *Bundestag* was constituted and had already left parliament before the last day of that parliament (2). Figure 8.2 by comparing the shares of all four categories – substitutes, short-termers, returning and re-elected MPs – shows that the short-termers are only of marginal importance, their average being 1.75 per term. The figure also shows a strong increase in substitutes caused by the 144 MPs sent to the *Bundestag* from the East German Volkskammer in September 1990. As can be seen, return and re-election-rates develop in close parallel, and oscillate around 70 per cent (the only instance, where they differed significantly, was again caused by the strong increase in MPs in 1990).

But coming back to the differing return- and re-election rates in the Matland and Studlar study, and in my replication, the question remains: what might explain the differences in the reported rates? A lot can be explained by the different time span covered by the Matland and Studlar study (for Germany: 1976–1987) and my own (1949–2009). First, as can be read from Table 8.1 and Figure 8.2, the early terms of the German *Bundestag* were characterised by a relatively high level of legislative turnover. This might have a simple cause. From the 1st to the 4th parliament, the number of parties represented in the German *Bundestag* decreased from nineteen to three (plus three independent MPs), a consolidation that presumably had an influence on the overall legislative turnover. Secondly, the period after German unification saw higher levels of legislative turnover – although the first all-German elections in 1990 produced an exceptional high return rate of slightly more than 80 per cent.[8] Increased post-unification turnover might partly be explained by the fact that the majority of East German voters were only slowly becoming 'politically socialised' into an all-German party system dominated by West German parties. Lower party affiliation results in a greater willingness to switch votes, and voter volatility is considerably higher in the 'new'

---

8. The reason for this high return rate is that on 28 September 1990 the East German *Volkskammer* sent 144 Members of Parliament to the *Bundestag*. General elections in unified Germany were held on the 2nd of December. In other words, these MPs enjoyed tenure of little more than two months. Yet, short terms lead to high return rates (Matland and Studlar 2004: 102). At the same time, the total number of seats in the *Bundestag* increased from 519 in the 11th term to 662 seats in the 12th term as a reflection of the larger Germany.

eastern German states (cf. Rattinger 1994). Higher voter volatility, in turn, is likely to lead to higher legislative turnover.[9]

However, increased turnover is not driven by lower party affiliation in the East alone. Although electoral volatility is undoubtedly higher there, volatility is not only a regional but also a secular phenomenon that affects the West as well (Becker and Saalfeld 2005). It is therefore questionable whether increased turnover after 1990 can be explained solely by German unification. If we assume the dissolution of traditional socio-economic 'milieus' and the weakening of ties between voters and parties to be a trend that all Western democracies share, a comparative study risks underestimating legislative turnover in Germany when it restricts analysis of German elections to the pre-unification period, while taking into account elections up to the mid-1990s in other Western democracies (see Matland and Studlar 2004: 92, note 34, and 108).

Finally, an additional reason for the higher reported German return rate in the Matland and Studlar study seems to lie in the authors' specific choice of elections. The three elections analysed (elections to the 9th, 10th and 11th term of the *Bundestag*, with the 1976 election as the base year) have all led to higher than average return rates, with the election to the 10th German parliament standing out among all sixteen elections as the one with the highest return rate ever. This election was a remarkable outlier because the 9th term of the German *Bundestag* ended with an early dissolution of parliament after only twenty-nine months instead of the regular forty-eight months. But the shorter the term, the higher, *ceteris paribus*, the return rate (Matland and Studlar 2004: 102). In fact, the shortest term in the post-war period produced the highest return rate of that period of time.[10]

However, taking into account all seventeen German post-war elections does not alter Matland and Studlar's findings about the determinants of legislative turnover – on the contrary, it reinforces them. Since Professors Matland and Studlar were so kind as to provide their original data set (see opening footnote) I was able to replicate their results and rerun their multivariate analysis with the additional data on 13 German elections. Table 8.3 compares the original findings with the results of the replication.

The replication strengthens all findings of the original study, with two exceptions: as was to be expected, with higher turnover in German elections the double-listings coefficient loses a little in strength (Hypothesis three), although it remains statistically

---

9. The relatively high return rates in September 2005 do not really indicate a reversal of this trend because the 15th term of the German *Bundestag* ended early, after only thirty-six months. Given that the decision of Chancellor Schröder to call new elections was challenged before the German Constitutional Court, and the Court did not issue its ruling before early August (the election was held in September), the election campaign was extremely short, and neither parties nor candidates had much time to prepare themselves. It seems safe to assume that these factors contributed to the relatively high return rate. Apart from the 2005 election, post-unification elections reveal relatively low return rates.

10. Selecting the election to the 10th German *Bundestag* is unproblematic for a multivariate analysis, such as the one on page 104 of the Matland and Studlar study, in which the authors can control for the time that has elapsed between two general elections.

Table 8.3: Determinants of turnover: a replication of the analysis of Matland and Studlar with the additional data of 13 German elections[11]

		Original model	Replication with additional data
	(Constant)	4.198 (1.33)	4.706 (1.61)
H1	PR system	9.852 (3.98)***	10.948 (4.55)***
H2	PR-STV (single transferable vote)	−3.580 (1.37)	−5.460 (2.30)**
H2	SNTV (single non-transferable vote)	−3.097 (1.00)	−3.872 (1.32)
H2	PR-preferential vote	−0.259 (0.16)	−0.597 (0.40)
H3	Double listings	−8.493 (2.49)***	−5.148 (2.50)**
H4	Electoral volatility	0.254 (5.66)***	0.257 (6.11)***
H5	Time (months)	0.365 (7.23)***	0.370 (7.88)***
H6	Seats controlled by traditional conservatives	−0.020 (0.42)	−0.030 (0.69)
H7	Seats controlled by leftist parties	0.034 (0.76)	−0.000 (0.00)
H8	Canada	14.883 (4.31)***	14.969 (4.55)***
	New democracy	6.135 (2.46)**	6.860 (2.87)***
	Portugal	11.267 (3.17)***	9.120 (2.71)***
	Observations	116	129
	Adjusted R-squared	0.70	0.70

Note: Absolute value of *t* statistics in parentheses; ** significant at the 5%-level; *** significant at the 1%-level.

significant (at the one per cent level).[12] Most of the other electoral system variables gain in strength.[13] The major findings of the comparative study are therefore confirmed: list PR leads to higher legislative turnover, the length of the parliamentary terms varies positively with turnover, and double listing increases re-election prospects.

11. Cf. Matland and Studlar (2004: 104, Table 3).
12. The other change is that the STV-variable becomes significant.
13. Some of the changes in the coefficients are not simply due to the integration of the additional German data. I have also corrected some errors in the M/S 'time' variable (see Matland and Studlar 2004: 108, Table A): the period between the 3rd and 4th Danish elections was forty-four not thirty-four months; the period between the 2nd and 3rd French elections was thirty-nine not twenty-seven months; the period between the 5th and 6th elections in Portugal was fifty-one not thirty-nine months; the period between the 5th and 6th elections in Japan was forty-three not thirty-one months; and the 4th German election was in January 1987 and not in November, so, therefore, the period between the 3rd and 4th elections was forty-seven not fifty-six months. I have also made some minor changes for Austria (the 2nd election was in May), Italy (the 4th election was in June), the UK (the 5th election was in April), and Portugal (the 1st election was in October). See Mackie and Rose (1991), and Internet resources.

Table 8.4: The return rate of list candidates

Term	Returned MPs	Returned via the party list	Per cent
1st (1949–1953)			
2nd (1953–1957)	262	113	43.13
3rd (1957–1961)	352	171	48.58
4th (1961–1965)	386	190	49.22
5th (1965–1969)	376	197	52.39
6th (1969–1972)	346	175	50.58
7th (1972–1976)	368	180	48.91
8th (1976–1980)	394	203	51.52
9th (1980–1983)	379	186	49.08
10th (1983–1987)	419	208	49.64
11th (1987–1990)	394	191	48.48
12th (1990–1994)	403	183	45.41
13th (1994–1998)	453	206	45.47
14th (1998–2002)	491	244	49.69
15th (2002–2005)	420	206	49.05
16th (2005–2009)	449	194	43.21
17th (2009–2013)	419	212	50.60
Average			**48.44**

The following section investigates whether list candidates in Germany's mixed-member electoral system are at a higher risk of not returning to the *Bundestag* than district candidates, and whether the possibility of double listing lowers turnover rates.

District-, list- and double-listed candidates: do their electoral fates differ?

Since the comparative evidence suggests that electoral rules have a quite substantial impact on legislative turnover, we should expect the different types of candidates in Germany's mixed member electoral system to face different electoral fates, too. This is indeed confirmed by candidate-type-specific return rates. As Table 8.4 shows, list candidates are much less likely to be re-elected than district candidates. The share of list candidates among all *Bundestag* members is 54.9 per cent, but their share among those who return to parliament is, on average, only 48.4 per cent (*see* Table 8.4; see footnote 76 for an explanation of why the mix between list and district candidates is not 50:50).

Table 8.4 is in line with what we already know about the different lengths of parliamentary tenure of list and district candidates reported above. If we subsequently want to compare survival estimates for list-, district- and double-candidates, calculating these is a less simple exercise than one might think at first. As will be discussed in more detail in the next chapter, as soon as we take the individual as our unit of analysis, we are confronted with a number of intricate questions as to how to classify single MPs: who is a district-MP, who is a list-MP, and who a double-listed one? For each single election, this question is easy to answer, but how are we to determine this for entire political careers? One strategy would be to look at extreme cases: somebody who in all elections always ran for office only on a state party list or only in a district. But looking at categories with rather few observations will, of course, lead to problems with respect to generalisability. On the other hand, the group of the more than 80 per cent of all MPs who ran as double candidates are not sufficiently differentiated to identify distinctive effects of electoral rules.

Does being double-listed improve re-election prospects? Clearly, being double-listed ought to never hurt, but only improve, a candidate's chance of being re-elected. But effects may be negligible because list ranks are unsafe or district races unpromising for the respective candidate. Parties often place candidates on unsafe list ranks or nominate them in unpromising districts out of symbolic or 'aesthetic' reasons: parties want to submit 'complete' lists and want to be present in every electoral district, even in those districts where their candidate has virtually no chance of winning (*see* Chapter Four). To what extent being double-listed improves re-election prospects is, therefore, an empirical question.

To answer this question, we are mainly dependent on indirect evidence, since classifying MPs as double listed-, district- or list-MPs is itself a controversial exercise (*see* Chapter Nine). One piece of indirect evidence for the protective character of the double candidacy is the longer parliamentary survival of those MPs who switched their status during their political career, i.e. those candidates who always ran both on a party list and in a district, but sometimes were elected into the *Bundestag* via the list, sometimes in the district (*see* Figure 8.3). This reflects exactly the supposed insurance-function of double candidacy, providing candidates in contested districts and states with close margins for both of the larger parties the possibility to shift between 'elected in the district' and 'elected on the party list' – and thereby to survive external electoral shocks. Of course, in order to not bias the analysis, we have to restrict the comparison to all MPs with at least two terms in parliament, since a MP who has switched his or her status is by definition someone with more than one term of *Bundestag* membership. As expected, parties' and candidates' strategies to hedge against electoral uncertainty by placing candidates both on lists and in districts result in better survival chances of these double-listed politicians (*see* Figure 8.3).

As becomes evident, being able to use both tracks into parliament significantly extends the time of membership in the *Bundestag*. The increase in use of this

Figure 8.3: Survival estimates for German MPs, 1949–2009 (in days), double candidates with at least two terms in parliament and change or no change of elections modus (list vs. district)

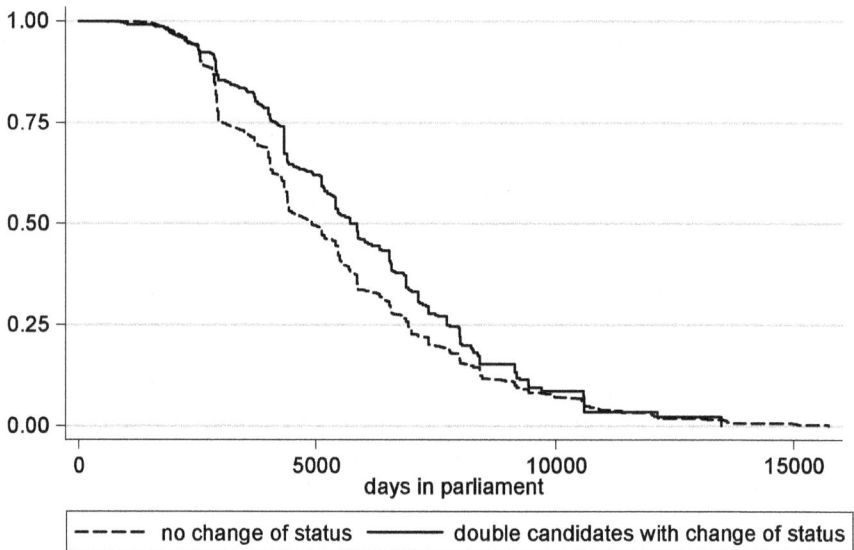

hedging instrument then has to be understood against the background of increased political uncertainty, i.e. a significant reduction in the number of safe seats and safe list positions (*see* Chapter Seven). As we have seen, double listing has become very widespread. Around 40 per cent of all candidates in German general elections run both in a district and have a place on a party list (Bundeswahlleiter 2005: 16–17; *see* Figure 7.1). This share has oscillated between 30 and 40 per cent since the first *Bundestag* elections. Once we look only at those actually elected, however, the number of double-listed MPs increases strongly, from around 50 per cent in the 1950s and 1960s to more than 80 per cent today (*see* Figure 6.3). This might already indicate higher chances of double-listed candidates to be elected – and re-elected.

To some extent, the better survival chances of double-listed candidates might point to a 'celebrity effect'. On the one hand, the more prominent and well-known a politician is, the more he or she is likely to win his or her district directly. Prominent politicians are, on the other hand, too important for the party to risk their failure of re-entering parliament. Therefore, they will also occupy a relatively safe position on the regional party list. Given their prominent names, listing them on a high list rank will also help in attracting list votes. Here, parties' nomination strategies interact with the electoral rules 'as such'. Relevant in this context is also a detail of the German election law which stipulates that the first five list positions on each state party list appear on the ballot with full name (including the title, both

Figure 8.4: Survival estimates for German MPs, 1949–2005, list vs. district candidates (in days)

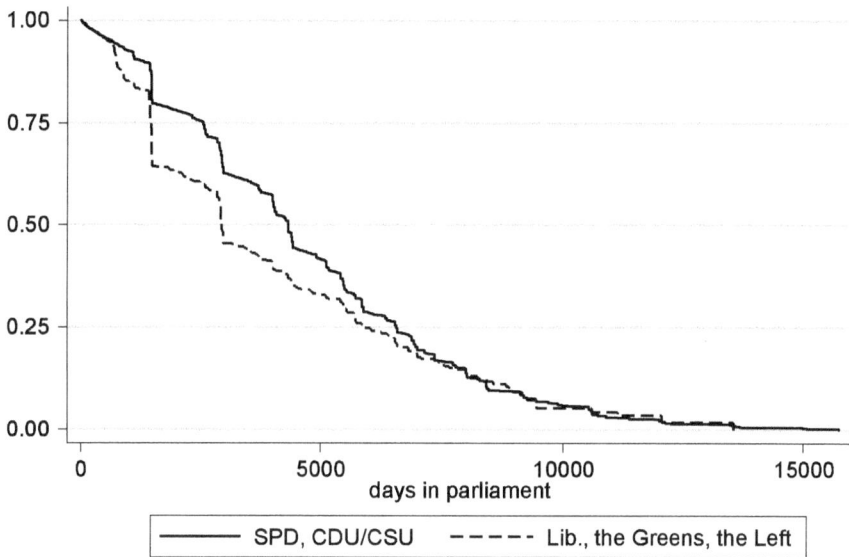

academic and noble).[14] Consequently, placing members of the party elite among the first five list positions may attract votes.

A second piece of indirect evidence is provided by the comparison between small (the Liberals, the Greens and the Left) and large parties (Social and Christian Democrats, including the Bavarian CSU). This comparison is mainly one between parties with and without chances of winning district seats, and therefore a comparison between two different uses of the double candidacy: for the larger parties double listing has exactly the insurance function that was argued above. For smaller parties, it cannot have this function, since they have almost no chance of winning a district in the first place. For them (*see* Chapters Two, Three and Four) double candidacies have a different function: by nominating district candidates, the parties expect their candidates to engage in active campaigning and hope to boost the parties' list votes at the district level (regardless of the fact that the candidate has practically no chances of winning the seat). Comparing small and big parties therefore also, if indirectly, means comparing the effects of electoral rules.

14. This seems to have had an effect on the frequency with which candidates with an academic or noble title are listed among the first five ranks on state party lists (Schneider and Tepe 2011; Manow and Flemming 2011a).

Table 8.5: Median parliamentary tenure for pure list- and pure district-MPs, i.e. those who always exclusively ran on a list or in a district

	Subjects	50%	Std. Err.	[95% Conf. Interval]
Pure list MPs	399	**1461**	7.19	1421–1461
Not pure list MPs	3084	4319	36.38	4175–4319
Pure district MPs	364	**3377**	248.29	2951–4019
Not pure district MPs	3119	4019	62.85	3995–4127
Total	3483	4019	65.82	3993–4073

As Figure 8.4 shows, members of either the Social or Christian Democrats enjoy significantly higher prospects of parliamentary survival than their colleagues from smaller parties who have no chance of ever winning a district.

These differences are confirmed if we compare the median tenure of two polar, but rather rare cases: those who always exclusively ran for office either on a list or in a district (*see* Table 8.5).

We see that both categories of MPs show a significantly higher risk of having to leave parliament early.

Electoral rules and re-election chances

Let me now sum up: In this chapter, I analysed legislative turnover in a prototypical mixed-member electoral system, the German one. I reported return rates for German members of parliament for all seventeen elections that have so far taken place in the Federal Republic. One central finding is that legislative turnover is significantly higher than reported in previous studies. Whereas Germany was qualified as an outlier in previous comparisons of legislative turnover, it now seems to be much more in line with countries with similar electoral systems. Generally, the German case seems to confirm most findings from the comparative study of legislative turnover: firstly, list-PR leads to higher legislative turnover; secondly, district candidates have higher chances of being re-elected to the *Bundestag*; thirdly, being double-listed apparently enhances the electoral chances of members of parliament; and finally that shorter terms increase incumbency return rates. The empirical evidence further revealed that, in the German electoral system, the nomination seems to be far more important than the election itself. Given that parties have more authority when compiling a party list than when nominating district candidates, the different electoral fate of district and list candidates might be determined to a higher degree by party strategies than by voter decisions.

Chapter Nine

Characteristics: Electoral pathways to the *Bundestag* and MPs' parliamentary strategies[1]

Every introductory text on the political system of the Federal Republic of Germany describes two kinds of representatives participating in the *Bundestag*: those who are directly elected from their district with the relative majority of the constituency votes and those who win a seat in parliament via the party list of their federal state (*Land*). Often, these two formal ways of gaining a seat in the *Bundestag* are also assumed to correspond to two specific types of representatives, each displaying distinctive behaviour (Bawn and Thies 2003; Shugart and Wattenberg 2001b; Stratmann 2006; Sieberer 2010; Stratmann and Baur 2002, Herron 2002). Those sceptical of this role differentiation thesis, however, are quick to point out that over 80 per cent of all members of the *Bundestag* run for office as both district and list candidates. Since the 'probability for double-candidacy politicians to win a seat via the district or the list mode is almost equal, [...] [this] should provide an incentive for double-candidacy candidates to seriously consider interests and demands of the local constituency' (Klingemann and Wessels 2001b: 291). Should double-listed representatives also prove to gear their service to 'their' electoral district, however, even if they have been elected to parliament via the party list, then a clear role differentiation between district and list representatives would be improbable.

In the empirical validation of the mandate-divide thesis, relevant studies regularly classify the MP's *type* according to his or her current *status*. This seems problematic for two reasons. On the one hand, such a classification disregards the mode of candidacy. On the other, it does ignore the course of the representative's career (possibly) before and after the election. If the mode of candidacy is not accounted for, this would imply, for example, that a 'pure' list representative is treated as if (s)he is confronted with just the same electoral incentives as a list representative who also ran for a mandate in an electoral district. When we neglect to consider the *course* of a political career (including *both* candidate- and MP-episodes), we imply that the past and the future are thoroughly irrelevant for the current political and parliamentary behaviour of a representative. Yet, if the main interest of a representative is re-election, then it is plausible to assume his/her current parliamentary behaviour also to be dependent on the mode of election sought by this person for future elections. At the same time, we can

---

1. Section six in this chapter is based on joint work with Peter Flemming.

plausibly assume that past experience has an impact on present behaviour. Therefore, testing for the effect of electoral rules on parliamentary behaviour renders it necessary to both look at the mode of candidacy as well as at previous and subsequent career episodes of a representative. This is the aspiration of the following chapter.

The central question examined in this chapter is whether typical career patterns that would clearly justify referring to them as either district- or list-representatives can be discerned. To answer this question I again, as in Chapters Six and Seven, apply sequence analysis (Brüderl and Scherer 2006; Scherer and Brüderl 2010, among others). Sequence analysis helps us to identify career patterns of *Bundestag* members. Once this analysis of the typical paths into the *Bundestag* has been provided in a clearer classification of the various types of representatives, I ask whether we can detect possible differences in parliamentary behaviour. For this purpose, I have replicated a study investigating the strategic calculations of committee membership: do district MPs sit more often in committees relevant to the interests of their constitutive districts and do list MPs sit disproportionally, often in committees that enhance their individual party-political profile (Stratmann and Baur 2002; Gschwend, Shugart and Zittel 2009; Heinz 2010)? In replicating the study by Stratmann and Baur, albeit with a significantly larger dataset, I test whether this pattern can also be verified when we take into account the previous episodes of a legislator's career and his, or her, mode of election. Furthermore, I study the committee membership of those representatives who entered the *Bundestag* via the party list but who had campaigned in an electoral district. Are there indications that such legislators focus their efforts as well on serving the interests of 'their' district?

The next two sections offer a brief summary of the positions, both pro and contra, in the debate over German parliamentarians' role differentiation and the impact of modes of election on the behaviour of legislators. The fourth section subsequently offers an analysis of the most frequent ways of being elected to parliament. In the fifth section, I will investigate the parliamentary behaviour of those MPs who contested a district but were elected to the *Bundestag* in the PR-tier. The section will focus on whether we see evidence that these representatives care for 'their' constituency's interest in parliament. After showing that there is indeed ample evidence that MPs have mixed roles, taking into account both their party's and their district's interests, one final piece of evidence is still lacking. Above, I have shown that the electorate has indeed only very limited means to deselect list-MPs (*see* Chapter Six) - the question remains why these MPs have an interest in cultivating a local reputation. In the sixth section, I will argue that parties will deselect those MPs who have shown a poor electoral performance in the district.

List versus district

With respect to the impact of different electoral rules on German MPs' parliamentary strategies, the literature offers diametrically opposed opinions. On the one hand, Stratmann and Baur state: 'In the German electoral system [...] some legislators are elected through PR and others are elected through FPTP [First-past-the-post; PM]. Thus, '*two legislator types* exist simultaneously in Germany' (Stratmann and Baur 2002: 506–507; italics added; see also Bawn 1999: 490; Bawn and Thies 2003). It is exactly this which is flatly denied by Burkett and Padgett: 'Contrary to widespread opinion, it is of absolutely no importance whether a mandate is obtained through the constituency or the *Landesliste*' (Burkett and Padgett 1987: 130; cf. Jesse 1988: 120).[2] Who is right?

The presumption that list and district MPs take up different roles is often countered by citing the fact that over 80 per cent of all MPs run as double candidates. Studies have pointed out that a candidature in an electoral district is, today, usually the prerequisite for a promising spot on the respective party list. As a rule, the chance to obtain a place on the party list is only given to a person 'who was also nominated as a district candidate by the party base and is willing to perform 'grunt work' in the electoral district' (Ismayr 2000: 86, own translation; see also Schüttemeyer and Sturm 2005). This is reflected in the chronological order of the electoral district nominations and the delegate convention, which decides on the lists for that particular *Land*. That the 'selection of the district candidates almost always precedes the delegate convention in the *Land*' – deciding on the party list – 'supports the assumption [...] that the district candidature is a key, if not even mandatory, prerequisite for a promising place on the list. Only the person who is willing to toil at the electoral base will apparently gain the trust and approval of the delegates' (Schüttemeyer and Sturm 2005: 548, own translation).

The parties expect their constituency candidates to campaign actively and engage in work on behalf of the electoral district 'regardless of which tier they are elected from' (Klingemann and Wessels 2001b: 291; see also Patzelt 2007: 83; Lundberg 2007). As early as the 1970s, Schweitzer detected that in 'most of the state parties, it has become the rule that somewhat promising list candidates are put up as district candidates in unsafe electoral districts not the least because, without a district mandate, they [...] as list representatives, should also serve an electoral district for their party as an MdB' (Schweitzer 1979: 12, own translation – MdB stands for *Mitglied des Bundestags*, Member of the German Parliament). Therefore, the district MPs almost always compete against one or more 'shadow representatives' (Lundberg 2007: 46–9). Consequently, district MPs do not hold a monopoly on representing the interests of their respective electoral districts in parliament (Patzelt 2007; Saalfeld

---

2. Many more similar judgments could be cited. For instance, Uwe Kitzinger notes in his study on the first two legislative terms: 'by and large, there was little difference in the *Bundestag* between the two types of members, and many probably were not sure which of their colleagues held constituency seats, and which did not. When local work was concerned the difference between constituency and list members was also less than might be thought' (Kitzinger 1960: 60–61) 'There is practically no difference – once elected – in the status or behavior of constituency candidates and list candidates. Constituency candidates may have certain additional engagements and duties in the constituency, but, since most list candidates have contested constituencies – and perhaps hope to do so again – they, too, will 'nurse' constituencies and undertake engagements there' (Roberts 1988: 114).

2005: 219; Schweitzer 1979). By the 1960's the literature on the German electoral system had already assessed that the system ensures 'that many electoral districts are represented both by a representative from the CDU/CSU as well as by a representative from the SPD' (Hermens and Unkelbach 1967: 16, own translation). From time to time, the list representative even becomes the more preferred person to address for matters concerning the electoral district, especially when the shadow representative belongs to a ruling party and is 'able, all things considered, to achieve more for the electoral district when dealing with Bonn [meaning federal, P.M.] authorities than the [directly elected, P.M.] man from the opposition' (Schweitzer 1979: 185, own translation).

It is worth highlighting that the argument levelled against the differentiation-hypothesis does not consider that district MPs do not feel committed to the interests of their electoral district, but states that list MPs, who also ran for the district mandate, should, in many regards, behave like district representatives. Therefore, it is not enough to produce proof that district MPs actually represent the interests of their constituency. Instead, the decisive question is whether this isn't also true for list MPs who held a double candidature. To answer this question, it becomes necessary to examine, simultaneously, the type of mandate *and* the mode of election.

The commitment to serve the electoral district does not just pertain to the two major parties, but also to the small parties, even though district candidates from these parties almost never have a realistic chance to actually win the seat (with the exception of the PDS/*die Linke* in the 'new' Eastern states). Small parties, themselves, have a strong interest in being represented in an electoral district by their own, locally active candidate, although they harbour no illusions about their chances to win on the district level, because the constituency candidature has a positive effect on the results of the second-vote tallies (Cox and Schoppa 2002; Ferrara *et al.* 2005; Hainmüller, Kern and Bechtel 2006; Hainmüller and Kern 2008). With regard to first and second votes, the electoral district performance of the prior election often becomes the criterion for placing candidates in promising spots on the party lists for the next election (Gschwend and Zittel 2008). Against the backdrop of these possible incentives and sanctions, it is not surprising that studies on the time schedules of elected representatives can only find slight differences between district- and list-MPs when it comes to the hours that both types of legislators invest in work for their electoral districts (Patzelt 2007: 55, Table 3).

While several observers emphasize the loyalty also of the list representatives (by double candidature) to 'their' electoral districts, others depict a contrasting scenario that stresses the selection effect of different electoral rules on different types of candidates. Schreiber, for example, maintains that different types of politicians arrive in the *Bundestag* via two alternative paths:

> Because some legislators are elected by way of proportional representation according to closed lists that voters cannot influence and other legislators are elected by plurality vote, parties have the option to use the party-list mode of

election to bring individuals into parliament who are less popular or less skilled at winning the voters' favour but whose presence is wanted for other reasons pertaining to parliamentary work (e.g. experts, representatives from certain geographical regions in which experience has proven that the opposing party usually wins all of the electoral districts). On the other hand, the plurality vote enables candidates who are very familiar with the matters of their respective electoral district, and have particularly close contact to the electorate, to get elected (plurality voting as the election of individual candidate personalities as opposed to the election of entire rows of candidates 'en bloc' from a certain list)' (Schreiber 1994: 144–45, own translation).

Schreiber does acknowledge the possibility of the election of a list candidate who, as a legislator, represents regional interests, however, in this view, the main concept is not that a legislator plays a double role and exhibits a twofold loyalty, but that two distinct types of legislators exist, each with a specific role (see also Bawn and Thies 2003).

Opponents and advocates of the role differentiation thesis seldom attempt to present empirical evidence to support their position. In the few cases where studies do try to prove differences in legislative behaviour empirically, the distinction applied between district and list representatives seems too crude to be fully convincing (Stratmann and Baur 2002; Lancaster and Patterson 1990). The question to be clarified empirically in the following, based on the career path of German members of parliament, is therefore, whether a closer examination of the mode of election and the entire course of a person's political career, enables us to confirm or reject the assumption that the different paths to a *Bundestag* seat determine different legislative behaviours.

Paths into the *Bundestag*

Of course it is indisputable that two kinds of MPs sit in the *Bundestag* in every legislative period: those who received their mandate through a successful candidature on a party list and those who won their mandate in a district. In this strictly formal sense, it is certainly unproblematic to speak of list- and district-MPs. Yet, with regard to the behaviour of legislators, this terminology does seem imprecise because it diverts attention from the fact that assertions about behaviour, parliamentary strategies, role differentiations, etc. are not based on mandates, but on the individual mandate holders. At this point, as can be easily demonstrated, things are more complicated.

Let's take two hypothetical cases: in the first, a legislator who had been elected by her district constituency to the *Bundestag* for the first time, loses the district mandate in a close race during the next election. Since she was a candidate for both a district mandate and a party-list mandate – i.e. a double candidate like more than 80 per cent of her colleagues – she does win a *Bundestag* seat via the list ranking. In the following election, she also campaigns again in 'her' electoral district. In view of the closeness of the race in the previous election, she is justifiably hopeful to win back the district mandate. Does it make sense to classify this legislator as a list-MP, and if so, which behavioural hypothesis should be linked to such a classification? Patzelt labels this representative a 'defeated direct list member' (Patzelt 2007: 53) and emphasises that this type of legislator has strong incentives to work on behalf of her electoral district.[3] The second case is that of a legislator who has won a district mandate in the *Bundestag* in the last four consecutive elections. Yet each time the race has been extremely close. Since the electoral district is not safe, the legislator is also assured by a promising ranking on the party list. Is it plausible to classify this legislator as a district MP? Should we assume that he would act exclusively, or at least primarily, in the interests of his electoral district and perhaps even against his own party in order to enhance his own local reputation and standing – even if he could depend on a good list position should the very close district race happen to turn out against his favour?

These cases demonstrate that the seemingly self-evident and unproblematic differentiation between list and district MPs does, indeed, require some clarification. Whom do we want to classify and as what? Is a list representative a person who *always* enters the *Bundestag* via the party list and *always only* runs as a list candidate? This would be the most restrictive but also the most unequivocal definition. Or should we – somewhat more generously – also count all those double candidates who, so far, *always* won their seats via the lists, and those who were *always* voted directly into the *Bundestag* as list- and district-MPs, respectively? Or do we only want to be so generous for those double candidates who either always had a *secure* spot on the party list or always had a *safe* electoral district (Manow and Nistor 2009)? How often do we even find people who have only held seats as either a district or a list representative? How often does a change of status occur within a legislator's career? Do the categories of district and list mandates actually define a type of legislator or, rather, an episode in a longer sequence of a legislator's career?

Whichever definition might be used, a first inference becomes clear: if studies that seek to prove differences in the behaviour of district and list representatives code the representative type as an independent, explanatory variable based solely on the MP's respective official status at the time, they neglect the respective mode of election. Consequently, these studies only translate unsatisfactorily the latent theoretical construct – election rules as incentive structures for legislative behaviour – into a measurement concept.

---

3. Klingemann and Wessels concur: 'The probability for double-candidacy politicians to win a seat via the district or the list mode is almost equal. This should be an incentive for double-candidacy candidates to seriously consider interests and demands of the local constituency. This should, of course, be particularly true for candidates with insecure list-positions. If this is indeed the case, even double-candidates should form some kind of district orientation which impacts on their district performance in order to reduce uncertainty about re-election chances' (2001: 291).

The danger of comparing list and district representatives, and their legislative behaviour, is that the actual core of the controversy concerning the idea of role differentiation will be missed – even if we study legislators who are always elected to the *Bundestag* exclusively by way of a district mandate from their electoral district, or via a place on the party list of their federal state. This core can be summarised as follows: on the one side, advocates of the differentiation thesis assume that the legislative behaviour of district representatives is determined primarily by their aim for re-election in their electoral district. List representatives are, at the same time, assumed to work chiefly toward a promising spot on their party list and, therefore, orient themselves first and foremost to their party and not on an electoral district (so argue, for example, Bawn and Thies 2003). The expectation at hand is that the mode of election leads to clearly distinctive legislative behaviour. On the other side, critics of the differentiation argument do *not* maintain that such calculations do not matter, but argue that the legislative behaviour of a significant number of list representatives, namely those who are double candidates, resembles in essential aspects the behaviour of district candidates, in that their legislative behaviour is also geared toward the interests and issues of the electoral district.

In order to assess these two theses, it is therefore imperative to take the mode of election into consideration likewise. The proof that the legislative behaviour of district representatives and list representatives differs (Stratmann and Baur 2002) *does not, in itself, provide sufficient evidence* to affirm the role differentiation thesis. For example, should district candidates belong disproportionately often to *Bundestag* committees that are highly relevant to their electoral districts, this fact itself does not tell us anything about the presumed role differentiation. Instead, it should be inquired whether those list representatives belonging to the committees in question (and who, as well, ran for a district mandate) also perhaps represent the issues and concerns of their home district, meaning that they select these *Bundestag* committees precisely because of the specific interests of their electoral districts.

In yet another way, the simple coding of district and list representatives according to their current status as legislators appears deficient. If we assert that re-election is the chief motive for the actions of a legislator, then not only should the past mode of election be reflected in a MP's behaviour, but also, and especially, the mode of election *targeted for the future*. A rational legislator should anticipate in her current behaviour the future retrospective judgment of her selectorate/ electorate concerning her parliamentary performance. As we know, a double candidature increases re-election chances (Manow 2007). Therefore, rational MPs should find this mode of election particularly attractive. In this case, however, list- or district-only candidatures should often be evaluated as transitory episodes. Again a sequence analysis would help in confirming or refuting such a presumption by observing the relative frequency of certain episodic sequences during longer parliamentary careers.

In the following, I will thus examine complete sequences of membership in the *Bundestag* for all legislators from 1949–2009. Once we have thereby clearly identified the (pure) list and district representatives, I examine whether we can confirm the finding in the literature that the membership in various types of *Bundestag* committees (district versus party committees) differs systematically between the two types of representatives.[4] In a second step, I subsequently inquire whether there are also any indications that list representatives with double candidatures gear their legislative activity toward the interests of the electoral district in which they – unsuccessfully – ran for office. Yet, let us begin by reconstructing, in the following section, the political incentive structure that represents the district, list, or double candidature for the individual representative.

A sequence analysis of parliamentary careers: members of the *Bundestag*, 1949 – 2009

Methods and the operationalisation of variables

The appropriate tool for assessing the influence of the various political career paths on the behaviour of elected legislators is an analysis of career *sequences* (cf. Chapter Five). Unlike in survival or event history analysis, the focus of interest in sequence analysis is not the length of time until the event occurs, but the pattern in which individual episodes or elements occur within a longer sequence. A sequence is an orderly succession of individual episodes or elements (Brzinsky-Fay, Kohler and Luniak 2006; Scherer and Brüderl 2010). The case presented here involves a certain candidature (list candidate, district candidate, double candidate) and the subsequent status of the legislator (list representative, district representative). Together, the three modes of candidacy and two types of mandates create four possible combinations of episodes: in the first, a person runs as a list candidate and subsequently becomes a list representative; the second consist of a district candidate and subsequent district representative; the third combines a double candidacy with a *Bundestag* mandate won via the party list ranking; and finally the fourth combines a double candidacy with a district mandate. The observation is expanded to also codify the episode 'no mandate', whereby the data base does not permit us to determine whether the person ran for office and was not elected or did not run. The status variable, therefore, can take on five different values (*see* Table 9.1).

The shortest sequence consists of one episode – a candidate who runs for a *Bundestag* seat just once and is elected just once. Since we are not observing

---

4. Stratmann and Baur also compare the committee membership of 'pure' list and district representatives, but only for one legislative period. For the period studied, the number of observations is so small that the authors have to pool party and district committees (2002: 511).

Table 9.1: Sequence elements for analysing German MPs' political careers

Status	Coding
No candidature *or* no mandate	0
List candidate / representative	1
District candidate / representative	2
Double candidate with list mandate	3
Double candidate with district mandate	4

candidates but representatives, a sequence that consists only of zero-episodes cannot occur. As mentioned, a zero-episode cannot be interpreted.[5]

Longer sequences are combinations of these individual episodes. Each of the seventeen legislative periods from 1949–2009, that I observe, is an episode featuring five possible variations, resulting in the number of possible different sequences equalling from five[17] to one.[6] Depicted are the courses of individual political careers of each legislator over time. A list representative, in the more narrow sense, would be a legislator whose career sequence consists solely of a series of episodes containing the element one (except for the time in which this person was not a member of the *Bundestag*). Likewise, the classification of a politician whose sequence only consists of the element two would be that of a strict district representative. As was shown in the previous section, the interpretation of sequences containing either only the element three (double candidature with list mandate) or the element five (double candidature with district mandate) is already much more controversial. Sequences in which the various episodes change are characteristic of legislators who would be grouped neither as district nor as list representatives.

To demonstrate this point, Table 9.2 shows three different exemplary career sequences for three legislators over the time span of six legislative periods. The first case is that of a legislator who did not run in the first legislative period, but was elected in the second, third, and fourth periods as a list candidate (one) after which this person left the *Bundestag*. The second case is that of a legislator who ran as a constituency candidate exclusively, starting in the second electoral period and held a *Bundestag* seat for four legislative periods (two). The third case represents a legislator who also did not have a seat in the first legislative period, but then ran four times as a double candidate for a *Bundestag* mandate

---

5. This is the case because the status of 'no candidature' is derived from the status of 'no mandate' (even without the information about whether a representative ran or not). Not until the data set is expanded to include information on candidatures – as is currently being done – will it be possible to ascertain whether candidates did not run for office and are, therefore, not participating in the *Bundestag*, or whether they ran but were not elected.

6. One because a sequence of only zeros is not possible.

Table 9.2: Three examples of political career sequences

Legislative period					
First	Second	Third	Fourth	Fifth	Sixth
No Candidature	*List Candidate / List Mandate*			*No Candidature*	
0	1	1	1	0	0
No Candidature	*District Candidate / District Mandate*				*No Candidature*
0	2	2	2	2	0
No Candidature	*Double Candidate / List Mandate / District Mandate*				*No Candidature*
0	3	3	4	4	0

Legend: No candidature *or* no mandate: 0; List candidate / representative: 1; District candidate / representative: 2; Double candidate with list mandate: 3; Double candidate with district mandate: 4.

and won a seat the first two times via the party list (three), followed by two times via district election (four). This legislator also did not run for a seat in the sixth electoral period.

For the following analysis, I use data from the biographical reference book on members of the *Bundestag* from 1949–2002 (Vierhaus and Herbst 2003) as well as my own compilation of data up to 2009. I include all legislators from 1949–2009, a total of 3,581 persons, with 60,877 observations (17 terms × 3,581 persons = 60,877 observations). If we only consider the times in which these people were actually members of the *Bundestag* (that is, ignoring the zero-episodes), the dataset still consists of 10,125 observations. This corresponds roughly to an average length of membership in the *Bundestag* of 2.8 legislative periods per legislator (10,125/ 3,581) and confirms earlier findings for the average re-election chances and length of membership of German MPs (see Manow 2008).

In the following, I apply the sequence analysis module for Stata (Brzinsky-Fay *et al.* 2006; Kohler *et al.* 2011). It offers considerable opportunities to prepare, analyse, and graphically present the various courses of event sequences – in our case, the careers of elected representatives. Not the least does it enable us to generate variables that indicate specific patterns of sequences. This is a prerequisite for testing the idea that different types of representatives display different types of legislative behaviour. In the following section, I evaluate the data on the basis of sequence analysis.

Empirical Findings

When the purpose is to identify distinct types of representatives, then one strictly descriptive finding is initially of interest: how often do career sequences occur in which the (exclusive) district candidature is always linked to the district

Table 9.3: Frequency of sequences with identical elements, all parties

Sequence	Number	Per cent	Cumul. Per cent
3	1,239	36.58	36.58
4	492	14.53	51.11
1	399	11.78	62.89
34	394	11.63	74.52
2	364	10.75	85.27
24	221	6.52	91.79
13	130	3.84	95.63
14	56	1.65	97.28
12	50	1.48	98.76
134	42	1.24	100.00
Total	3,387[a]	100.00	

[a] The lower number of cases is due to an analysis limited to only the ten most frequent sequences.
Legend: List candidate / representative: 1; District candidate / representative: 2; Double candidate with list mandate: 3; Double candidate with district mandate: 4.

mandate and the (exclusive) list candidature to the list mandate? The following frequency table (Table 9.3) shows the frequency of sequences *with identical elements*. For the question at hand, the third row (list representative) and the fourth row (district representative) and their corresponding sequences one or two are particularly interesting. These rows combine all representatives who exhibit such a candidature/mandate sequence, be it once, twice, or many times. As becomes evident in Table 9.3, among the population of all legislators, we have 485 that we can classify as list-only representatives and 384 as district-only representatives. Together, they represent about 23 per cent, nearly one fourth, of all legislators. Thus, we arrive at the first important intermediary result in the sequence analysis of the careers of German *Bundestag* legislators: *in an indisputable (restrictive) sense*, our differentiation between district and list representatives only holds true for one fourth of all *Bundestag* legislators (if we do not apply this distinction in the strictly formal and static sense that classifies the representatives of a certain legislative period according to the way they entered the *Bundestag*).

By far, the most frequent sequence is three, the double candidature with list mandate (row one). More than a third of all *Bundestag* legislators enter the parliament in this manner. In particular, legislators from the smaller parties run as double candidates and enter the *Bundestag* via the state party list. As we saw in the third section, the classification of these legislators as list representatives is not unproblematic since there are obvious incentives for them to represent the interests of their constituency in their legislative and general political behaviour

Table 9.4: Frequency of sequences with identical elements, CDU/CSU and SPD

Sequence	Number	Per cent	Cumul. Per cent
3	562	22.23	22.23
4	472	18.67	40.90
34	382	15.11	56.01
2	347	13.73	69.74
1	310	12.26	82.00
24	221	8.74	90.74
13	91	3.60	94.34
14	55	2.18	96.52
12	50	1.98	98.50
134	38	1.50	100.00
Total	2,528	100.00	

Legend: List candidate / representative: 1; District candidate / representative: 2; Double candidate with list mandate: 3; Double candidate with district mandate: 4.

as well. This is even more relevant for the group of double candidates who win a district mandate in their electoral district (sequence four). In this category we also have to include those legislators who ran sometimes only as a district candidate and sometimes as a double candidate, but always won a district mandate (sequences two to four). Finally, those double candidates, who in some cases entered the *Bundestag* via the party list and in others through district election in an electoral district (sequences three and four), are also to be included in this group. Nearly three-fourths of all legislators never undergo a change of status during their career.

When we limit our observation to the large parties, whose members of parliament actually have a realistic chance of entering the *Bundestag* in both ways – that is, for the legislators of the CDU/CSU and the SPD (*see* Table 9.4) – we observe the expected shifts in the frequency of sequences. The number of double candidates winning list mandates drops noticeably, while the number of double candidates who successfully win a district mandate increases, as does the number of those who enter parliament sometimes via the party list and in other times via an electoral district (row three, sequence three to four). However, the relative number of list-only or district-only representatives remains nearly unchanged. Moreover, for the legislators of these two major parties, of which the overwhelming number actually has the chance to win an electoral district, the number of legislators who can be classified as clearly list or district members of parliament, does not increase.

An index plot illustrates this quite clearly (*see* Figure 9.1 and 9.2), whereby Figure 9.1 depicts the frequency of different sequences for all parties, and Figure 9.2 limits its observations to the Christian (CDU/CSU) and Social

Figure 9.1: Index plot, all parties, 1949–2009

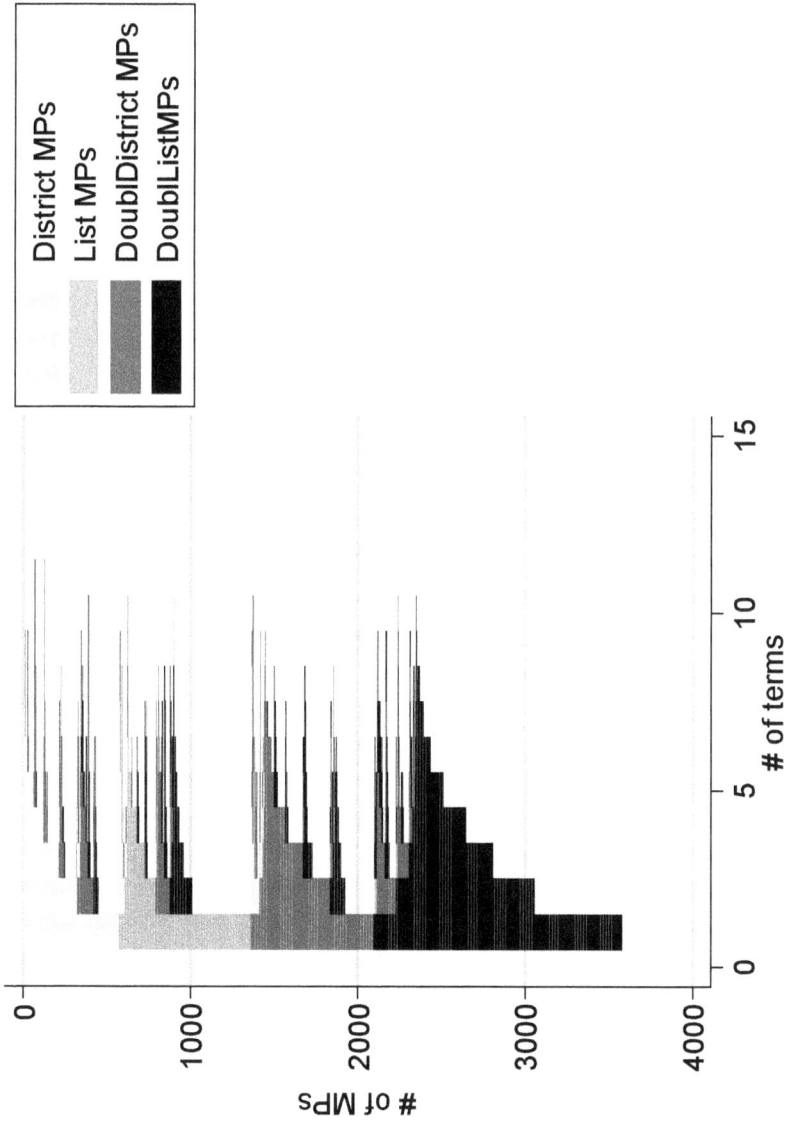

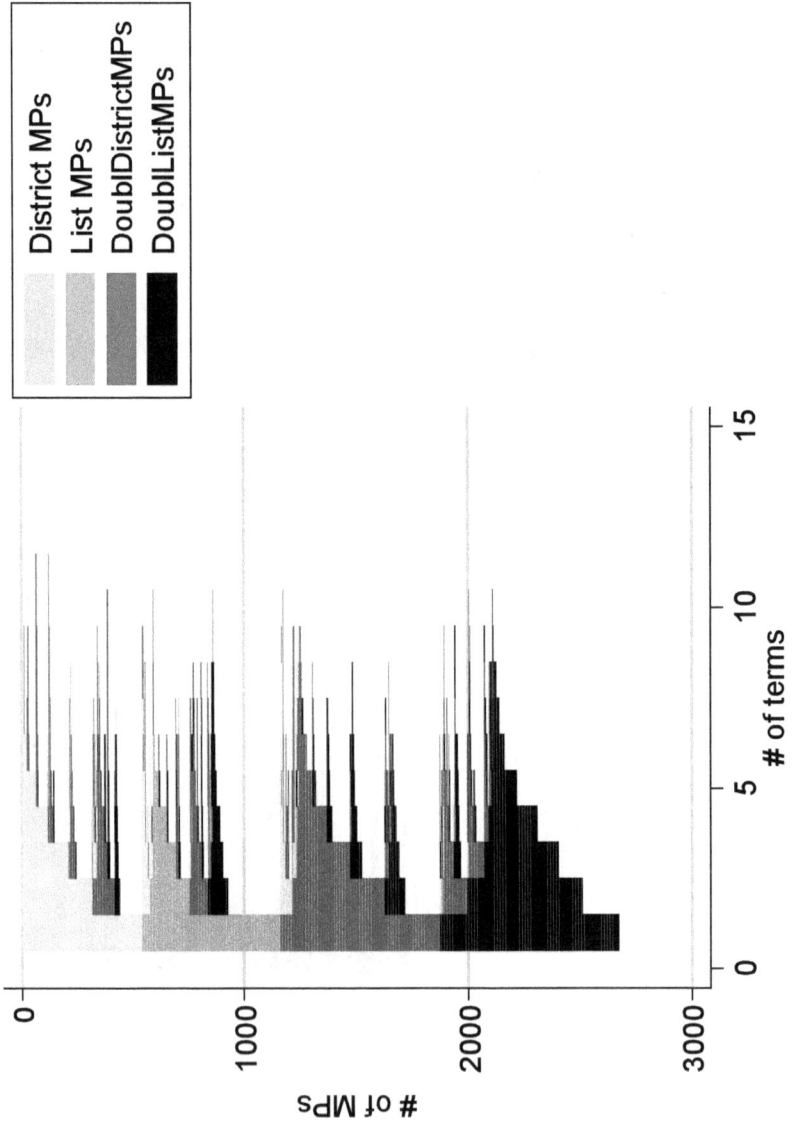

Figure 9.2: Index plot, CDU/CSU and SPD, 1949–2009

Democrats (SPD). The x-axis lists the number of episodes; the y-axis displays the number of representatives with the same career sequence. Both figures depict the dominant political sequence as being the one in which the double candidature leads to either a list or district mandate. When observing all parties, the most frequent sequence is the one in which a one-time double candidature is linked to a one-time list mandate.

With regard to the question about the importance of the *future* mode of candidature as opposed to the *past*, we observe that sequences in which legislators switch from a double to a single candidature (be it the party list or the electoral district) are extremely rare. Among the thirty most frequent sequences, only eighty-five legislators of all 3,581 MPs have followed this path, while 362 legislators – that is, about four times as many – moved in the opposite direction (2.4 per cent from double to single candidatures as opposed to ten per cent in the opposite direction).

Once we have generated a specific dummy variable for all representatives whom we can clearly identify as either list or district representatives, we are able to test the hypothesis of differing legislative behaviour for these two types of representatives. In the literature, proponents of this differentiation thesis cite disparities in committee memberships between list and district representatives as proof of their distinct orientations and strategies (see Stratmann and Baur 2002). Consequently, I will first investigate, in the next section, whether we can actually determine systematic differences once we limit the observation to those representatives whom we can classify undoubtedly as district or list representatives – in other words, those who *always* and *exclusively* ran on the party list or in an electoral district.

According to the role differentiation theses, we should expect to find (exclusive) district representatives more often in committees that have distinct relevance to affairs affecting their electoral district (e.g., Committee for Transport, Building and Urban Development or Committee for Food, Agriculture and Consumer Protection), while (exclusive) list representatives are primarily members in committees in which they can develop their political profile in a general political sense (such as Committee for Foreign Affairs or Committee for Affairs of the European Union). In a second step, I will inquire whether we find list MPs with double candidatures also deciding to join *Bundestag* committees for reasons of representing local interests. Proceeding in this way, I expand the study to include the mode of election for *Bundestag* MPs.

List and district representatives and their committee memberships

In the following, I replicate the study on committee membership of *Bundestag* MPs by Stratmann and Baur (2002). In their study, the authors ask whether significant differences can be discovered between list and district representatives with regard to the *Bundestag* committees to which they belong (for a recent replication, see also

Gschwend, Shugart and Zittel 2009).[7] For their study, the authors distinguish three types of *Bundestag* committees: 'district,' 'party', and neutral committees. District committees are those that serve specific material interests of electoral districts, like the agriculture committee 'where funds can be channelled to the home district' (Stratmann and Baur 2002: 508). The expectation is that district representatives should be represented above average in this type of committee because critical decisions affecting districts are made here. So-called party committees, such as the committees for foreign affairs or for health issues, offer individual legislators either the chance to develop their political reputation politically or to serve group-specific redistributive functions. In this type of committee, the authors expect to find a disproportionate number of list representatives as members. With regard to a third class of committees, which Stratmann and Baur classify as 'neutral' (e.g. committees on voting rights or parliamentarian immunity), no clear expectation can be expressed concerning the committee membership. Stratmann and Baur code district and list representatives according to their current status as *Bundestag* members, even though they also use a robustness test to check whether representatives with exclusive list or constituency candidatures also engage in different *Bundestag* committees (Stratmann and Baur 2002: 511). What is not taken into consideration in Stratmann and Baur's study are previous episodes as a candidate or mandate holder. Likewise, they do not consider the possibility that any indication of a 'local' pattern of representing interests could be found among list representatives in district committees.

My replication of the study uses a significantly enlarged database.[8] First, I analyse whether the findings of the Stratmann and Baur study can be substantiated when the types of representatives are more distinctly defined, as outlined above. To do this, I follow the authors' classification and consider the Transportation Committee[9] and the Committee for Food and Agriculture as typical district committees (Stratmann and Baur 2002: 508). In addition, I include the Defence Committee as a district committee – coded as a party committee by Stratmann

---

7. With respect to committee-assignment, Werner Patzelt provides a very concise description of the process: 'Committee seats are allocated among parliamentary parties according to the percentage of seats held in the parliament. Thus, all committees are to some degree politically representative 'samples' of the plenary. But in no sense are they 'random' samples. Rather, committee seats are sought and filled according to the individual MP's personal preferences and skills. At the beginning of a legislative session, members are asked by the management of their parliamentary parties, the whips, to apply for committee seats of their choice, or at least to declare their preferences. Then the whips transform these applications or preferences into an overall proposal for the assignment of members to committee seats. This proposal requires at least informal, sometimes even formal, consent by the plenary of the parliamentary party. [...] Sometimes there are contested committee seats; then intra-party negotiations and compensations are required. But the parliamentary party's management usually succeeds in evolving a politically satisfactory list' (Patzelt 1999: 29–30). For the process of committee assignment, see also (Ismayr 2000).

8. The Stratmann-Baur study features 1,600 observations for three legislative periods, while my study covers the total of 3,581 members of the *Bundestag* for seventeen legislative periods. My unit of analysis however is not 'membership episode', but the single MP.

9. Labelled 'Traffic Committee' in Stratmann and Baur.

Table 9.5: Chances of being a member in the Transportation, Agriculture, Defence Committees, 1949–2009, logistic regression odds ratios

Odds Ratios	Agriculture	Transportation	Defence
'Pure' List-MPs	0.47**	0.49**	1.30
	(0.16)	(0.16)	(0.21)
'Pure' District-MPs	1.40	1.71***	1.00
	(0.31)	(0.33)	(0.18)
Observations	3,437	3,430	3,581

p-values in parentheses; * significant at the 10%-level; ** significant at the 5%-level *** significant at the 1%-level.

and Baur (2002: 508). In the Defence Committee, many political decisions of considerable local significance are made, concerning the location of military bases, military training areas, and regions being affected by the armaments industry (see Berg 1985). It is therefore plausible that district interests drive committee membership here, too. I finally ask whether list representatives with double candidatures might not also belong, disproportionately often, to district committees like the three under investigation here: agriculture, transportation and defence. The issues specific to the electoral district are surveyed in part indirectly – by way of geographical information – and in part directly, e.g. via the presence of military bases in a district.

We can first observe the relative probability of committee membership according to each type of representative with a logistic regression (*see* Table 9.5).

Table 9.5 strongly substantiates the general expectation that district (list) MPs have a greater (lesser) probability of belonging to the three constituency committees. This higher probability however fails to meet the conventional standards of significance in the case of the defence committee. Even so, more important in our context is the question whether the list MPs, who also ran in a district, are found, likewise, in disproportionate numbers in those *Bundestag* committees that are politically relevant for the districts that such legislators (indirectly) represent.

The fact that the agriculture committee tends to be made up of district representatives from the CDU/CSU and list representatives from the SPD, is interpreted by Stratmann and Baur as proof that agricultural interests are represented prominently in the CDU/CSU but not in the SPD.[10] Yet, there is an

---

10. 'In German politics, the farm population tends to support the CDU/CSU overwhelmingly, and this party has a reputation of working for farm interests. Thus we predict that CDU/CSU FPTP [First-past-the-post; PM] members, as opposed to SPD FPTP members, are on the Agriculture Committee. SPD FPTP members are elected primarily from urban areas, and they cannot dispense special benefits to urban areas if they are on the Agriculture Committee. Thus, we predict that FPTP SPD members will avoid membership on the Agriculture Committee' (Stratmann and Baur 2002: 508).

alternative and, in my view, more plausible explanation for this pattern. Due to the socioeconomic composition of the electorate, SPD representatives rarely win many district mandates in rural regions (see Gudgin and Taylor 2012 [1979]). This, however, does not mean that the SPD abandons the representation of rural interests. Via list representatives, the party can guarantee parliamentary representation of 'certain regions in which experience has shown that the opponent wins all of the electoral districts' (Schreiber 1994: 145, see above). Therefore, the critical question is whether we also find evidence for representation of district interests among list representatives, especially among those who held a double candidature. Such evidence could be a specific regional pattern of recruitment, which, in the case of the agriculture committee, could be an overrepresentation of SPD list representatives with double candidatures from rural regions (like Bavaria, Baden-Wurttemberg or Lower Saxony).

As long as detailed (digitally readable) socioeconomic district level data are unavailable, we are left to answer this question primarily with approximate values and indirect evidence. A first (rough) approximation is possible simply using the district numbers, because these contain a geographic dimension (roughly: district one 'Flensburg' in the North, Danish border, to district 242 or 243 'Kempten' or 'Kaufbeuren', in the South, Austrian border). This geographic dimension remained essentially unchanged during the observed time span despite smaller redistricting.[11] Should we find clear geographic patterns in the committee membership of list representatives, this has to be interpreted as an obvious indication of the strategic selection of committee membership, one that aims to represent regional and local interests. Should the assumption of the role differentiation thesis, that list representatives do *not* gear themselves to such interests, be correct, the regional pattern of recruitment among list representatives should be primarily random, meaning that it corresponds foremost with the frequency in which certain regions/electoral districts are represented by list representatives in the *Bundestag*.

Figures 9.3 and 9.4 show the regional pattern of CDU- and SPD-MPs, those elected in a district or via the list, and finally the regional recruitment pattern of those who ran a double candidature, were elected via the party list and became a member in the transportation- or agriculture-committee, respectively. A clear regional pattern becomes apparent. The CDU fails to win districts especially in the old industrial areas of North-Rhine Westphalia and Northern Hesse (district numbers 75 to 140), and therefore, CDU list-MPs are overrepresented in these regions, as well as in the Northern city-states of Bremen and Hamburg. In these places, public infrastructure is of importance (e.g. harbours) and CDU-list MPs who become members in the transportation committee are recruited from these areas. The SPD is particularly unsuccessful in Germany's south, in Baden-Wurttemberg, Bavaria and parts of Rhineland Palatine (district numbers 160 to 240). Therefore

---

11. The period under investigation is restricted to 2002, since district numeration changed only when the new German states were integrated into the old system of district numbers.

Figure 9.3: Regional representation of CDU district- and list-MPs and of double candidate list-MPs in the Transportation Committee, 1953–2009

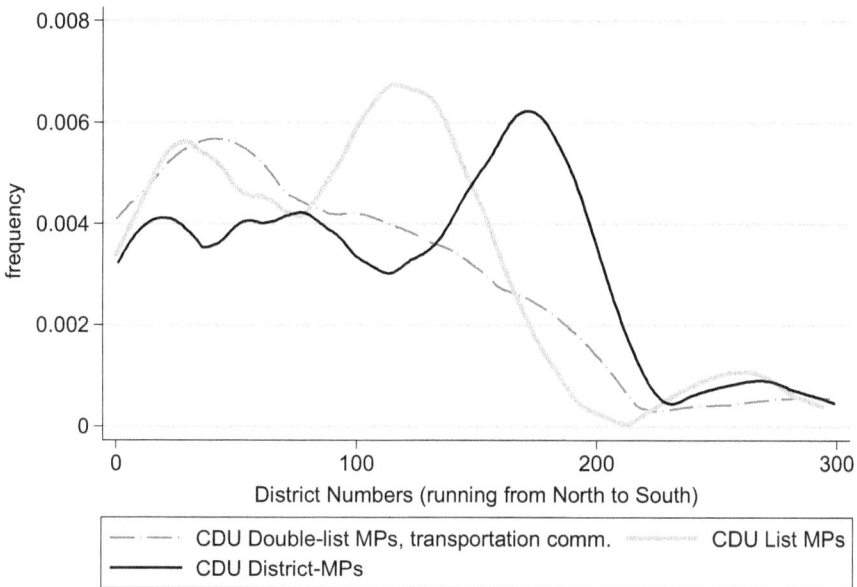

SPD list-MPs are overrepresented in these regions. Figure 9.4 shows the density plot for the SPD membership in the agriculture committee for legislators with list mandates and double candidatures. As becomes clear, being unsuccessful in southern districts does not mean that the SPD has to forego the representation of rural interests. The party can employ its double candidates in regions where it is unsuccessful in winning districts, and as Figure 9.4 shows, this is exactly what the party does.

The picture that emerges from observing regional recruitment patterns of MPs with membership in the *Bundestag* committees for Agriculture or Transportation can be supported by additional district-level information. Although we lack socioeconomic time-series data at the district level, at least for the last two *Bundestag* elections, the German election-office does provide district data in digitalised form.[12] This data allows checking, at least for these last two terms, whether the committee recruitment of list-MPs with a double candidacy shows regional variation that would indicate the representation of district interests by list-MPs. I code a dummy variable for those districts in which list-MPs who were

---

12. See http://www.bundeswahlleiter.de/de/bundestagswahlen/BTW_BUND_09/strukturdaten/ und http://www.bundeswahlleiter.de/de/bundestagswahlen/BTW_BUND_05/strukturdaten/.accessed 22 July 2014.

Figure 9.4: Regional representation of SPD district- and list-MPs and of double candidate list-MPs in the Agriculture Committee, 1953–2002

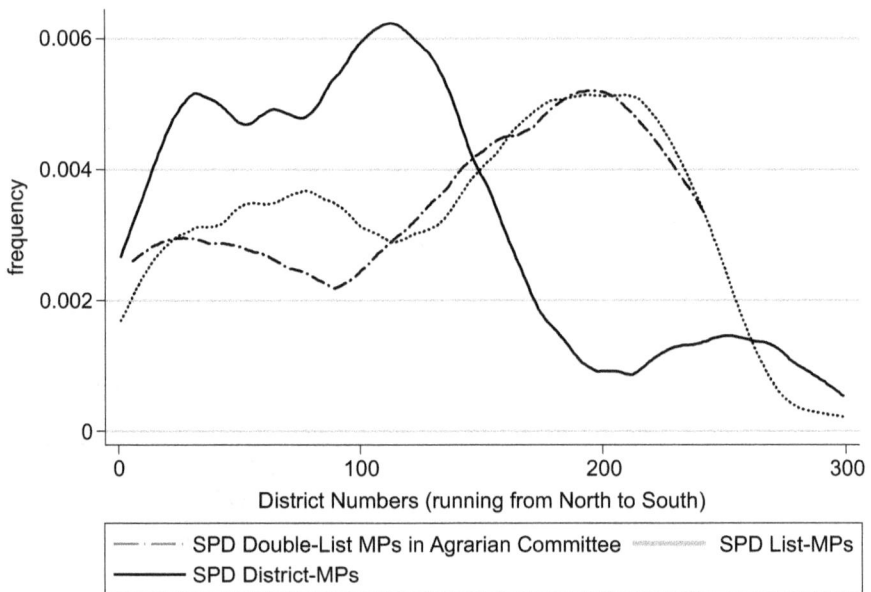

members of the transportation or agriculture committee had run unsuccessfully.[13] Unfortunately, the reported indicators are not identical over time. As variables indicating a rural district, I employ the number of agricultural firms, the employment share of the agricultural sector (for the 2005 *Bundestag* election) or simply the area of the district (for the 2009 election) as proxies. As an indicator for the relevance of public infrastructure, I take the absolute number of people commuting to and from work per district (for the 2009 election). I expect districts which are represented via list-MPs in the agriculture-committee to be more rural than other districts, and I expect districts which are represented via list-MPs in the transportation-committee to have a higher number of commuters (in these cases, list MPs would represent their district in the according committee).

Regressing the area, agricultural employment or the number of farms in a district on the variable indicating membership in the agriculture committee by list-MPs with double candidature, leads to the following results: in 2009 a district was on average 710 km^2 bigger (significant at the $p < 0.01$ level), i.e. more rural, if it was represented by a list-MP in the agriculture committee – with

13. These are districts like Herzogtum Lauenburg – Stormarn-Süd, Unterems, Delmenhorst – Wesermarsch – Oldenburg-Land, Prignitz – Ostprignitz-Ruppin – Havelland I, Märkisch-Oderland – Barnim II, Potsdam – Potsdam-Mittelmark II – Teltow-Fläming II, Börde – Jerichower Land, Lippe I, Olpe – Märkischer Kreis I, etc.

the average district having a size of 1194 km^2. The net number of commuting persons per district[14] increases by 27.5 per 1,000 inhabitants (significant at the $p < 0.05$ per cent level) if represented in the transportation committee by a list-MP (the average being 62 commuters per 1,000 persons in a district). For the 2005 election, we have even more detailed data, since the German election office reported the number of farms per district as well as the employment share of the agricultural sector for this election. The employment share in the district increases significantly (at the ß < 0.005 level) by one per cent (the average employment share for all 299 districts being 1.4 per cent), if the district is represented by a list-MP in the agriculture committee during the 16th term. The same finding turns up when looking at the number of farms, which increases by 3.3 per 1000 persons and an average of 5.5 farms in all 299 districts. Unfortunately, we cannot calculate the number of commuters for the 2005 election since the German election office did not report this indicator for this election. Overall, each variable indicating either a rural district or a district with a high importance of public infrastructure increases significantly if the district is represented by list-MPs in the agriculture or transportation committee, respectively.

An analogous examination of regional patterns of representation (measured on the numbering of electoral districts or state party lists) is less suitable for studying the defence committee, because military bases or military training grounds (or defence-industry firms) are not clearly clustered geographically. Therefore, for each individual list representative among the members of the defence committee, I inquired whether the military maintained a base in the district in which he or she was running for office. This far more demanding coding had to be limited to the period from 1972–2002, but it did still submit an informative finding from the observation of 120 list representatives with double candidatures.

For seventy-two of the 120 list representatives who have been members of the defence committee – that is, for nearly two-thirds of them –we find that the military does indeed maintain a base (garrison, hospital, administrative office, etc.) in the electoral district of their (unsuccessful) district candidature. Moreover, eight of these list representatives also have a professional link to the military (usually as a career soldier), as do fourteen other list representatives who were, or are, members of the defence committee but do not have any military facilities in their district. This analysis has not taken into consideration the location of the arms industry in each of the districts, nor does it include military training areas and bases of allied armed forces (due to the unavailability of data). However, by only considering base locations of the German military, this analysis already finds evidence of a direct connection of district interests for more than 60 per cent of all districts represented in the defence committee by list representatives. For district representatives, such a connection to the local interests of their districts can be derived from their prominent participation in the defence committee (*see* Table 9.5).

---

14. See (Bundeswahlleiter 2009b, 2005).

Mixed rules, mixed roles

Does the German mixed member electoral system produce two types of representatives – the one type directly elected legislators who aim primarily to represent the interests of his/her district, and the other type, list-elected legislators who are primarily loyal to his/her party and seek to serve 'functional' interest groups? The study presented here has addressed this controversial question in two steps. The first was to use sequence analysis in order to assess empirically just how prominent the exclusive 'path to the *Bundestag*' was by way of either the party list or the electoral district, as compared to the careers of all *Bundestag* members. The sequence-analytical examination of the 'path to the *Bundestag*' allowed, in the second step, to limit the comparative analysis of legislative behaviour (defined here as the membership in *Bundestag* committees) of list and district representatives to those legislators whose classification can be considered indisputable because they have always run for office as either list candidates or district candidates. Subsequently, the examination of the pattern of committee membership was expanded to those legislators, to whom the critics of the role differentiation thesis attribute a strategy of district-interest representation in their legislative behaviour likewise, namely to list representatives who simultaneously run for a district mandate (usually regardless of how promising this candidature is or not).

Both of these steps reinforced scepticism of the role differentiation- or mandate-divide thesis (cf. Herron 2002). For one, career paths leading to a *Bundestag* mandate, exclusively via the party list or the electoral district, are to be found rarely: only 23 per cent of all members of parliament can be classified as such, namely as a list or district representative. This number is certainly too small to assert in anything else than a formal sense, that the German mixed member electoral system produces two types of legislators ('two legislator *types* exist simultaneously in Germany', Stratmann and Baur 2002: 506, author's emphasis). Furthermore, the analysis clearly proved that legislators who unsuccessfully run for a district mandate still use their status as a list member to represent the local interests of that same district in parliament – independent of any realistic prospect of ever winning a district mandate there in the future. Evidently, the incentive structures created by the combination of plurality voting and proportional representation in the German electoral system function in a way in that parties reward active district work with a promising ranking on the state party list (Hainmüller, Kern and Bechtel 2006). Therefore, *Bundestag* legislators who held a double candidature – which accounts for more than 80 per cent of them – are faced with strong incentives to direct their legislative and general political work toward benefitting both the party and their electoral district. As the empirical findings presented here indicate, the German mixed member electoral system leads to role consolidation rather than to role differentiation (Shugart 2001b; Shugart and Wattenberg 2001c).

Chapter Ten

Conclusion

The elections to the 18th German *Bundestag* on 22 September 2013 saw 44.3 million German voters turning out, 71.5 per cent of those 61.9 million, eligible to vote. They elected 631 *Bundestag* Members. For the first time in post-war history, the liberal party (FDP) is not part of the new *Bundestag* since it failed to meet the legal threshold of 5 per cent of list votes (with 4.8 per cent, equalling around 2.1 million votes). At the same time, the newly founded Eurosceptic AfD (*Alternative für Deutschland*; Alternative for Germany) very narrowly failed to enter parliament, too, with 4.7 per cent or around 2 million votes. The upshot is an unprecedented level of 'wasted votes'. In 2013, 15.7 per cent of all those German voters who turned out and cast a valid vote did so in vain – the party of their choice did not make it into parliament.

Both outcomes – the failure of the FDP as well as that of the new protest party *Alternative für Deutschland* – appear to be related to the recent change in the electoral law that was implemented after the German constitutional court had twice ruled the existing law as 'unconstitutional'. Due to a new provision in Germany's reformed election law, surplus seats for one party now have to be counterbalanced by compensation seats for other parties so that overall proportionality is secured (apart from the disproportionality due to the legal threshold, which – not surprisingly, with two parties failing entry so narrowly – was again controversially debated in the aftermath of the 2013 election). As a consequence, the new German *Bundestag* surpasses the regular 598 seats by thirty-three members, due to four surplus plus twenty-nine compensation seats, adding up to the 631 MPs mentioned above. Given that the previous elections in 2009 had resulted in a total of twenty-four surplus seats, the marked reduction of these mandates is surprising. Worst case scenarios had predicted an overall size of the *Bundestag* of almost 700 MPs, given that a higher number of surplus seats would very likely have resulted also in a much higher number of compensation seats.

That this scenario did not materialise can partly be explained by the high number of 'wasted votes'. As a consequence, of the many ballots that did not count for the distribution of seats, the Christian Democrats gained about 49 per cent of all seats with only roughly 41 per cent of all valid votes. Yet, with a higher seat share, it is more unlikely to win more district seats than the list-vote share would assign to a party. With a seat share of 49 per cent, a party would usually need to win all of the districts in a state in order to generate surplus seats (*see* Chapters Two and Three). In 2013, this only happened in Bavaria and Thuringia. So, the small number of surplus seats in this latest election is mainly explained by the narrow failure of both the FDP and the AfD due to the five per cent threshold. The next election might turn out quite differently, then possibly leading to a much more substantial increase in surplus and compensation seats (and in anticipation of this, parties are well aware of the need for yet another electoral reform).

But how does this relate to the electoral fate of the liberal party? With compensation seats securing near proportionality, the new electoral rules weaken the incentives for 'coalition' or 'threshold insurance'-voting. In the German electoral systems, voters split their votes mainly out of two strategic considerations (*see* Chapter Five): voters feeling close to a small party might want to avoid wasting their nominal vote by casting that vote for the candidate of the larger prospective coalition partner. For instance, an FDP voter might cast his or her *Erststimme*, nominal vote, for the candidate of the CDU or CSU. Correspondingly, voters close to a larger party sometimes split their vote in order to secure the chance that the smaller prospective coalition party will pass the legal threshold. For example, an SPD-voter might cast his or her second vote, i.e. the party-list vote, for the prospective smaller coalition partner, for instance the Greens (Pappi *et al.* 2006; Pappi and Thurner 2002). Under the previous electoral rules, i.e. without compensation for surplus seats, the electoral costs of vote splitting were partially counterbalanced for supporters of larger parties. The 'threshold-insurance'-strategy of vote splitting translated into a smaller party-list vote share, and therefore, *overall* fewer seats for either the CDU or the SPD. Yet with an increasing discrepancy between nominal and party-list votes, the larger parties, at the same time, had a higher chance of gaining surplus seats, thereby offsetting some of the loss incurred by vote splitting. With full compensation, however, threshold insurance voting has become more costly for supporters of large parties. As a consequence, in 2013, the share of voters that split their ticket was lower than in previous elections (20.6 per cent of those who gave their party vote to one of the established parties, Christian- or Social-Democrats, Liberals, the Left or the Green party cast their nominal vote for another party; this is almost five per cent lower than in 2009 and about 3.4 per cent lower than in 2002)[1] – a further reason for the small number of surplus seats in the most recent elections. When in the last days of the campaign the liberals, in the light of their deteriorating prospects, started a 'second votes'-initiative targeted at CDU voters and their interest to keep the liberals in parliament, the CDU party leadership officially stated that the party 'could not afford to give away votes'.

Apart from these small, but quite consequential changes, Germany's election law remained much as it was in the past. Consequently, central effects and outcomes closely resembled earlier elections. Take, for instance, a look at the translation of nominal votes into district mandates (*see* Figure 10.1 and Table 10.1): the familiar picture of high disproportionality in the plurality tier is displayed.

---

1. Own calculations according to www.bundeswahlleiter.de.

Figure 10.1: Vote-seat translation in the plurality tier, federal elections 2013

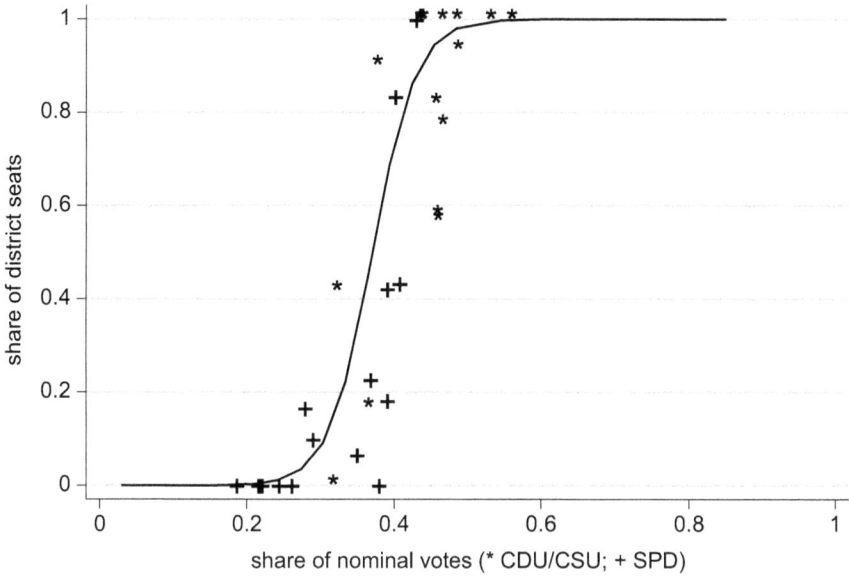

Table 10.1: rho (ρ) and beta (β) in 2013 as compared to previous federal elections

election	ρ	β
1987	8.057 (1.217)***	0.061 (0.003)***
1990	6.204 (1.424)***	0.094 (0.008)***
1994	6.361 (1.487)***	0.088 (0.008)***
1998	3.590 (1.166)***	0.096 (0.018)
2002	6.760 (1.627)***	0.097 (0.008)***
2005	3.536 (1.013)***	0.125 (0.016)***
2009	6.502 (1.419)***	0.166 (0.074)***
2013	8.422 (2.104)***	0.130 (0.0076)***

To win a district in the latest election, on average, a 37 per cent district vote share was enough. Compared to the election in 2009, this is a slightly lower, but in a longer perspective, clearly still a high degree of disproportionality (*see* Table 10.1, Figure 10.2; compare Figure 2.6).

As Figure 10.3 shows, with a vote share of 29.4 per cent and 58 districts (19.4 per cent of all 299 districts), the 2013 election counts as one of the most disastrous for the Social Democrats, comparable to their poor performance in 2009 and in the 2nd and 3rd federal elections, in 1953 and 1957.

The electoral rules' persisting effects in the 2013 election might explain why the electoral reform debate continues as well (Nohlen 2014). In general, it seems as if the German electoral system has more admirers abroad than at home (Capoccia 2002). Whereas it has served as a reform blueprint in many countries recently, from New Zealand to Japan, from Italy to Venezuela, from Hungary to Lesotho (Shugart and Wattenberg 2001b; Shugart 2001c; Massicotte 2011), a flourishing German reform debate features a surprisingly wide variety of proposals: more or less every conceivable alternative to Germany's mixed system has been introduced to the debate at some point.[2] Yet, given the partisan-political redistributive consequences, it is hard to imagine any of those proposals having the slightest chance of finding a parliamentary majority – apart from the fact that none of them seem particularly persuasive on its own.

In the light of this book's findings, the energy and passion of the German electoral reform debate must appear astonishing. Part of the explanation is certainly the activism of the *Bundesverfassungsgericht*, Germany's constitutional court, which has repeatedly ruled certain aspects of the electoral system as 'unconstitutional' (Lang 2014; Nohlen 2014: 390–394) and has forced politicians into several rounds of electoral reform. Yet, the court's judicial activism has not always been well advised and based on a thorough understanding of the functioning logic of Germany's MMP-electoral rules. In particular, the court's obsession with the equal weight of each single vote (*gleicher Erfolgswert*) mirrors the long-held misconception that the German electoral system is just a more complicated proportional, but not a mixed system.

The preceding chapters sketched the picture of a complex, but overall quite balanced institutional arrangement that, indeed successfully, combines those two features that elsewhere in the post-war period have been attempted to be achieved jointly: fairness, i.e. proportionality, and personalisation (Renwick 2011, 2010; Moser and Scheiner 2012). Germany's mixed electoral rules also have regularly

---

2. The latest elections provoked Paul Nolte, a Berlin-based historian, to propose a switch to a first-past-the-post system, a position shared by many others, including the former member of the constitutional court (and former *Bundestag* MP), Hans-Joachim Jentsch, as well as the ex-chancellor Helmut Schmidt. Another former member of Germany's constitutional court, and previously president of the Federal Republic, suggested introducing a French-style majority runoff system (Roman Herzog in *Sueddeutsche Zeitung*, 17th May 2010), whereas others pleaded for parallel voting (i.e. a Mixed-member majoritarian [MMM] or superimposition system), i.e. abolishing any compensation between the plurality- and the PR-tier (Linhart 2009).

Figure 10.2: The 'left-shift' of the cube rule curve over seventeen Bundestag elections

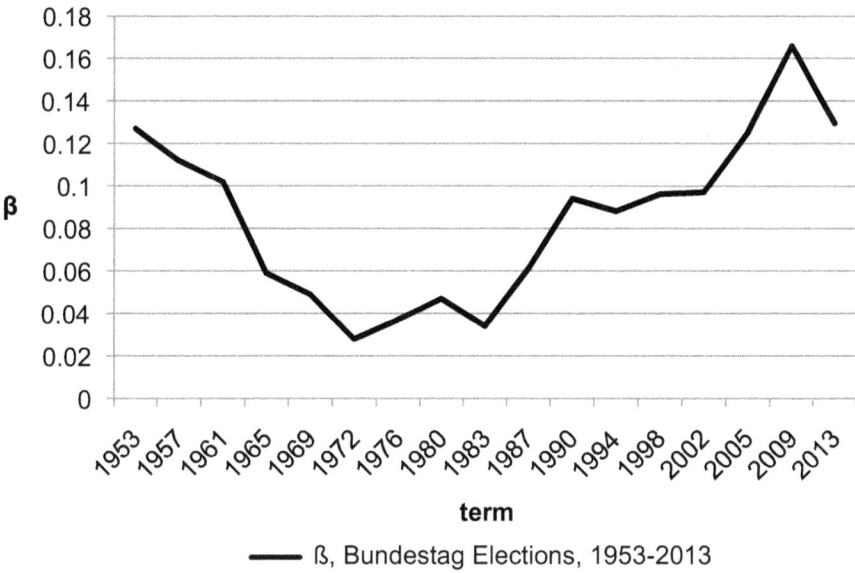

β

term

ß, Bundestag Elections, 1953-2013

Figure 10.3: Constituency votes shares and shares of district mandates in the Bundestag elections, 1953 to 2013 for the CDU/CSU and SPD (cf. Figure 2.3)

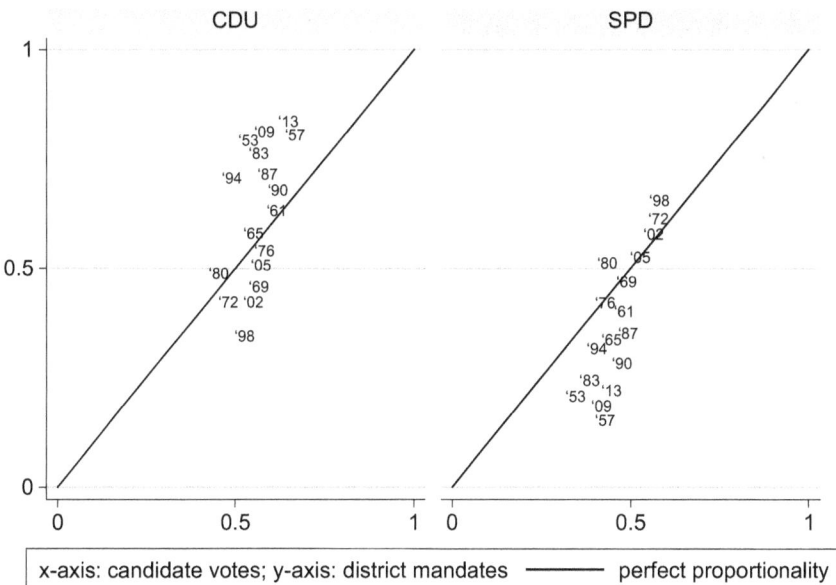

x-axis: candidate votes; y-axis: district mandates ——— perfect proportionality

secured parliamentary majorities and have not precluded government stability – something which the comparative perspective evinces quite clearly (*see* Table 1.1 and Figure 1.1).

Germany's MMP-system leads to largely proportionate outcomes – but personalisation has always been another important second objective and regarding MPs' representational roles, apparently it has been successfully achieved. As Chapters Four and Nine showed, the incentive structure of Germany's mixed system does actually make sure that MPs both act as disciplined and committed party representatives *as well as* spokespersons of 'their' districts – no matter whether they were actually elected in a constituency or whether they had 'only' run as a candidate in it. The findings I presented strongly suggest that German MPs indeed combine these two roles, while there is little evidence for a mandate-divide between MPs elected into the *Bundestag* via the party-list or via the district. Confronted with mixed rules, members of parliament employ mixed strategies – as do their parties when nominating them. This becomes evident with more than 80 per cent of all MPs running as double candidates. Furthermore, even those MPs who have been elected to parliament via the list, have strong interests in building a local reputation. They care for 'their' district and value a district- more than a list-mandate. Parties evidently share these interests: they want their MPs to engage in constituency service and, therefore, condition the placement in a promising list position on engagement at the district level. This applies for large as well as small parties.

The question of proportionality is somewhat more complex. On the one hand, parliamentary representation is quite fair, particularly in a comparative perspective (*see* Table 1.2). On the other hand, small deviations from proportionality are intended – as in the case of the legal thresholds (five per cent of the nationwide PR-vote or three district mandates), which were introduced against the background of the high party fragmentation from which the functioning of the Weimar Republic was perceived to have suffered. Yet, the disproportionality due to surplus seats has become a more recent phenomenon. The recent (2013) electoral reform which introduced full compensation for surplus seats has made this a problem of the past, but only at the cost of an increased *regional* disproportionality and a high likelihood that the combined number of surplus and compensation seats will inflate the number of parliamentary seats to an unacceptable extent. So, yet another reform of Germany's election system is in the offing.

The preceding chapters were, however, not exclusively directed toward the German electoral system. Rather, the analyses were meant to benefit from the many methodologically advantages that a mixed-electoral systems offers. They were, thereby, able to shed light on a couple of current debates in electoral studies and comparative politics more generally, like the *mandate-divide debate* on the impact of electoral rules on parliamentary behaviour; like the *contamination debate* on the effects that the two tiers of a mixed electoral system have on each other, modifying the 'pure' effects of either majoritarian or proportional rules; like the *descriptive representation debate* on the causes of women's very uneven electoral chances in districts or on party lists, respectively; or like the *debate on electoral accountability* or on the *cartel party thesis* about the relative weights of selectorates (parties) vs. electorates (voters) in selecting and sacking members of parliament. The preceding chapters presented little evidence in support of the mandate-divide thesis. To the contrary, much points in the direction of a dual representational role of German *Bundestag* members, with them being oriented both toward the party and the district. This has to do with parties' interest in their candidates' district service even if candidates have no chance of winning the district seat. As the preceding analysis showed, there is a robust positive effect of candidates' district presence on a party's list-votes in this district. This also explains why the increase in the number of parties at the federal level translates itself almost one-to-one into an increase in the number of district candidates at the local level – with the effect of an increasing disproportionality in the vote-seat translation in the plurality tier. The German data also confirms the prevailing wisdom about the very different career chances of female candidates under majoritarian or proportional electoral rules. This, however, seems to be mainly due to different career requirements in both tiers, not due to 'gender stereotyping' by reactionary voters. The promotion of women via the proportional tier also indicates to what extent party elites manage to pursue overall programmatic goals at the expense of the local nomination logic in the district and at the expense of individual (local) careers. In line with this finding, the empirical evidence also shows how much the selection of candidates by the party leadership dominates the election of candidates by the voters. The power to re-nominate, which of course includes the possibility and threat not to re-nominate, is a potent instrument in the hands of party elites and, therefore, a strong instrument to establish party discipline.

Where does this all leave us? Gudgin and Taylor's classic analysis of majoritarian systems – to which the preceding analysis owes so much – had been undertaken with the explicit aim to provide a *'technical statement* about how a particular system works, and no more' (Gudgin and Taylor 2012 [1979]: xliii;). Yet, in the end, the two authors could not refrain from also giving a normative assessment, and in fact a quite harsh one. Majoritarian rules in their view have the 'important weakness that the relationship between total votes gained and number of seats won is uncontrolled, arbitrary, sometimes unpredictable, and in some circumstances open to abuse' (2012 [1979]: xli). With increasing evidence that the British two-party system – in particular under influence of the PR-ruled European elections – might lastingly change into a multi-party system, the preceding analysis also contains important insights for the working of a first-past-the-post system in a multi-party setting. One prediction seems safe: with a higher (effective) number of district parties the disproportionality of the vote-seat translation will increase, possibly rendering the relationship between votes and seats even more 'arbitrary and unpredictable' than before. And this might trigger a revival of a reform debate that, already in the 1970s, had looked at the German system as a potential template (Hansard Society 1976). Quite a similar development of increased disproportionality can be expected for the French two-round, two-ballot majoritarian system – again since French parties represented in the European Parliament due to the PR-electoral rules for

EP-elections, but not, or only scarcely, represented in the *Assemblée National*, will have an interest in filing candidates in national elections in as many districts as possible. The effects on disproportionality and volatility, highlighted above, can then be expected to be similar in France, too.

Gudgin and Taylor, in their last chapter (ch. 7 'Beyond Pluralities'), devoted an insightful section also to the analysis of the German mixed-member electoral system with an eye to possible British reforms. Again, the two authors could not abstain from a normative judgement: 'The West German electoral system does seem to have justified the hopes of its proponents in producing both proportionality in results while preventing multiplication of parties' (Gudgin and Taylor 2012 [1979]: 191). And they recommend a slightly modified version of the German system (with a higher share of constituency than list seats) for the British debate: 'The additional-member vote system is simply the most reliable tool available for the respectable electoral engineer; it takes the geography out of elections' (2012 [1979]: 199). While the preceding analysis does disagree in two respects with this assessment – namely that mixed electoral rules succeed in taking 'the geography out of elections' and that German electoral rules have prevented the 'multiplication of parties' – Gudgin and Taylor's overall positive evaluation of the German electoral system is largely shared here.

Appendix to Chapter Two

That votes in majoritarian systems are translated into seats according to a regular pattern that is quite well captured by the cube rule, has been demonstrated in numerous studies. But why exactly do we observe this regularity? Answers have remained controversial (Taagepera 1986). While the cube rule has been applied very successfully in countless electoral studies, the causal mechanisms behind it have seemed to be not fully clear for a long time. The rule is regularly used, but rarely understood: 'the cube law is usually plucked from nowhere' (Gudgin and Taylor 2012 [1979]: 30). In the preceding chapter I, likewise, applied, but didn't explain the cube rule. In this appendix I would like to briefly discuss – in my view – the most convincing theoretical derivation of the cube rule. I will also show that the German data do support this derivation.

Within the debate about the mechanisms behind the cube rule, Graham Gudgin and Peter Taylor in an important contribution have already, in 1979, pointed to the nexus between the cube rule and a cumulative normal distribution of vote shares (Gudgin and Taylor 2012 [1979]). They showed that the cube rule approximates a cumulative density function of a normal distribution (with a standard deviation (SD) in the range between ten to 15 per cent of the votes). A variation of vote shares in that range can be found in many different electoral systems. We, therefore, can understand the cube rule as a function that approximates the cumulative density function (CDF) of a normal distribution with a SD in that range. All that is necessary for calculating the proportionality of the vote-seat translation are, then, the distribution of vote shares and its exact standard deviation.

The standard deviation measures the degree of similarity or dissimilarity of electoral districts. It therefore captures essential information on a country's political geography. Its lower limit is zero: in this case, all districts would have the exactly identical vote shares – they would be absolutely homogeneous with respect to their socio-economic, cultural, ethnic, linguistic etc. composition. The upper limit of the standard deviation is not defined, but bound by the fact that vote shares may vary between zero and 100 per cent. Empirically, the standard deviation of vote shares in majoritarian electoral systems like the British, or that of New Zealand, has often been between ten and 15 (cf. Tables 2.2 and 2.3 Gudgin and Taylor 2012 [1979]: 24–25).

The size of the SD results from the interaction of the (average) district size and the prevalent settlement patterns: how segregated do different groups of voters (i.e. different socio-economic groups) live from each other? And to what extent do the boundaries of electoral districts match with these settlement patterns? Both dimensions interact: with larger district size it becomes less likely that we see

Table A2.1: Standard deviations for Christian and Social Democrats

Federal election	CDU Standard Deviation of Nominal Votes	SPD Standard Deviation of Nominal Votes
1953	18.96	9.46
1957	14.71	10.59
1961	12.24	9.55
1965	18.47	9.55
1969	10.42	10.19
1972	10.51	10.13
1976	10.37	9.73
1980	10.34	9.73
1983	9.59	9.64
1987	8.91	9.65
1990	8.52	10.08
1994	9.03	9.23
1998	9.51	8.86
2002	11.27	9.28
2005	10.58	9.54
2009	8.32	8.65
Ø	11.36	9.62

'extreme' or 'mono-cultural districts' with an almost exclusive party followership for one party – at a given level of segregation. With higher levels of segregation, we are more likely to see 'extreme' or 'mono-cultural' districts – at a given district size. Jonathan Rodden (2005) has recently shown that densely populated industrial regions tend to be very homogeneous socio-economically and therefore politically. This feature carries over to their post-industrial successor regions. Gudgin and Taylor state:

> The standard deviation of the CPD [Cumulative Probability Distribution] constitutes a link between the spatial organization (electoral geography) and the electoral outcome (seats won) through its implicit measurement of marginal seats in the normal-distribution model. It does this because, in measuring the spread of a CPD, the standard deviation indicates the degree to which party support varies between constituencies' (Gudgin and Taylor 2012 [1979]: 24).

In Germany, the average standard deviation of district votes for the CDU and the SPD over all elections from 1953–2009 was 11.4 (CDU) and 9.6 (SPD), respectively (*see* Table A2.1) – smaller than the SDs we observe for the UK or New Zealand.

Table A2.2: OLS, regression of ρ at the election level on the standard deviation of the vote for Social or Christian Democrats, 1953–2009

	ρ at the election-level
Effect. Number of District Parties	−1.305
	(0.094)*
Number of Districts	0.207
	(0.168)
SD SPD District votes	−0.771
	(0.243)
SD CDU District Votes	−0.162
	(0.148)
Constant	14.355
	(0.048)**
Observations	32
Adjusted R-squared	0.236

Robust p-values in parentheses; * significant at the 10%-level; ** significant at the 5%-level; *** significant at the 1%-level.

In other words, inter-district vote differences are smaller and districts are more homogeneous in Germany compared to in the UK or New Zealand, but as expected with greater homogeneity for the SPD than the CDU. A smaller standard deviation means a steeper slope of the cumulative normal distribution, i.e. a more disproportionate vote-seat translation. If the (socio-economic) voter composition is very similar across districts, small vote shifts trigger major seat shifts.

Regressing the ρ of the federal elections, i.e. the disproportionality of the vote-seat translation in the plurality tier, on the standard deviations (*see* Table A2.2) does indeed show a negative relation between both measures, even if both coefficients miss conventional standards of significance.

One empirical expectation following from the 'political geography'-argument is that 'all other things being equal, smaller constituencies will tend to produce larger variances' (Gudgin and Taylor 2012 [1979]: 47). This can be tested by looking at different levels of aggregation for the same election – i.e. holding the socio-economic composition and territorial distribution of the electorate, its voting behaviour as well as parties' nomination and coalition strategies completely constant and only varying the district size. Figures A2.1 and A2.2 show the cumulative density functions for the electoral results of the Social Democrats and the Christian Democrats in the 2009 federal election in the state of North Rhine-Westphalia. Both figures display the distribution of vote shares for each party, first at the level of the sixty-three *electoral districts* (Wahlkreise) and second at the level of the 16.244 *voting districts* (Wahlbezirke) in this state. Table A2.3 displays

Table A2.3: Summary statistics for CDU and SPD vote share in the 2009 federal election in the state of North Rhine-Westphalia

	Obs	Mean	Std. Dev.	Min	Max
CDU votes (%), voting districts	16244	38.796	11.346	7.919	83.333
CDU votes (%), electoral districts	63	38.796	7.888	24.764	54.528
SPD votes (%), voting districts	16244	34.887	9.756	3.468	71.601
SPD votes (%), electoral districts	63	34.887	7.030	23.364	53.361

summary statistics for both levels and both parties. That smaller districts lead to higher variance is instantly apparent both from the table and the figures. What also becomes very clear from the graphical presentation is the family resemblance between the cube rule and the cumulative density function of a normal distribution (*see* Figures A2.1 and A2.2). The steeper slope of the CDF with a smaller number of districts confirms our previous finding that disproportionality increases with fewer districts.

Figure A2.1: Cumulative density function of the SPD (nominal) vote shares at the district and voting district level

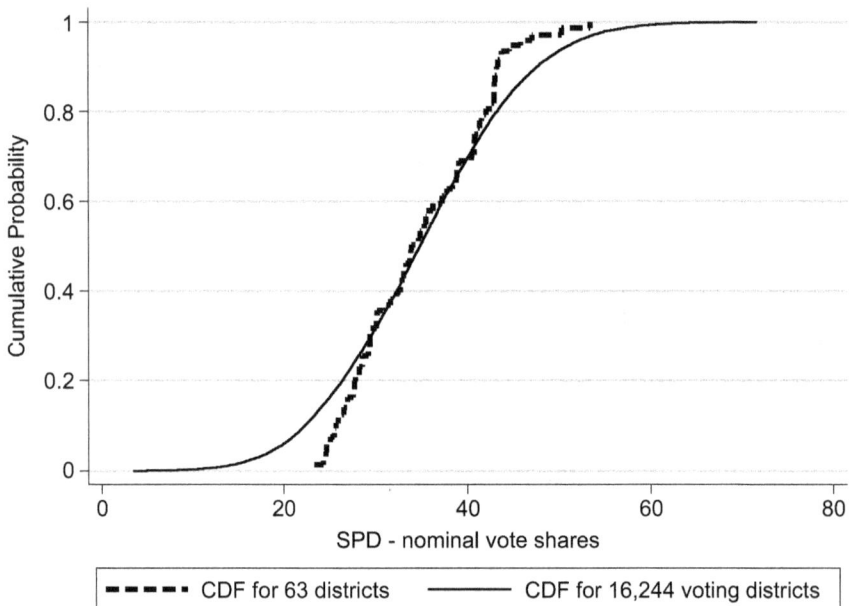

Figure A2.2: Cumulative density function of the CDU (nominal) vote shares at the district and voting district level

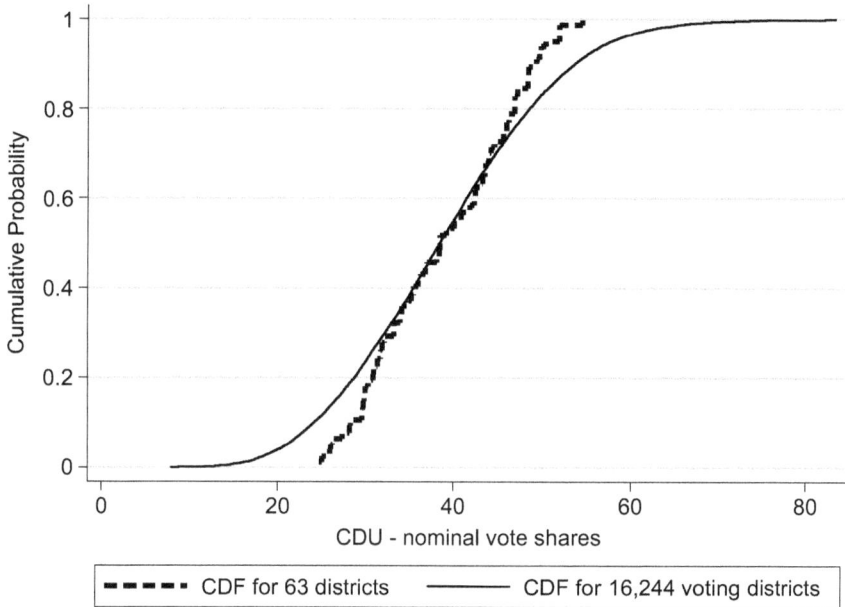

Bibliography

Abraham, D. (1988) *The Collapse of the Weimar Republic*, Princeton: Princeton University Press.

Andeweg, R. B. and Thomassen, J. J.A. (2005) 'Modes of political representation: towards a new typology', *Legislative Studies Quarterly* 30(4): 507–528.

Armin, H. H. von (2002) 'Wählen wir unsere Abgeordneten unmittelbar?', *Juristenzeitung* 57(12): 578–588.

— (2004) 'Wahl ohne Auswahl. Die Parteien und nicht die Bürger bestimmen die Abgeordneten', *Zeitschrift für Rechtspolitik* 37(4): 115–119.

Bailer, S., Meißner, P. *et al.* (2013) *Seiteneinsteiger im Deutschen Bundestag*, Wiesbaden: Springer VS.

Bailer, S., Meißner, P., Ohmura, T. and Selb, P. (2011) *Rekrutierung und Kompetenzen von Bundestagsabgeordneten*, unpublished manuscript.

Bartolini, S. and Mair, P. (1990) *Identity, Competition, and Electoral Availability: The stabilisation of European electorates 1885–1985*, Cambridge: Cambridge University Press.

Bawn, K. (1993) 'The logic of institutional preferences: German electoral law as a social choice outcome', *American Journal of Political Science* 37(4): 965–989.

— (1999) 'Voter responses to electoral complexity: ticket splitting, rational voters and representation in the Federal Republic of Germany', *British Journal of Political Science* 29(3): 487–505.

Bawn, K. and Thies, M. F. (2003) 'A comparative theory of electoral incentives: representing the unorganized under PR, plurality and mixed-member electoral systems', *Journal of Theoretical Politics* 15(1): 5–32.

Becker, R. and Saalfeld, T. (2005) 'Entwicklung der Parteiidentifikation im Lebensverlauf, Deutschland 1984–2000', Bern/Kent, unpublished manuscript.

Behnke, J. (2003a) 'Überhangmandate: Ein behebbarer Makel im institutionellen Design des Wahlsystems', *Zeitschrift für Politikwissenschaft* 13(3): 1235–1269.

— (2003b) 'Von Überhangsmandaten und Gesetzeslücken', *Aus Politik und Zeitgeschichte* B52/2003: 21–28.

— (2003c) 'Ein integrales Modell der Ursachen von Überhangmandaten', *Politische Vierteljahresschrift* 44(1): 41–65.

— (2007) *Das Wahlsystem der Bundesrepublik Deutschland: Logik, Technik und Praxis der Verhältniswahl*. Baden-Baden: Nomos.

— (2009) 'Überhangmandate bei der Bundestagswahl Eine Schätzung mit Simulationen', *Zeitschrift für Parlamentsfragen* 40(3): 620–636.

— (2012) 'Ursachen und Wirkungen - Überlegungen zur Beibehaltung der Überhangmandate im neuen Wahlgesetz', *Zeitschrift für Parlamentsfragen* 43(1): 170–184.

Behnke, J. and Grotz, F. (2011) 'Das Wahlsystem zwischen normativer Begründung, empirischer Evidenz und politischen Interessen', *Zeitschrift für Parlamentsfragen* 42(2): 260–278.

Berg, H.-J. (1985) *Der Verteidigungsausschuss des Deutschen Bundestages. Kontrollorgan zwischen Macht und Ohnmacht,* München: Bernard und Graefe.

Blais, A. (ed.) (2008) *To Keep or to Change First Past the Post? The politics of electoral reform*, Oxford: Oxford University Press.

Blossfeld, H.-P., Golsch, K. and Rohwer, G. (2007) *Event History Analysis with Stata*, Mahwah, N.J./London: Lawrence Erlbaum Associates.

Bormann, N.-C. and Golder, M. (2013) 'Democratic electoral systems around the world, 1946–2011', *Electoral Studies* 32 (2): 360–369.

Box-Steffensmeier, J. M. and Jones, B. S. (2004) *Event History Modeling: A guide for social scientists*, New York: Cambridge University Press.

Brockmann, H. (2012) 'Frauen und Mütter im Deutschen *Bundestag*: Eine explorative Längsschnittstudie', *Zeitschrift für Parlamentsfragen* 43(4): 727–738.

Brüderl, J. and Scherer, S. (2006) 'Methoden zur Analyse von Sequenzdaten', in A. Diekmann (ed.) *Methoden der Sozialforschung* (Sonderheft 44 der *Kölner Zeitschrift für Soziologie und Sozialpsychologie*), Wiesbaden: VS-Verlag, pp. 330–347.

Brzinsky-Fay, C. and Kohler, U. (2010) 'New developments in sequence analysis', *Sociological Methods & Research* 38(3): 359–364.

Brzinsky-Fay, C., Kohler, U. and Luniak, M. (2006) 'Sequence analysis with Stata', *The Stata Journal* 6(4): 435–460.

Bücking, H.-J. (1998) 'Der Streit um Grundmandatsklausel und Überhangmandate', in E. Jesse and K. Löw (eds) *Wahlen in Deutschland*, Berlin: Dunker & Humblot.

Bundeswahlleiter (2005) *Wahl zum 16. Deutschen Bundestag am 18. September 2005. Heft 1: Ergebnisse und Vergleichszahlen früherer Bundestags-, Europa- und Landtagswahlen sowie Strukturdaten für die Bundestagswahlkreise,* Wiesbaden: Statistisches Bundesamt.

— (2009a) *Wahl zum 17. Deutschen Bundestag am 27. September 2009, Sonderheft, Die Wahlbewerber für die Wahl zum 17. Deutschen Bundestag*, Wiesbaden: Statistisches Bundesamt.

— (2009b) *Wahl zum 17. Deutschen Bundestag am 27. September 2009. Heft 1: Ergebnisse und Vergleichszahlen früherer Bundestags-, Europa- und Landtagswahlen sowie Strukturdaten für die Bundestagswahlkreise,* Wiesbaden: Statistisches Bundesamt.

— (2010) *Wahl zum 17. Deutschen Bundestag, Ergebnisse der Wahlbezirksstatistik,* Wiesbaden: Statistisches Bundesamt.

Burkett, T. and Padgett, S. (1987) *Political Parties and Elections in West Germany: The search for a new stability,* London: Palgrave Macmillan.

Butler, D. (1953) *The Electoral System in Britain, 1918–1951,* Oxford: Clarendon Press.

Butzer, H. (1991) *Immunität im demokratischen Rechtsstaat. Verfassungsgrundlagen und Parlamentspraxis des Deutschen Bundestages,* Berlin: Duncker & Humblot.

Cain, B., Ferejohn, J. and Fiorina, M. (1987) *The Personal Vote: Constituency service and electoral independence,* Cambridge, MA: Harvard University Press.

Calvo, E. (2009) 'The competitive road to proportional representation: partisan bias and electoral regime change under increasing party competition', *World Politics* 61(2): 254–295.

Capoccia, G. (2002) 'The political consequences of electoral laws: the German system at fifty', *West European Politics* 25(3): 171–202.

Carey, J. M. (2009) *Legislative Voting and Accountability,* New York: Cambridge University Press.

Carey, J. M. and Shugart, M. S. (1995) 'Incentives to cultivate a personal vote: a rank ordering of electoral formulas, *Electoral Studies* 14(4): 417–439.

Caselli, F. and Morelli, M. (2004) 'Bad politicians', *Journal of Public Economics* 88(3–4): 759–782.

Caul, M. (2001) 'Political parties and the adoption of candidate gender quota', *The Journal of Politics* 63(4): 1214–1229.

Cazzola, F. (1988) *Della Corruzione: fisiologia e patologia di un sistema politico,* Bologna: Il Mulino.

Chang, E. C. C. and Golden, M. (2004) 'Electoral systems, district magnitude and corruption', *British Journal of Political Science* 37(1): 115–137.

Cleves, M. A., Gould, W. W. and Gutierrez, R. G. (2004) *An Introduction to Survival Analysis using STATA,* College Station, Texas: Stata Press.

Cox, G. W. (1987) *The Efficient Secret: The Cabinet and the development of political parties in Victorian England,* New York: Cambridge University Press.

—— (1997) *Making Votes Count: Strategic coordination in the world's electoral systems,* New York: Cambridge University Press.

Cox, G. W. and Rosenbluth, F. (1993) 'The electoral fortunes of legislative factions in Japan', *American Political Science Review* 87(3): 577–589.

—— (1995) 'Anatomy of a split: the Liberal Democrats of Japan', *Electoral Studies* 14(4): 355–376.

—— (1996) 'Factional competition for the party endorsement: the case of Japan's Liberal Democratic Party', *British Journal of Political Science* 26(2): 259–269.

Cox, K. E. and Schoppa, L. J. (2002) 'Interaction effects in mixed-member electoral systems: theory and evidence from Germany, Japan, and Italy', *Comparative Political Studies* 35(9): 1027–1053.

Crisp, B. F. (2007) 'Incentives in mixed-member electoral systems: general election laws, candidate selection procedures, and cameral rules', *Comparative Political Studies* 40 (12): 1460–85.

Cross, W. (2008) 'Democratic norms and party candidate selection', *Party Politics* 14(5): 596–619.

Dalton, R. J. (2008) 'The quantity and the quality of party systems, party system polarization, its measurement, and its consequences', *Comparative Political Studies* 41(7): 899–920.

Davidson-Schmich, L. K. (2006) 'Implementation of political party gender quota: evidence from the German Länder 1990–2000', *Party Politics* 12(2): 211–232.

Diaz, M. M. (2008) *Representing Women: Female legislators in West European Parliaments*, London: Routledge, ECPR Press.

Döring, H. and Manow, P. (2015) *Parliaments and governments database (ParlGov): Information on parties, elections and cabinets in modern democracies*, Bremen University (www.parlgov.org).

Eder, C. and Magin, R. (2008) 'Wahlsysteme', in M. Freitag and A. Vatter (eds) *Die Demokratien der Deutschen Bundesländer*, Stuttgart: UTB, pp. 33–62.

Edinger, M. and Schwarz, B. (2009) *Leben nach dem Mandat. Eine Studie zu ehemaligen Abgeordneten*, SFB 580 Gesellschaftliche Entwicklungen nach dem Systemumbruch (H. 35).

Estevez-Abe, M. (2006) 'Gendering the varieties of capitalism: a study of occupational segregation by sex in advanced industrial societies, *World Politics* 59(1): 142–75.

Falter, J. W. and Rattinger, H. (1983) 'Parteien, Kandidaten und politische Streitfragen bei der Bundestagswahl 1980: Möglichkeiten und Grenzen der Normal-Vote-Analyse', in M. Kaase and H.-D. Klingemann (eds) *Wahlen und politisches System: Analysen aus Anlaß der Bundestagswahl 1980*, Opladen: Westdeutscher Verlag, pp. 320–421.

Falter, J. W. and Schoen, H. (2005) *Handbuch Wahlforschung: Ein einführendes Handbuch*, Wiesbaden: VS Verlag. (2nd edition 2014).

Fearon, J. D. (1999) 'Electoral Accountability and the Control of Politicians: Selecting good types versus sanctioning poor performance, in A. Przeworski, S. C. Stokes, and B. Manin (eds) *Democracy, Accountability, and Representation*, New York: Cambridge University Press, pp. 55–97.

Feldkamp, M. (2005) *Datenhandbuch zur Geschichte des Deutschen Bundestages, Ergänzungsband 1994–2003*, Baden-Baden: Nomos.

— (2006) 'Deutscher *Bundestag* 1987 bis 2005: Parlaments- und Wahlstatistik', *Zeitschrift für Parlamentsfragen* 37(1): 3–19.

Ferrara, F. (2004) 'Electoral coordination and the strategic desertion of strong parties in compensatory mixed systems with negative vote transfers', *Electoral Studies* 23(3): 391–413.

Ferrara, F. and Herron, E. S. (2005) 'Going it alone? Strategic entry under mixed electoral rules', *American Journal of Political Science* 49(1): 16–31.

Ferrara, F., Herron, E. S. and Nishikawa, M. (2005a) The Logic of Contamination: District-Level Party Systems, *Mixed member electoral systems. Contamination and its Consequences*, New York: Palgrave Macmillan, 33–48.

— (2005b) *Mixed Member Electoral Systems: Contamination and consequences*, New York: Palgrave Macmillan.

Fisman, R. and Gatti, R. (2002) 'Decentralization and corruption: evidence across countries', *Journal of Public Economics* 83(3): 325–345.

Forschungsgruppe Wahlen (1990) Sieg ohne Glanz: Eine Analyse der Bundestagswahl 1987, *Wahlen und Wähler: Analysen aus Anlaß der Bundestagswahl 1987*, in M. Kaase and H.-D. Klingemann (eds), Opladen, Westdeutscher Verlag: 699–734.

— (1994) Gesamtdeutsche Bestätigung für die Bonner Regierungskoalition: Eine Analyse der Bundestagswahl 1990, *Wahlen und Wähler: Analysen aus Anlaß der Bundestagswahl 1990*, in M. Kaase and H.-D. Klingemann (eds), Opladen, Westdeutscher Verlag: 615–665.

Fürnberg, O. and Knothe, D. (2009) 'Wahlsiege ohne Stimmenmehrheit: Auswirkungen von verstärktem "Lagersplitting" auf Mandatsverteilung und Koalitionsoptionen', *Zeitschrift für Parlamentsfragen* 40(1): 56–74.

Gallagher, M. (1991) 'Proportionality, disproportionality and electoral systems', *Electoral Studies* 10(1): 33–51.

Gallagher, M. and Mitchell, P. (2005) *The Politics of Electoral Reform*, Oxford: Oxford University Press.

Gamson, W. A. (1961) 'A theory of coalition formation', *American Sociological Review* 26(3): 373–382.

Gelman, A. and Hill, J. (2007) *Data Analysis using Regression and Multilevel/ Hierarchical Models*, New York: Cambridge University Press.

Gerring, J. and Thacker, S. C. (2004) 'Political institutions and corruption: the role of unitarism and parliamentarism', *British Journal of Political Science* 34(2): 295–330.

Gibowski, W. G. and Kaase, M. (1986) 'Die Ausgangslage für die Bundestagswahl am 25. Januar 1987', *Wahlen und politischer Prozeß: Analysen aus Anlaß der Bundestagswahl 1983*, in M. Kaase and H.-D. Klingemann (eds), Opladen, Westdeutscher Verlag: 509–543.

Golden, M. (2003) 'Electoral connections: the effects of the personal vote on political patronage, bureaucracy and legislation in postwar Italy', *British Journal of Political Science* 33(2): 189–212.

Golden, M. and Chang, E. C. C. (2001) 'Competitive corruption: factional conflict and political malfeasance in postwar Italian Christian Democracy', *World Politics* 53(4): 588–622.

Golder, S. N. (2005) 'Pre-electoral Coalitions in Comparative Perspective: A Test of Existing Hypotheses', *Electoral Studies* 24(4): 643–663.

— (2006a) 'Pre-electoral coalition formation in parliamentary democracies', *British Journal of Political Science* 36(2): 193–212.

— (2006b) *The Logic of Pre-Electoral Coalition Formation*, Columbus: The Ohio State University Press.

Grotz, F. (2000) 'Die personalisierte Verhältniswahl unter den Bedingungen des gesamtdeutschen Parteiensystems. Eine Analyse der Entstehungsursachen von Überhangmandaten seit der Wiedervereinigung', *Politische Vierteljahresschrift* 41(4): 707–729.

—— (2009) 'Verhältniswahl und Regierbarkeit – Das deutsche Wahlsystem auf dem Prüfstand', *Zeitschrift für Politikwissenschaft* (Sonderband 'Wahlsystemreform'): 155–181.

Gschwend, T. (2007) 'Ticket-splitting and strategic voting under mixed electoral rules: evidence from Germany', *European Journal of Political Research* 46(1): 1–23.

Gschwend, T. and Zittel, T. (2008) 'Individualised Constituency Campaigns in Mixed-Member Electoral Systems: Candidates in the 2005 German Elections', *West European Politics* 31(5), 978–1003.

Gschwend, T. , Shugart, M. S. and Zittel, T. (2009) 'Assigning Committee Seats in Mixed-Member Systems - how important is 'Localness' as compared to Mode of Election?', Manuscript.

Gudgin, G. and Taylor, P. J. (2012 [1979]) *Seats, Votes, and the Spatial Organisation of Elections*, Colchester: ECPR Press.

Hainmüller, J. and Kern, H. L. (2008) 'Incumbency as a source of spillover effects in mixed electoral systems: evidence from a regression discontinuity design', *Electoral Studies* 27(2): 213–27.

Hainmüller, J., Kern, H. L. and Bechtel, M. (2006) 'Wahlkreisarbeit zahlt sich doppelt aus - Zur Wirkung des Amtsinhaberstatus einer Partei auf ihren Zweitstimmenanteil bei den Bundestagswahlen 1949 bis 1998', *Jahrbuch für Handlungs- und Entscheidungstheorie*, T. Bräuninger and J. Behnke (eds), Wiesbaden: VS Verlag, 11–45.

Hansard Society (1976) *The Report of the Hansard Commission on Electoral Reform*, London: The Hansard Society for Parliamentary Government.

Hazan, R. Y. and Rahat, G. (2010) *Democracy Within Parties: Candidate selection methods and their political consequences*, Oxford: Oxford University Press.

Heinz, D. (2010) 'Mandatstypen und Ausschussmitgliedschaften der Mitglieder des Deutschen *Bundestags* – Eine empirische Untersuchung von 1949 bis 2005', *Zeitschrift für Parlamentsfragen* Volume 41(3): 518–527

Henning, C., Linhart, E. and Shikano, S. (eds) (2009) *Parteienwettbewerb, Wählerverhalten und Koalitionsbildung*, Baden-Baden: Nomos.

Hermens, F. A. and Unkelbach, H. (1967) 'Die Wissenschaft und das Wahlrecht', *Politische Vierteljahresschrift* 8(1): 2–22.

Herrmann, M. (2012) 'Voter uncertainty and failure of Duverger's law: an empirical analysis', *Public Choice* 151(1/2): 63–90.

Herron, E. C. (2002) 'Electoral influences on legislative behaviour in mixed-member systems: evidence from Ukraine's Verkhovna Rada', *Legislative Studies Quarterly* 27(3): 361–382.

Herron, E. C. and Nishikawa, M. (2001) 'Contamination effects and the number of parties in mixed-superposition electoral systems', *Electoral Studies* 20(1): 63–86.

Hoecker, B. (1994) 'The German Electoral System: A barrier to women?', in W. Rule and J. F. Zimmerman (eds) *Electoral Systems in Comparative Perspective: Their impact on women and minorities*, Westport, CT: Greenwood Press, pp. 65–77.

Huddy, L. and Terkildsen, N. (1993) 'Gender stereotypes and the perception of male and female candidates', *American Journal of Political Science* 37(1): 119–47.

Imbens, G. W. and Lemieux, T. (2008) 'Regression discontinuity designs: a guide to practice', *Journal of Econometrics* 142 (2): 615–635.

Ismayr, W. (2000) *Der Deutsche Bundestag im politischen System der Bundesrepublik Deutschland*, Opladen: Leske + Budrich.

Iversen, T. and Rosenbluth, F. (2006) 'The political economy of gender: explaining cross-national variation in the gender division of labor and the gender gap', *American Journal of Political Science* 50(1): 1–19.

— (2010a) *Women, Work, and Politics: The political economy of gender inequality*, Yale: Yale University Press.

— (2010b) 'Gender and Political Careers: A comparative labor market analysis of female political representation' in T. Iversen and F. Rosenbluth (eds) *Women, Work & Politics: The political economy of gender inequality*, New Haven: Yale University Press, pp. 134–161.

Jesse, E. (1988) 'Split-voting in the Federal Republic of Germany: an analysis of the federal elections from 1953 to 1987', *Electoral Studies* 7(2): 109–124.

— (1990) *Elections: The Federal Republic of Germany in Comparison*, New York, Oxford, Munich: Berg.

— (1998) 'Grundmandatsklausel und Überhangmandate. Zwei wahlrechtliche Eigentümlichkeiten in der Kritik' in M. Kaase and H.D. Klingemann (eds) *Wahlen und Wähler. Analysen aus Anlass der Bundestagswahl 1994*, Opladen: Westdeutscher Verlag, 15–41.

— (2009) 'Verhältniswahl und Gerechtigkeit', *Zeitschrift für Politikwissenschaft* 19 (Sonderheft 'Wahlsystemreform'): 105–132.

Kaack, H. (1969) *Wer kommt in den Bundestag? Abgeordnete und Kandidaten 1969*, Opladen: Leske.

Kaiser, A. (2002) 'Gemischte Wahlsysteme. Ein Vorschlag zur typologischen Einordnung', *Zeitschrift für Parlamentsfragen* 32(4): 1547–1574.

Katz, J. and King, G. (1999) 'A statistical model for multiparty electoral data', *American Political Science Review* 93(1): 15–32.

Katz, R. S. and Mair, P. (1995) 'Changing models of party organizations and party democracy: the emergence of the cartel party, *Party Politics* 1(1): 5–28.

— (2009) 'The cartel party thesis: a restatement', *Perspectives on Politics* 7(4): 753–766.

Kendall, M. G. and Stuart, A. (1950) 'The law of cubic proportions in electoral results, *British Journal of Sociology* 1(3): 183–197.

— (1952) 'La Loi de Cube dans les Elections Britanniques', *Revue Française de Science Politique* 2(2): 270–276.

King, G. (1990) 'Electoral responsiveness and partisan bias in multiparty democracies', *Legislative Studies Quarterly* 15(2): 159–81.

King, G. and Browning, R. X. (1987) 'Democratic representation and partisan bias in Congressional elections', *American Political Science Review* 81(4): 1251–73.

Kitzinger, U. (1960) *German Electoral Politics: A study of the 1957 campaign*, Oxford: Claredon Press.

Klein, H. H. (1989) '§17 Indemnität und Immunität', in H.-P. Schneider and W. Zeh (eds) *Parlamentsrecht und Parlamentspraxis*, Berlin: de Gruyter, pp. 555–592.

Kleinert, H. (2012) 'Anmerkungen zum Wahlrechtsstreit - Ein Problem gelöst, ein anderes bleibt. Oder: Ein Blick über die Grenzen lehrt Gelassenheit', *Zeitschrift für Parlamentsfragen* 43(1): 185–192.

Klingemann, H.-D. and Wessels, B. (2001) 'The Political Consequences of Germany's Mixed-Member System: Personalization at the grass roots? in M. S. Shugart and M. P. Wattenberg (eds) *Mixed-Member Electoral Systems: The best of both worlds?*, Oxford: Oxford University Press, pp. 279–296.

Koch, J. W. (2002) 'Gender stereotypes and citizens' impressions of house candidates' ideological orientation', *American Journal of Political Science* 46(2): 453–62.

Kohler, U., Luniak, M. and Brzinsky-Fay, C. (2011) *SQ: Stata module for sequence analysis*, Boston College Department of Economics.

Kunicova, J. and Rose-Ackerman, S. (2005) 'Electoral rules and constitutional structures as constraints on corruption', *British Journal of Political Science* 35(4): 573–606.

Laakso, M. (1979) 'Should a two-and-a-half law replace the cube law in British elections?, *British Journal of Political Science* 9(3): 355–384.

Laakso, M. and Taagepera, R. (1979) 'Effective number of political parties: a measure with application to West Europe, *Comparative Political Studies* 12(1): 3–27.

Lancaster, T. D. (1986) 'Electoral structures and pork barrel politics', *International Political Science Review* 7(1): 67–81.

Lancaster, T. D. and Patterson, W. D. (1990) 'Comparative pork barrel politics perceptions from the West-German-*Bundestag*, *Comparative Political Studies* 22(4): 458–477.

Lang, H. (2014) *Wahlrecht und Bundesverfassungsgericht: Eine Skizze aktueller wahlrechtlicher Entscheidungen und Probleme*, Baden-Baden: Nomos.

Lee, D. S. (2008) 'Randomized experiments from non-random selection in U.S. House Elections, *Journal of Econometrics* 142(2): 675–697.

Lee, D. S. and Lemieux, T. (2010) 'Regression discontinuity designs in economics', *Journal of Economic Literature* 48(June): 281–355.

Lewis, J.B. and Linzer, D.A. (2005) 'Estimating Regression Models in which the Dependent Variable is based on Estimates', *Political Analysis* 13(3): 345–364.

Lijphart, A. (1990) 'The political consequences of electoral laws, 1945–85', *American Political Science Review* 84(2):481–496.

Linhart, E. (2009) 'Mögliche Auswirkungen von Grabenwahlsystemen in der Bundesrepublik Deutschland. Theoretische Überlegungen und Simulationen', *Zeitschrift für Parlamentsfragen* 40(3): 637–660.

Lundberg, T. C. (2007) *Proportional Representation and the Constituency Role in Britain*, Houndmills, Basingstoke: Palgrave Macmillan.

Lundell, K. (2004) 'Determinants of candidate selection: the degree of centralization in comparative perspective, *Party Politics* 10(1): 25–47.

Mackie, T. T. and Rose, R. (1991) *The International Almanac of Electoral History*, 3rd rev. edn, Houndmills, Basingstoke: Macmillan.

Mager, U. and Uerpmann, R. (1995) Überhangmandate und Gleichheit der Wahl, *Deutsches Verwaltungsblatt* 110(6): 273–280.

Mann, G. H. (1995) 'Die unumgängliche Umkehr bei der Berechnung von Überhangmandaten: Reformvorschläge', *Zeitschrift für Parlamentsfragen* 27(3): 398–404.

Manow, P. (2007) 'Electoral rules and legislative turnover: evidence from Germany's mixed electoral system, *West European Politics* 30(1): 195 – 207.

— (2008) 'Wiederwahlchancen im deutschen System der personalisierten Verhältniswahl – eine empirische Untersuchung der sechzehn Bundestagswahlen, 1949–2005', *Zeitschrift für Politikwissenschaft* 18(2): 147–166.

— (2010) 'Disproportionalität und ihre Folgen - Die Mehrheitswahlkomponente des deutschen Mischwahlsystems', *Zeitschrift für Politikwissenschaft* 20(2): 149–178.

— (2011) 'The cube rule in a mixed member electoral system: the plurality tier in German *Bundestag* elections', *West European Politics* 34(4): 773–94.

— (2013) 'Mixed Rules, different Roles? An Analysis of the Typical Pathways into the *Bundestag* and of MPs' Parliamentary Behavior', *Journal of Legislative Studies* 19(3), 287–308.

Manow, P. and Flemming, P. (2011a) 'Der Titel als politisches Distinktionsmerkmal? Eine Untersuchung der Wahlbewerber zum Deutschen *Bundestag* seit 1949', *Zeitschrift für Politikwissenschaft* 21(4): 531–551.

— (2011b) *Kandidaten- und Abgeordnetendatensatz Bundestag, 1949–2009*, Universität Bremen, Technische Universität Dortmund.

Manow, P. and Nistor, M. (2009) 'Wann ist ein Listenplatz sicher? Eine Untersuchung der Bundestagswahlen 1953 bis 2002', *Zeitschrift für Parlamentsfragen* 40(3): 588–605.

Mansbridge, J. (2003) 'Rethinking representation', *American Political Science Review* 97(4): 515–528.

Martin, L. W. and Stevenson, R. T. (2001) 'Government formation in parliamentary democracies', *American Journal of Political Science* 45(1): 33–50.

Massicotte, L. (2011) 'Mixed Systems', in J. M. Colomer (ed.) *Personal Representation. The neglected Dimension of Electoral Systems*, Colchester: ECPR Press, pp. 99–117.

— (forthcoming) *Mixed Member Proportional Systems: How they work in Germany, New Zealand and Britain*, Manuscript.

Massicotte, L. and Blais, A. (1999) 'Mixed electoral systems: a conceptual and empirical survey, *Electoral Studies* 18(3): 341–366.

Matland, R. E. (1998 [2002]) 'Enhancing women's political participation: legislative recruitment and electoral systems', in IDEA (ed.) *Women in Parliament: Beyond numbers*, Stockholm: IDEA.

Matland, R. E. and Montgomery, K. (eds) (2003) *Women's Access to Political Power in Post-Communist Europe*, Oxford: Oxford University Press.

Matland, R. E. and Studlar, D. T. (1996) 'The contagion of women candidates in single-member district and proportional representation electoral systems: Canada and Norway, *Journal of Politics* 58(3): 707–733.

— (2004) 'Determinants of legislative turnover: a cross-national analysis, *British Journal of Political Science* 34(1): 87–108.

McDermott, M. L. (1997) 'Voting cues in low information elections: candidate gender as a social information variable in contemporary United States elections, *American Journal of Political Science* 41(1): 270–83.

Mitchell, P. (2000) 'Voters and their representatives: electoral institutions and delegation in parliamentary democracies, *European Journal of Political Research* 37(3): 335–351.

Moncrief, G. *et al.* (2004) 'Time, term limits and turnover. trends in stability in U.S. state legislatures, *Legislative Studies Quarterly* 29(3): 357–381.

Moser, R. G. and Scheiner, E. (2004) 'Mixed member electoral systems and electoral system effects: controlled comparison and cross-national analysis', *Electoral Studies* 23(4): 575–599.

— (2012) *Electoral Systems and Political Context: How the effects of rules vary across new and established democracies*, New York: Cambridge University Press.

Naundorf, C. (1996) 'Der überflüssige Überhang: Reformvorschläge', *Zeitschrift für Parlamentsfragen* 27(3): 393–397.

Nishikawa, M. and Herron, E. S. (2004) 'Mixed electoral rules' impact on party systems', *Electoral Studies* 23(4): 753–768.

Nohlen, D. (1978) *Wahlsysteme der Welt. Ein Handbuch*, München: Piper.

— (2000) *Wahlrecht und Parteiensystem*, Opladen: Leske + Budrich.

— (2009) 'Wahlsysteme in Reformprozessen', *Zeitschrift für Politikwissenschaft* 19(1; Sonderheft Wahlsystemreform): 45–80.

— (2014) *Wahlrecht und Parteiensystem,* 7th edn, Stuttgart: UTB.

Nolte, P. (2013) 'Absolute Mehrheit? Ja, bitte!' *Spiegel* 25th September 2013: 46–47.

Ordeshook, P. and Shvetsova, O. (1994) 'Ethnic heterogeneity, district magnitude, and the number of parties', *American Journal of Political Science* 38(1): 100–123.

Panizza, U. (2001) 'Electoral rules, political systems, and institutional quality', *Economics and Politics* 13(3): 311–342.

Panizza, U. and Bertok, J. (2004) 'Electoral rules and corruption: managing conflicts of interest in OECD countries', *Global Corruption Report 2002. Special Focus: Political Corruption*, Transparency International, London: Pluto Press, pp. 317–322.

Pappi, F. U. and Thurner, P. W. (2002) 'Electoral behaviour in a two-vote system: incentives for ticket splitting in German *Bundestag* elections', *European Journal of Political Research* 41(2): 207–232.

Pappi, F. U., Herzog, A. and Schmitt, R. (2006) 'Koalitionssignale und die Kombination von Erst- und Zweitstimme bei den Bundestagswahlen 1953 bis 2005', *Zeitschrift für Parlamentsfragen* 37(3): 493–513.

Patzelt, W. (1997) 'German MPs and their roles', *Journal of Legislative Studies* 3(1): 55–78.

— (1999) 'What can an individual MP do in German parliamentary politics?', *Journal of Legislative Studies* 5 (3):23–52.

— (2007) 'The constituency roles of MPs at the federal and Länder levels in Germany, *Regional and Federal Studies* 17 (1):47–70.

Persson, T., Tabellini, G. and Trebbi, F. (2003) 'Electoral rules and corruption', *Journal of the European Economic Association* 1(4): 958–989.

Peters, H. (1956) *Zur Kandidatenaufstellung für freie demokratische Wahlen. Vom Bonner Grundgesetz zur gesamtdeutschen Verfassung*, FS für Hans Nawiasky, T. Maunz, München, pp. 341–358.

Phillips, A. (1995) *The Politics of Presence: The political representation of gender, ethnicity, and race*, Oxford: Oxford University Press.

Porter, S. R. (1995) *Political Representation in Germany: The effects of the candidate selection committees*, Rochester: Ph.D.

Powell, G. B. (2000) *Elections as Instruments of Democracy: Majoritarian and proportional visions*, New Haven, London: Yale University Press.

Rahat, G. (2007) 'Candidate selection: the choice before the choice', *Journal of Democracy* 18(1): 157–170.

— (2009) 'Which candidate selection method is the most democratic?', *Government and Opposition* 44(1): 68–90.

Rahat, G. and Hazan, R. Y. (2011) 'The barriers to electoral system reform: a synthesis of alternative approaches', *West European Politics* 34(3): 478–494.

Rahat, G. *et al.* (2008) 'Democracy and political parties: on the uneasy relationships between participation, competition and representation', *Party Politics* 14(6): 663–683.

Rattinger, H. (1994) 'Parteiidentifikationen in Ost- und Westdeutschland', in O. Niedermayer and K. von Beyme (eds) *Politische Kultur in Ost- und Westdeutschland*, Berlin: Edition sigma, pp. 77–104.

Reibel, C.-W. (2007) *Handbuch der Reichstagswahlen 1890–1918: Bündnisse, Ergebnisse, Kandidaten*, Düsseldorf: Droste.

— (2011) 'Bündnis und Kompromiss: Parteienkooperation im Deutschen Kaiserreich 1890–1918', *Historische Zeitschrift* 293(1): 71–114.

Renwick, A. (2010) *The Politics of Electoral Reform: Changing the rules of democracy*, New York, Cambridge University Press.

— (2011) 'Electoral reform in Europe since 1945', *West European Politics* 34(3): 456–477.

Roberts, G. (1988) 'The German Federal Republic: The two-lane route to Bonn, candidate selection in comparative perspective', in M. Gallagher and M. Marsh (eds) *The Secret Garden of Politics*, London: Routledge, pp. 94–118.

— (2000) 'By decree or by design? The surplus seats problem in the German electoral system: causes and remedies', *Representation* 37(3–4): 195–202.

Rodden, J. (2005) *Red States, Blue States, and the Welfare State: Political Geography, Representation, and Government Policy Around the World.* Unpublished Manuscript, Chicago.

— (2010) 'The geographic distribution of political preferences', *Annual Review of Political Science* 13: 321–340.

— (2011) *The Long Shadow of the Industrial Revolution: Political geography and the representation of the Left*, Stanford: Manuscript.

Rudzio, W. (2003) *Das politische System der Bundesrepublik Deutschland*, 6, Auflage ed. Opladen: Leske + Budrich.

Rule, W. (1987) 'Electoral systems, contextual factors and women's opportunity for election to parliament in twenty-three democracies, *Western Political Quarterly* 40(3): 477–498.

Saalfeld, T. (2005) 'Germany: Stability and strategy in a mixed-member proportional system', in M. Gallagher and P. Mitchell (eds) *The Politics of Electoral Systems*, Oxford: Oxford University Press, pp. 209–229.

Salmond, R. (2006) 'Proportional representation and female parliamentarians', *Legislative Studies Quarterly* 31(2): 175–204.

Samuels, D. J. (1999) 'Incentives to cultivate a party vote in candidate-centric electoral systems: evidence from Brazil', *Comparative Political Studies* 32(4): 487–518.

Scarrow, S. E. (2001) 'Germany: The mixed-member system as a political compromise', in M. S. Shugart and M. P. Wattenberg (eds) *Mixed-Member Electoral Systems: The best of both worlds?*, Oxford: Oxford University Press, pp. 55–69.

Scherer, S. and Brüderl, J. (2010) 'Sequenzdatenanalyse' in C. Wolf and H. Best (eds) *Handbuch der sozialwissenschaftlichen Datenanalyse*, Wiesbaden: VS-Verlag.

Schindler, P. (1984) *Datenhandbuch zur Geschichte des Deutschen Bundestages 1949 bis 1982*, Baden-Baden: Nomos.

— (1998) *Datenhandbuch zur Geschichte des Deutschen Bundestages*, Baden-Baden: Nomos.

— (1999) *Datenhandbuch zur Geschichte des Deutschen Bundestages 1949–1999*, Baden-Baden: Nomos.

Schmidt, M. G. (2003) *Political Institutions in the Federal Republic of Germany*, Oxford: Oxford University Press.

Schneider, S. and Tepe, M. (2011) 'Dr. Right and Dr. Wrong: Zum Einfluss des Doktortitels auf den Wahlerfolg von Direktkandidaten bei der Bundestagswahl 2009', *Politische Vierteljahresschrift* 52(2): 248–85.

Schreiber, W. (1989) '§12 Wahlkampf, Wahlrecht und Wahlverfahren,' in H.-P. Schneider and W. Zeh (eds) *Parlamentsrecht und Parlamentspraxis*, Berlin: de Gruyter, pp. 401–440.

—   (1994) *Handbuch des Wahlrechts zum Deutschen Bundestag: Kommentar zum Bundeswahlgesetz*, Köln, Berlin, Bonn, München: Heymanns.

Schröder, H. J. (1971) *Die Kandidatenaufstellung und das Verhalten des Kandidaten zu seiner Partei in Deutschland und Frankreich*, Berlin: Duncker & Humblot.

Schröder, V. and Manow, P. (2014) 'Elektorale Koordination, legislative Kohäsion und der Aufstieg der modernen Massenpartei: Die Grenzen des Mehrheitswahlrechts im Deutschen Kaiserreich, 1890–1918', *Politische Vierteljahresschrift* 55(3): 518–554.

Schüttemeyer, S. S. and Sturm, R. (2005) 'Der Kandidat - das (fast) unbekannte Wesen. Befunde und Überlegungen zur Aufstellung der Bewerber zum Deutschen *Bundestag*', *Zeitschrift für Parlamentsfragen* 36(3): 539–53.

Schweitzer, C. C. (1979) *Der Abgeordnete im parlamentarischen Regierungssystem der Bundesrepublik*, Opladen: Leske + Budrich.

Shikano, S. (2007) *Interactive Mechanism of mixed-electoral systems: a theory-driven comparative analysis via computational modelling and Bayesian statistics*. Habilitationsschrift, Mannheim.

Shugart, M. S. (2001a) 'Electoral 'efficiency' and the move to mixed-member systems', *Electoral Studies* 20(2): 173–193.

—   (2001b) 'Extreme' Electoral Systems and the Appeal of the Mixed-Member Alternative, in: M. S. Shugart and M. P. Wattenberg (eds) *Mixed-Member Electoral Systems: The Best of Both Worlds?*, Oxford: Oxford University Press, pp. 25–51.

Shugart, M. S. and Wattenberg, M. P. (2001a) 'Mixed-member electoral systems: a definition and typology', in M. S. Shugart and M. P. Wattenberg (eds) *Mixed-Member Electoral Systems: The best of both worlds?*, Oxford: Oxford University Press, pp. 9–24.

—   (eds) (2001b) *Mixed-Member Electoral Systems: The best of both worlds?*, Oxford: Oxford University Press.

—   (2001c) 'Introduction: The electoral reform of the twenty-first century', in M. S. Shugart and M. P. Wattenberg (eds) *Mixed-Member Electoral Systems: The best of both worlds?*, Oxford: Oxford University, pp. 1–6.

Shugart, M. S., Wattenberg, M. P. and Sieberer, U. (2007) *Erklärungen zur Abstimmung und innerfraktionelle Geschlossenheit im Deutschen Bundestag*, Mannheim: unpublished manuscript.

—   (2010) 'Behavioral consequences of mixed member electoral systems: deviating voting behavior of district and list MPs in the German *Bundestag*', *Electoral Studies* 29(3): 484–96.

Stata (2003) *Survival Analysis and Epidemiological Tables*, Texas: Stata Press.

Stratmann, T. (2006) 'Party-Line Voting and Committee Assignments in the German Mixed-Member System', in R. D. Congleton and B. Swedenborg (eds) *Democratic Constitutional Design and Public Policy: Analysis and evidence*, Cambridge, MA: MIT Press, pp. 111–130.

Stratmann, T. and Baur, M. (2002) 'Plurality rule, proportional representation, and the German *Bundestag*: how incentives to pork-barrel differ across electoral systems', *American Journal of Political Science* 46(3): 506–514.

Strohmeier, G. (2009) 'Vergangene und zukünftige Reformen des deutschen Wahlsystems', *Zeitschrift für Politikwissenschaft* (Sonderheft Wahlsystemreform): 11–44.

Taagepera, R. (1986) 'Formulating the cube law for proportional representation elections: a generalization of the cube law, *American Political Science Review* 80(2): 489–504.

Taagepera, R. and Shugart, M. S. (1989) *Seats and Votes: The effects and determinants of electoral systems*, New Haven: Yale University Press.

Taylor, P. J. and Johnson, R. J. (1979) *Geography of Elections*, Harmondsworth: Penguin.

Tomz, M., Tucker, J. A. and Wittenberg, J. (2002) 'An easy and accurate regression model for multiparty election data', *Political Analysis* 10(1): 66–83.

Treisman, D. (2000) 'The causes of corruption: a cross-national study', *Journal of Public Economics* 76(3): 399–457.

— (2002) *Decentralization and the Quality of Government*. Working paper, Department of Political Science, UCLA.

Vierhaus, R. and Herbst, L. (2003) *Biographisches Handbuch der Mitglieder des Deutschen Bundestages 1949–2002,* 3 vols, München: K.G. Saur.

Wängnerud, L. (2009) 'Women in parliaments: descriptive and substantive representation', *Annual Reviews of Political Science* 12: 51–69.

Weber, M. (1918 [1988]) *Parlament und Regierung im neugeordneten Deutschland. Gesammelte Politische Schriften*, Tübingen: Mohr (Siebeck), pp. 306–443.

Wissenschaftliche Dienste des Deutschen *Bundestags* (1998) *Die Mitglieder des Deutschen Bundestages, 1.–13. Wahlperiode*, Berlin: Deutscher Bundestag.

Wüst, A., Schmitt, H., Gschwend, T. and Zittel, T. (2006) 'Candidates in the 2005 *Bundestag* election: mode of candidacy, campaigning and issues', *German Politics* 15 (2006) 4: 421.

Zeuner, B. (1970) *Kandidatenaufstellung zur Bundestagswahl 1965*, Den Haag: Martinus Nijhoff.

— (1973) 'Wahlen ohne Auswahl', in W. Steffani (ed.) *Parlamentarismus ohne Transparenz,* Opladen: Westdeutscher Verlag.

Zittel, T. and Gschwend, T. (2007) 'Individualisierte Wahlkämpfe im Wahlkreis. Eine Analyse am Beispiel des Bundestagswahlkampfes von 2005', *Politische Vierteljahresschrift* 48(2): 293–321.

Index

www.ingramcontent.com/pod-product-compliance
Lightning Source LLC
Chambersburg PA
CBHW072119020426
42334CB00018B/1647